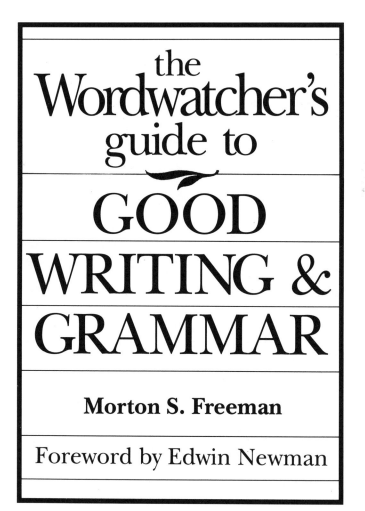

the Wordwatcher's guide to

GOOD

WRITING &

GRAMMAR

Morton S. Freeman

Foreword by Edwin Newman

Writer's Digest Books   Cincinnati, Ohio

The Wordwatcher's Guide to Good Writing & Grammar. Copyright © 1990 by Morton S. Freeman. Printed and bound in the United States of America. All rights reserved. No part of this book may be reproduced in any form or by any electronic or mechanical means including information storage and retrieval systems without permission in writing from the publisher, except by a reviewer, who may quote brief passages in a review. Published by Writer's Digest Books, an imprint of F&W Publications, Inc., 1507 Dana Avenue, Cincinnati, Ohio 45207. First edition.

94   5 4

Library of Congress Cataloging in Publication Data

Freeman, Morton S.
    [Handbook of problem words & phrases]
    The wordwatcher's guide to good writing & grammar / Morton S. Free-
man. — 1st ed.
        p. cm.
    Originally published as: A handbook of problem words & phrases.
c1987.
    Includes index.
    ISBN 0-89879-436-6
    1. English language—Usage—Dictionaries. I. Title.
PE1460.F654   1990
428'.003—dc20   90-12514
                                                                        CIP

Dedication

To Shirley Cole, my sister-in-law,
who encouraged me to become a wordwatcher

Foreword

For me, one of the by-products of coming to be regarded as an expert on the English language was meeting Morton Freeman. Birds of a feather, as you must have heard, flock together. But hold on: By-product, now that I think of it and of Morton Freeman, is not quite the right word. Bonus is more like it.

Morton Freeman is someone who cares about the English language, who wants to protect and nurture it, and, more important, enable others to use it more efficiently and more pleasurably. (The pleasure to be had—free—from using a language well is, sadly, often over-looked.) I know that some people regard those who worry about the state of the language as stuffy, and cranky, and boring. In fact, many of them are as lively and engaging as anyone you could want to meet— and, when it comes to English, as practical. So it is with Morton Free-man. When he offers advice on grammar and usage, he does not do it for obscure, crotchety, or what might be called technical, reasons. His advice is plain, specific, direct, and good-humored.

Behind that advice there is, of course, an attitude. One element of that attitude is the view that if we want the language to serve us well, we must serve it well, which is to say, use it correctly. Not, however, simply for the sake of using it correctly. There is more to it than that. Use it correctly and you are likely to use it economically, saving your-self time and effort. And you are more likely to be properly under-stood, the value of which need hardly be dwelt upon. You will also have more fun. As I have already suggested, there is a great deal of gratification to be had from using the language well in dealing with others or when you are alone with your own thoughts. Morton Free-man would like others to understand that and act on it.

So, when he sets out to give advice, he is not trying to demonstrate how much he knows or trying to intimidate or impress anyone. He is trying to be helpful.

On that last point, I defy anyone to read this book and not find in it questions—many questions—he or she would want to ask. For here are questions, on points of grammar, on spelling, on choice of words, on what is permissible and what is not—and why—that have troubled all of us.

By the way, I considered writing "each and every one of us" rather than "all of us," but I looked up that entry in this book. Also, in the second sentence of the first paragraph, I wrote that birds of a feather flock together. I could have let it go at "flock," but the "together" has the endorsement of time. That is desirable. So are Morton Freeman's endorsements. See for yourself.

—Edwin Newman

Preface

What makes *The Wordwatcher's Guide to Good Writing & Grammar* different from other books on the English language? And why the need for another such undertaking?

In the first place, this book is not a text. Nor is it a collection of fiats or a listing of grammatical rules. Instead, the *Guide* presents actual problems bothersome to those concerned with the intricacies and nuances of good writing and grammar. To resolve these problems, the book offers guidelines that are currently being observed by the most competent and careful users of the language.

For many years as a teacher of English, as the Director of Publications of the American Law Institute-American Bar Association (ALI-ABA), and as a newspaper columnist (my column appropriately titled "Word Watcher"), I made note of the errors in grammar, usage, punctuation, and related matters committed by students as well as lawyers and college professors whose manuscripts I edited. And daily I received questions on these various matters from my newspaper readers, many of whom asked whether a compilation had been made of the articles that appeared in their newspapers, so that between the covers of a book they could have the full assemblage.

A question bound to be asked is, Who determines the correct way to say or write something? Unfortunately, there is no Académie Anglaise to tell us in scholarly thunder what is right and what is wrong. The practical approach to authoritatively approved diction, it was thought, was through usage panels, groups of reputable writers and recognized grammarians. But unfortunately again, these English specialists to whom questions were addressed did not, in most cases, agree with one another. In fact, their diversity of opinion was so prevalent that readers were left in a quandary.

Morris Bishop pointed out that the 100 or more *American Heritage Dictionary* panelists agreed on only one reference — in disfavor of *simultaneous* as an adverb ("the referendum was conducted simultaneous with the election"). Even in such a clear-cut case as the word *unique*, with its accepted sense of one of a kind, 6 percent approved of "rather unique" and "most unique."

Despite this lack of absolute certainty, there is nevertheless a consensus among those with a feel for the language. This book espouses the practice of those speakers and writers because their standards consistently lead the way to the highest levels of communication. Without these usage conventions, we could just as well spell *fish* (as George Bernard Shaw, with tongue in cheek, suggested) as *ghoti*: "gh" as in tough, "o" as in women, and "ti" as in motion.

Regardless, a writer (or anyone else) may not wish to be bound by grammatical strictures. Fine. But, you may wonder, what is to be gained by saying, for example, "Hopefully, the train will arrive on time" when it is just as easy to say what many critics hold are the only correct forms — "It is to be hoped that" or "I hope that." And consider the rule that *less* applies to quantity and *fewer* to number. So why say, "There are *less* than six tulips in that bunch"?

Naturally, anyone may opt for a word or phrase that is popular or faddish if it seems suitable. But this practice is best exercised by a person who, through intellectual judgment, has decided to deploy a word or phrase that in this instance was preferable to conventional usage. That is an educated approach.

The Wordwatcher's Guide in effect says, "Here are the canons of usage that merit the respect of those qualified to judge which expressions are acceptable in an educated society." Although the principles of standard, or formal, usage are recommended, equal time has been given to the informal, which makes the decision which to use yours alone.

— Morton S. Freeman

Boca Raton, Florida
May 10, 1990

A

❋ a/an

1. What rule should one follow when choosing between *a* and *an*?
Authorities agree that *a* should be used before words that begin with
a consonant sound (*a* chair, *a* table). This means that the sound is the
key, not the kind of initial letter. Therefore, say *a unit, a eulogy,* since
they have consonant sounds. Conversely, words beginning with a
vowel sound take *an* (*an apple, an oyster*).

> **Note:** The question that bothers many people is whether *a* or *an* should
> be used before a word beginning with *h*. The trend is to use *a* before an
> aspirated *h*, one that is sounded (*a hotel, a historian, a historical moment*),
> and *an* before a silent *h* (*an hour, an heir, an honor*). Those who prefer the
> combination of, say, *an historic event,* may feel free to use it. Although not
> preferred, such usage is acceptable.

2. Is it proper to say, "Can anyone select a more competent a person"?
It is not. The second *a* is superfluous. Correct: "a more competent
person." The notion that the added *a* makes for emphasis is ground-
less.

3. What justifies the combination *many a*?
Many a (*many* has a plural sense and *a*, a singular) has idiomatic sanction. It is deeply entrenched in the finest literary works. The illogicality
of the combination has been ignored. We say, "*Many a* man has failed
to reach his goal." "*Many an* hour has been wasted shooting pool."

> **Note:** In negative comparisons, do not use *a* or *an*. For example, in "No
> easier *a* task, no brighter *an* hour," omit the *a* and *an*.

4. We speak of "a Federal Bureau of Investigation report," but what article is used if the name of the agency is abbreviated to FBI?
The article *an*—*an* FBI report. Treat abbreviations as corresponding
words and choose *a* or *an* accordingly, which means that it is the sound
of the initial letter in the abbreviated form that governs. FBI sounds
like EFF-B-I. And so we say, "*an* H.R. bill," "*an* M.I.T. student."

-able/-ible

Is there a way to tell when to use the suffix *-able* and when to use *-ible*?
There is none. The correct spelling of words with those terminations
is baffling. To be safe, one must consult a dictionary or a speller. Perhaps this vague guideline will help a little: More words end in *-able*

than in *-ible*. But what phonetic difference is there between the endings in "It is *definable* but not *comprehensible*"? None.

> **Note:** There have been many efforts to remedy the backward spelling of the English language, but to no avail. No one can see the usefulness of the letter *l* in *should* and *would* or the letter *g* in *thought, although,* and *enough.* And so with *-able* and *-ible.* Those suffixes are pronounced alike. The only excuse for their existence seems to be a trap in a spelling bee. Which is not much of an excuse. Everyone would benefit, and life would be pleasanter, if *-able* served as the ending wherever a suffix with this sound was called for.

about/around

1. Which is correct: "The temperature should be *around* (or *about*) sixty degrees"?

The latter: *about.* Use *about* to mean approximately and *around* to refer to motion — "The pole-vaulter wrapped his fingers *around* the pole and started down the runway."

2. Would you approve of this sentence: "Around five thousand people attended the rally"?

Used as a preposition, *around* is an unacceptable colloquialism. Better style calls for *about* (*about* five thousand people).

3. "The newspaper reported that it was estimated that about thirty thousand people paraded." Something is amiss in that sentence. Can you pinpoint it?

What is wrong is the use of *about* and *estimated* in the same sentence. Those words indicate approximation; therefore using both, as was done, is a redundancy. *About* should have been omitted.

> **Note:** *Around,* except informally, should not replace *about* in "I will meet you *around* three o'clock," the intended sense being at that approximate time. The combination *at about* is unacceptable, since *at* pinpoints and *about* approximates. Also avoid the use of *about* to mean almost, as in "The conductor is *about* ready to begin."

above

I have often seen something like "He wrote the above." Is that sentence written in good style?

The consensus among grammarians is that *above* should not serve as a noun, as in the example. It is more desirable to say *the above phrase, the above material, the above quotation,* or whatever, using *above* as an adjective, or to say *the material quoted above,* using *above* as an adverb. Some critics frown so much on the use of *above* in such a construction that they would avoid the word under any circumstance and instead would say *previously mentioned, in the figures cited,* and so forth. But they are a dying breed.

Note: Be careful not to overuse *above*, for it may make one's writing sound like a lawyer's brief—a good reason to avoid it. Another reason, but one less persuasive, is that if *above* appears on the top line of a page, it may be thought ludicrous by those who refuse to accept its sensible reference, that it refers to what preceded, not what is physically above.

absolute terms

May we say, correctly, that this is more perpendicular, or horizontal, or parallel than that?

The adjectives you mention have absolute meanings and therefore are incapable of comparison — they are complete unto themselves. We may not say, at least not properly so, that this is more perpendicular than that or that this is the most horizontal or parallel of all, because if something is perpendicular, it simply is that, just as something square or round cannot be squarer or rounder than something else. However, you may qualify these "absolutes" by the expression "more nearly." Something can be more nearly horizontal than another thing, just as one person's analysis can be more nearly accurate than someone else's. As with adjectives, when the meaning of an adverb is absolute, it too is logically incapable of comparison.

Note: Some grammarians are drifting away from the notion that absolute terms are really absolute and are therefore incapable of being compared. They would approve of such qualifiers as *totally (totally unique), absolutely (absolutely parallel), more (more perfect),* and so forth. For those writers who prefer not to be taken to task, the safest course to follow is the one established by tradition — absolutely (but not *most absolutely*).

acclimate/advertisement

Has each of these words, *acclimate* and *advertisement*, one simple pronunciation?

No. *Acclimate,* meaning to become accustomed to circumstances, is pronounced either uh-KLIE-miht or AK-luh-maet; *advertisement,* either ad-VUHR-tis-ment or AD-vhir-tiez-ment. In each case, the first is preferred.

account

How is the word *account* properly constructed?

We account *to a person* for what we did ("Ralph will *account to* the treasurer for the missing money"). We account *for an action* ("Tom will have to *account for* his misbehavior").

Note: The term *accountable* is governed by the same prepositional idiom; that is, *for* or *to* ("We are *accountable for* our fiduciary holdings"; "We are *accountable to* the treasurer for funds advanced").

accusation/recrimination

How do the words *accusation* and *recrimination* differ in meaning?
An *accusation* charges someone with wrongdoing ("An *accusation* of embezzlement was lodged with the grand jury"). *Recrimination* is a countercharge, an accusation brought against the accuser by the accused ("Be assured that if you accuse the mayor of malfeasance, there will be *recriminations*").

Achilles' heel

What is an Achilles' heel?
It is, figuratively, a weak, unguarded spot. Achilles, the hero of Homer's *Iliad*, when an infant, was dipped by his mother into the river Styx to make him invulnerable. She held him by his heel, which therefore did not touch the water. A poisoned arrow shot from the bow of Paris pierced Achilles' heel, fatally wounding him.

> **Note:** Ancient classical names that end in *s* take their possessive form differently from ordinary proper names. We say, "Mr. Davis's boat" but Achilles' heel (Moses' leadership, Jesus' sermon), in which an apostrophe only is added to the name.

acute/chronic

In medicine, how are the terms *acute* and *chronic* distinguished?
Chronic refers to a condition that lingers and cannot be quickly cured; *acute*, to one that has reached a crisis and requires immediate attention.

> **Note:** The terms *acute* and *chronic* are not the exclusive property of the medical profession. They are used in general discourse as well. Anything severe or significant may be said to be acute (an *acute* food shortage). *Chronic* denotes a habit that persists for a lengthy period (a *chronic* complainer).

ad

Is it now acceptable to use *ad* for "advertisement"?
Yes, except in formal usage *ad* is in good standing, and justifiably so, as are the clipped forms *taxi* for "taxicab," *auto* for "automobile," and *phone* for "telephone." Most people would say, "I'm hurrying to catch a plane" rather than an "airplane." These terms are solidly entrenched in approved usage.

> **Note:** Abbreviations are usually followed by a period. *Ad* is a clipped form, not an abbreviation, and therefore takes no period. And thinking of tennis, it would be hard for the scorekeeper to get along without *ad* for *advantage*.

adapt

Which preposition does the verb *adapt* take?

Adapt, which means to adjust to a special use or situation, takes *to* when "in accordance with" can be sensibly substituted, as in "This material is not *adapted to* our curriculum." It takes *for* when meaning made (over), revised, or expurgated ("The play was *adapted for* television"). It takes *from* when the product or outcome results from something to which it is attributed ("The model of the train was *adapted from* Tom Thumb's").

adjacent/contiguous

If my property abuts my uncle's, are our properties *adjacent* or *contiguous*?

They are contiguous. In exact usage *adjacent* means lying near, close at hand, perhaps (but not necessarily) touching. *Contiguous* means an actual contact, touching, sharing a common boundary or edge, in the way your uncle's lot abuts. Books loosely standing on a shelf are adjacent. If they actually touch one another, they are contiguous.

adjective/adverb

What is the basic difference between an *adverb* and an *adjective*?

An *adjective* is a word that qualifies nouns ("He is a *large* man") or pronouns ("He is *old*"). An *adverb* modifies verbs (spoke *quickly*), adjectives (an *extremely* witty man), and adverbs (*very* haltingly).

> **Note:** Copulative verbs, those that link subject and predicate, follow a special rule. Those verbs are in a class by themselves in that they are static, not active, verbs. The most frequently used copulative verbs are *be* ("He *is* tall"—*tall* is an adjective, called a predicate adjective) and verbs pertaining to the senses (*feel, look, smell, touch, taste,* and *seem, become, grow,* and *appear).*

admittance/admission

What distinction is made between the words *admittance* and *admission*?

Admission refers to permitted entrance, to which are attached certain rights and privileges (*admission* to the D.A.R.); *admittance,* to physical entry only, access. A burglar may gain admittance to a clubhouse but would not be granted admission as a member. Except for signs, "No admittance" "Admittance by badge only," the word *admittance* is not commonly used.

> **Note:** *Admission* is used figuratively to mean a confession of wrongdoing, as in admission of guilt, which may be followed by the admission of evidence.

adore

"I adore pizza" and "I adore subs" are my daughter's favorite expressions. How can I correct her?

Explain that *to adore* is to revere or to have a high regard for; it is not an acceptable emphatic for "like." Tastes and flavors are thus *liked,* not *adored.* But your daughter may rightly say she adores her grandparents.

> **Note:** Informally *adore* has come to mean to like very much ("Sammy *adores* bike-riding"). The term has reached such widespread colloquial usage that it is no longer objectionable on that level.

adverb, placement of

Where should an adverb be placed?

Immediately before the word it modifies. Be particularly alert to the placement of *almost, even, just,* and *only.* Note the difference between "*Even* Stu did not phone me on Monday" and "Stu did not phone me *even* on Monday." See the varied meanings of a sentence as *only* moves from an introductory position to one before each successive word. Try it in "Only the warden handed the monkey a ball."

advise

What do you think of the word *advise* in "The firm wishes to *advise* that we'll close on Tuesday"?

A better word would be *inform,* which means to tell or impart information to. To *advise* is to give advice, in the way a lawyer talks to a client. Although *inform* and *advise* are synonyms, they are best used in different contexts, with *advise* restricted to business or legal writing.

> **Note:** A question sometimes raised is the form preferred for one who gives advice: *adviser* or *advisor.* Dictionaries and other authorities lean toward the former, *adviser.* But note there is no variant for *advisory,* "empowered to advise." It is spelled only that one way.

affect/effect

I believe that some people who use *affect* for *effect* and vice versa know the meaning they intend but simply confuse the spelling. Do you think otherwise?

You are probably right. The cause of the problem may be that *affect,* meaning to influence or to feign, in general usage is only a verb. *Effect* is also a verb. It means to complete, to accomplish, or to bring about ("He *effected* a change in the scheduling"), but as a practical matter it is almost always used as a noun meaning result or impression ("Her new hairstyle had an electric *effect* on him"). A mnemonic device to keep the spellings of these words straight is to remember that some-thing must affect something to have an effect on it, just as *a* comes before *e* in the alphabet.

> **Note:** The noun *affect* is a term confined to psychology. The verb *affect* sometimes displaces more precise words: for example, "The engineer's illness *affected* the train's schedule" (delayed); "Hank was *affected* by his neighbor's death" (saddened).

afraid/frightened

1. My aunt frequently says, "I'm afraid," as in "I'm afraid we must leave" or "I'm afraid we can't attend." Is that phraseology accept-able?
Her usage is informal for "to think" or "to believe." She could just as well say, "I think we must leave" and "I'm sorry we can't attend." *Afraid* is preferably used when there is real cause for fear or alarm or at least some apprehension.

> **Note:** The use of *afraid,* as in "I'm *afraid* you're wrong," is so common as to lend some belief to its idiomatic acceptance. But no one has gone so far as to welcome it into standard English.

2. Grammatically, is a person *frightened of* thunder?
No. He is frightened *by* thunder, possibly because he has always been *afraid of* thunder. The sense of afraid is habitual fear. To *frighten* is to fill with sudden and extreme fear or terror. Idiomatically, a person is *frightened by* and is *afraid of*.

> **Note:** Some dictionaries sanction *frightened of*. Most do not, and certainly very few authorities approve of it. Not uncommonly one may hear some-thing like "Are you frightened of bull terriers?"

after the conclusion

"After the conclusion of the seminar," the chairman said, "refresh-ments will be served." May I have your comments?
The chairman wasted words. He needed to say only, "After the semi-nar, refreshments will be served" or "At the conclusion. . . ." That which is after occurs at the conclusion of something.

again

Is *again* properly used in this sentence: "My brother loaded the car trunk so poorly that my father had to reload it again"?
The word *again* is used superfluously, since reload means "to load again." Be careful not to use *again* after a word beginning with the prefix *re-* when it means *again*.

aggravate

If so many people use *aggravate* to mean irritate, why is that usage in ill repute?

The fact is that many authorities do accept *aggravate* to mean "annoy" ("Those pesky flies *aggravate* me"). But some hold fast to its traditional meaning, "to make a bad condition worse" ("Smoking *aggravates* a cold"). These traditionalists, however, are waging a losing battle, since the overwhelming majority of people use *aggravate* primarily to mean either "to annoy" or "to make angry." The point must be made that the informal use of *aggravate*, in the sense of exasperate, irritate, vex, or bother, may exasperate some critics. In formal writing, to play safe, stick with the meaning that everyone will regard as standard—to intensify.

agnostic/atheist

Help me clarify the terms *agnostic* and *atheist*.

An *agnostic* disclaims any knowledge of God, believing the existence and nature of God cannot be known. An *atheist* contends that there is no God.

> **Note:** The word *atheist* was derived from the Greek *a*, "against," and *theo*, "God." The word *agnostic* was an 1869 coinage of Thomas Huxley, an English biologist, who sought a word to describe his own feelings, that he did not know whether a god existed and would therefore not deny such a possibility. Huxley, it should be noted, was an ardent evolutionist of the Darwinian school.

ago/since

I vaguely recall getting advice on the use of *ago* and *since*. What restrictions on their use should we observe?

Do not use the words together, since each word refers to past time. In tandem they are redundant. Not "It was nearly twenty-two years *ago since* I met her," but "It was nearly twenty-two years *ago that* . . . ," or use *since* and drop *ago*.

> **Note:** An odd thing about this combination is that *ago* takes the mind back to a time, whereas *since* brings it up to the present. The kernel of the advice on the use of *ago* is to follow it with *that* or *when* or to use it by itself (without *since*).

agree

Please clarify the prepositions that *agree* takes. Sometimes they are confusing.

Agreed. Note these uses: "Although the delegates *agree in* principle, they could not *agree on* an agenda"; "The members *agreed among* themselves to *agree to* their opponent's plan"; "I *agree with* you that the prepositions can be confusing." The authorities put it thus: *agree* takes prepositions *with* (persons), *to* (suggestions), *in* (thinking), and *upon* (a course). But note that a thing may agree *with* another thing.

agreement of subject and verb

1. What accounts for the misusage in the following sentence: "A quartet of girls were heard singing 'America' "?
The writer failed to determine the true subject. The subject here is *quartet,* a singular noun. It is unaffected by the following prepositional phrase. Hence "A quartet. . . *was.*" A verb must agree with its subject in number and person.

2. Why is it that although we say, "Study and hard work *are* good for you," we say, "Pie and ice cream *is* my favorite dessert"?
Generally a subject containing two or more elements connected by *and* is plural (the boy *and* the girl *are,* the paper *and* pencil *are). But some compound subjects constitute a unit; that is, they have been compounded into a oneness, and as such, take a singular verb.* Hence we say, "Pie *and* ice cream *is* . . ." because their togetherness makes them a unit.

> **Note:** Be careful. Not all writers agree on whether two elements have become one. And there are reasonable grounds for differences of opinion. When writers decide to follow a compound subject with a singular verb, they ought to feel sure that readers would most likely agree with this usage. Although no one would object to these sentences—"Ham *and* eggs *is* one of America's favorite breakfast foods," "A horse *and* buggy *is* what my Grandpa used," "The wear *and* tear *was* more than expected"—one may disagree, as many have, with the form of the verb in Kipling's "the tumult *and* the shouting *dies.*" The thing to determine when deciding whether to use a singular verb in these cases is the unity of the elements.
>
> Keep in mind that compound subjects involving *anyone . . . anyone, everything . . . everything,* and *nobody . . . nobody* take a singular verb, although at first glance it would seem illogical. We say, "Anyone who is someone *and* anyone who would like to be someone *is* invited." "Everything on the shelf *and* everything on the desk *is* an antique." The answer to this oddity seems to be that since the second element is unnecessary to establish the basic point, it has no grammatical bearing on the verb.

3. Which is correct: "Eleven feet *are* all we need" or "Eleven feet *is* all we need"?
The latter. A unit of measurement is singular, even though denoted by a plural noun ("We thought 140 pounds *was* too heavy." "We know that ten dollars *is* all it's worth." "Four years *is* a long time"). A period of time is regarded as a unit.

4. Do we say, "The shipment we received today *was* (or *were*) canta-loupes"?

[handwritten: is - singular / are - plural]

The verb *was* is called for because the subject of the sentence (*shipment*) is singular. The verb agrees in number with the subject, not with the complement.

5. What is the number of the verb following *or* in a compound subject?

The governing rule is the same as that which applies to *neither . . . nor.* If the number of the elements is different, the number of the subject nearer the verb controls: for example, "Pencils or a pen *was* what he wanted"; "A pen or pencils *were* what he wanted."

[handwritten left margin: WAS -S / were -pl]

[handwritten right margin: controlled by the pen singular]

6. I often see sentences like this one: "Amoco is opening their newest unit next week." Is this given correctly?

[handwritten left margin: is-singular]

It is not. *Amoco,* a collective noun, is being regarded as a singular (Amoco *is*). Collective nouns may serve either as singular or as plural. The example, however, lost consistency when it used the pronoun *their* instead of *its.*

7. How do we know whether a verb following a fraction should be singular or plural?

The number of the verb is determined not by the fraction but rather by the noun following it. "One half of the *apple is* rotten"; "One half of the *apples are* rotten."

8. "Many a man and woman seek for themselves a better living." Is a correction needed?

Although a compound subject (two or more parts) connected by *and* requires a plural verb, an exception is made with *many a.* It takes a singular verb and pronoun. Therefore, substitute *seeks* and *himself* (or *herself*) for *seek* and *themselves.*

9. Was this news report wrongly worded: "Money and support for the community is needed"?

It was. Plural subjects (*money and support*) take a plural verb (*are*). Only if dual subjects have been blended into a oneness ("Apple pie and ice cream *is* my favorite") is a singular verb permitted.

10. Do we say, "No man and no woman *was* (or *were*) allowed to enter"?

A *no . . . no* construction is singular (*was*) if the following nouns are singular, even though joined by *and.* Here the sense is that *no one* was allowed to enter.

11. This sentence may be grammatically wrong but it makes sense: "No one talked; they all remained quiet." Do you agree?

Yes. Convention requires a singular pronoun; sense demands a plural (*they*). To avoid this grammatical contradiction, reconstruct: "No one talked; *everyone* remained quiet."

12. "No applicants will be interviewed this month but will be next

[handwritten: NO subject]

month." Is that sentence subject to criticism?

It is because the second clause lacks a subject. You may not refer to subject *no applicants* and transplant it, for it is not that *no applicants* will be interviewed next month. Say, "but *applicants* will be interviewed next month."

13. May one say, correctly, that five hundred police marched today and that three hundred police retired during the year?

Yes to the first. *Police* is being used as a collective noun, a group. No to the second. The policemen retired individually, not as a group. Say, "three hundred *policemen* retired during. . . ."

14. Should we say, "Three times three *is* (or *are*) nine"?

A multiple sum, or collection of units, is regarded as a singular. Just as we say, "Here *is* the four hundred dollars I owe you" and "Sixteen pounds *is* what it weighs," so we say, "Three times three *is* nine."

15. Why do we say, "His wages *meet* his needs" and not "*meets* his needs"?

True, *wages* are a single thing, just as *trousers* and *scissors* are single items. But they are all regarded as plurals, not as singulars — "His trousers *are* long"; "The scissors *are* in the drawer." Hence "His wages *meet* his needs."

16. Why is it wrong to say, "A red and green scarf *is* on the table"?

It is not. One scarf, although of two colors, takes the singular *is*. But in "A red scarf and a green scarf are on the table," *are* is required, for the reference then is to two scarfs.

17. Do we say, "The long and the short of the matter *is* (or *are*) that we're staying home"?

We say, "The long and the short of the matter *is* . . ." because *the long and the short* is a combination that means conclusion or result. The two subjects pertain to a single idea. Likewise, "Her love and devotion *is* more than one needs."

a hold/ahold

Which is preferable, *a hold* or *ahold*, in "We'll try to get . . . of him soon"?

The former. It is idiomatic to say, "I'll get *a hold* of him soon," which means, figuratively, "get in touch." Of course, "get a hold" sounds like "get ahold." However, *ahold* is not a word in the English language and certainly should not appear in writing. Someone who has grasped something, say a handle bar, has gotten a hold on it.

> **Note:** The two verbs that lead most often to substandard *ahold* are *get* and *take*. The caveat, therefore, is to let those verbs serve as a beacon when thinking of the noun *hold*.

aid/aide

It is hard for me to differentiate the meanings of *aid* and *aide*. Can you *aid/aide* me?

Yes. Note that an *aide* is a helper, and that the word *helper* has two *e*'s. If the word wanted does not mean a helper or an assistant, then use *aid*, a word with no *e*'s.

> **Note:** Do not be beguiled by newspaper headlines that speak of an *aid* who was indicted. It seems that some papers will accept ambiguity when it will save space.

alibi/excuse

Is it proper to use *alibi* to mean *excuse*?

Opinion among usage critics is divided. Most authorities say no, but many say yes. Therefore feel free to do as you like. *Alibi* is best used in its traditional sense, a plea that the accused person was somewhere else when the crime was committed. Colloquially, it is equated with *excuse*, but if you need a word to convey the sense of "excuse," why not simply say *excuse*. It may be, because of the persistent use of *alibi* to mean excuse, that with time *alibi* in this sense will be admitted into standard English. But today, when one says, "What is your *alibi* for coming late?" the implication is that you won't be believed anyway. Although it does not necessarily follow, an *excuse* is considered legitimate; an *alibi*, something tinged with fraud.

> **Note:** In Latin, *alibi* means "elsewhere." In formal English, it is a noun only. It should not be used as a verb ("They tried to *alibi* their mistakes").

all

When *all* is used as a noun, is it a singular or a plural?

It depends on the meaning ascribed to it. If *all* is the equivalent of everything or the only thing, it takes a singular verb ("*All is* not lost"; "*All* I want *is* to come home safely"). If *all* encompasses each person in a group, it takes a plural verb ("*All are* wishing you well"; "*All were* regarded as competent mechanics").

alleged

May one correctly speak of an *alleged robber*?

No. A suspected robber, yes. *Alleged* is properly used only of a crime or a condition, not of a person. To *allege* is to make a charge or statement without proof.

> **Note:** Some journalists believe that if they call the defendant an alleged criminal, the modifier *alleged* will act as a hedge against defamation. Not true. The word is no defense in a libel suit.

all kinds of

When my son refers to a rich man, he says, "He has all kinds of money." Does he express himself correctly?
The expression *all kinds of*, meaning much, should not be used in either formal or informal English. It is an unacceptable colloquialism.

all over

What may be said about the phrase *all over the world*?
It is good idiom, but in formal writing transpose *all* and *over*: *over all the world*. And never use *all over* for *everywhere*. Not "We looked *all over* for the pen," but "We looked *everywhere*."

all right

I have seen *all right* written several ways. A common one is *alright*. Is this spelling acceptable?
Alright is not an English word. It is good only for those who write *alwrong*. *All right* is correctly written this way, in two words. And while we are at it, the forms *allright* and *all-right* are also all wrong.

> **Note:** Perhaps *alright* is imitative of such words as *already* and *altogether*. Whether or not this is so, the misspelling has not been established, and with almost all authorities it is not all right.

all that

My little boy said that he didn't think the play was all that good. Did he use good English?
His English was not bad; it was informal. When *all that* is preceded by a negative (*not, didn't*), it is understood as making a comparison. Your son might have been comparing the play with one he had previously seen. In formal language the sentence might be phrased "He didn't think the play was good (or very good)."

all together/altogether

The words *all together* and *altogether* sometimes mix us up. We're never sure how to spell the one we want. Is there anything that can help us?
There may be a mnemonic aide, but I am not aware of one. You will have to remember that *all together* means all at once ("We'll now sing *all together*") or everyone in one place ("The family is *all together* on the front lawn") and that *altogether* means completely or all told ("My supervisor is *altogether* pleased that the department is working *all to-*

gether"; "Jill spent three dollars *altogether*"). One idea that might help is to remember that *all* in *all together* is not necessary to the sense of the sentence. "We'll now sing *together*" is as clear as "We'll now sing *all together*." If the sentence makes sense without *all* and you want the full expression, use *all together*. If the sentence is out of kilter using *all*, obviously the word wanted is *altogether*.

allude/refer

Aren't alluding to something and referring to it the same action?
The words *allude* and *refer* are not to be interchanged as though they were synonyms. To *allude* is to mention indirectly. It may be only a hint. To *refer* is to mention directly, to name a specific person or thing. You refer to an author when you state his name. You allude to his works if you speak about them without a direct reference.

alma mater/arctic

Two questions on pronunciation. How are *alma mater* and *Arctic* pronounced?
The first may be pronounced either al-mah MAY-ter or ahl-mah MAH-ter. The second allows no choice: ARK-tic. Note the *k* sound in the first syllable.

almost

I hear *almost* misplaced so frequently that I would like to know what rule governs its proper placement?
Place *almost*, with its sense of not quite, near the word it modifies. "Roger *almost* has a perfect record" needs a shifting of *almost*: "Roger has *almost* a perfect record."

> **Note:** A common failing is to use *most* for *almost* to mean very nearly in a sentence such as "*Most* everyone was there." The adverb *almost*, of course, is required (*most* is a pronoun, adjective, and adverb, but as an adverb, it serves only in the comparison of adjectives and adverbs). Since *almost* is an adverb only, it should not modify a noun, as in "It was an *almost* disaster." In "It was an *almost*-closed session," the hyphen should be omitted — "It was an *almost* closed session."

alone

1. I was criticized for ambiguity when I said, "I will handle this matter alone." Was the criticism deserved?
For the sake of clarity, bear in mind that *alone* may mean either unaccompanied (that is, by myself) or only. If you had said *by myself*, if that is what you meant, you would not have been criticized. Of course, if

you meant that you would handle only this matter, *only* should have replaced *alone*.

2. Is this sentence written clearly: "He bought that property alone"? It is not, since the sense might be either that he did not buy that property with others or that he bought just that one property. Say, "He *alone* bought . . ." or "He bought *only* that property."

along with

"The architect along with five assistants are coming early." Please criticize.

The parenthetical phrase introduced by "along with" does not create a grammatical plural when accompanying the subject. This means that the addition introduced by "along with" does not affect the number of the verb. Hence the need for the singular *is*. Commas, although unnecessary, help clarify: "The architect, along with his five assistants, *is* coming early."

> **Note:** The principle previously mentioned, that the number of a subject and verb is not altered by intervening words beginning with *along with*, applies to such parenthetical expressions as *together with*, *in addition to*, *as well as*, *besides*, and plain *with*. If the subject is plural ("The boys, *as well as* their father, *are* boarding the train"), naturally the verb is plural. If the subject is singular, the verb is singular, despite the number of the noun in the parenthetical phrase ("The coach, with all the gym teachers, *has* entered the field").

also → ADVERB

What may be said of this sentence: "He studied French, also Hebrew"?

Also, an adverb meaning in addition to, is being misused as a conjunction. The sentence is corrected by substituting *and* or *and also* for *also*.

> **Note:** Many grammarians frown on the use of *also* when it begins a sentence, even if used adverbially. Rather than "*Also* the schedule will have sessions listed," they would recommend "The schedule will *also* have. . . ."

alternate[ly]/alternative[ly]

1. Two of the most confusing words in the language are *alternate* and *alternative*. Would you distinguish between them?

As a verb *alternate* means to change back and forth ("Day *alternates* with night"). As a noun *alternate* means substitute ("Whitman will serve as an *alternate*"). As an adjective *alternate* means by turns, first one then the other ("There were *alternate* highs and lows in the market today").

Alternative means another choice. Originally it encompassed only two choices. The word derives from Latin *alter*, meaning "one of two" or "the other of two." Today most critics believe that the number should not be restricted to two, which makes *alternative* a synonym of "choice" ("We now have four *alternatives* from which to choose").

> Note: If you use *alternative* only in its traditional sense — one of two — you will be on solid ground. Although their number is declining, some critics do not accept the extended sense of *alternative* and still restrict its use to a choice between two. Bear in mind that the synonyms *alternative* and *choice* may have different connotations. A *choice* is made, or not made, of a person's free will. Inherent in *alternative* is a sense of compulsion. "Your *alternatives* are to pay the fine or go to jail." Usually the verb *alternate* is followed by *with*. The verb and the noun are stressed on the first syllable — AL-ter-nate. The stress of *alternative[ly]* is on the second syllable — al-TERN-a-tive[ly].

2. What pitfalls should one avoid when using the word *alternatives*?
Alternatives are joined by *and*, not *or*: "The *alternatives* are victory *and* (not *or*) surrender." And they are not to be modified by *other*: "The *alternative* (not *the other alternative*) is to visit France." The combination *the other alternative* is as redundant as *two alternatives*. Do not say, "They had no *alternatives*." Say, "They had no *alternative*."

although/whereas/while

Please distinguish among the uses of *although*, *whereas*, and *while*.
Although expresses concession ("*Although* you have not established your credit, we will honor your order"). *Whereas* expresses contrast ("For English you receive four credits, *whereas* for typing, only two"). *While* expresses time ("We will clean the shop *while* the boss is away").

> Note: The words *although* and *though* are synonyms and may be interchanged if either is suitable. *Although* is favored to introduce a sentence ("*Although* it is raining, we will leave"). *Though* is usually employed internally ("Busy *though* she was, she had time to pet her dog") and to link single words ("happy *though* broke"). Be careful not to use *while* to mean "although" or "whereas" if it might be confusing. In "*While* you slept, I read," *while* is apparently being used as a conjunction of duration. But if what was intended was "*Although* (or *whereas*) you slept, I read," *while* is being misused.

alumnae/alumni

1. How are *alumnae* and *alumni* pronounced?
Alumnae rhymes with knee. *Alumni* rhymes with nigh. These are anglicized pronunciations. The Latin pronunciation is the reverse.

> Note: Do not say, "Andy is an *alumni* of Lehigh University." Say, "Andy is an *alumnus* . . . ," the singular masculine form of *alumni*.

2. Are women graduates referred to as *alumnae* or *alumni*?
Alumnae is the Latin plural of *alumna*, a woman graduate. But the masculine form *alumni* now includes graduates of both sexes and therefore serves two functions — a masculine plural and a mixed plural.

always may

Is it correct to say, "The car always may be used on weekends"?
The adverb is misplaced. It should not precede but follow the first auxiliary. Make it "The car *may always be used* on weekends," placing the adverb between *may* and *be*.

> Note: Another common misplacement that comes to mind is the adverb *surely*, as in "He *surely* will come." Improved is "He will *surely* come."

amateur/novice

Are the words *amateur* and *novice* synonyms?
They are not. An *amateur* does the favored activity as a pastime, not as a profession, even though the skill involved may equal a professional's. A *novice* is a beginner in a field or an activity.

> Note: The derivation of *amateur* and *novice* leads to their current meanings. *Amateur* (Latin *amare*, "to love," through French *amateur*, "lover") is used to describe one who thoroughly enjoys a pastime. A *novice* (Latin *novus*, "new") is a beginner, a person who lacks experience. A close synonym of *novice* is *tyro* (Latin *tyro*, "a recruit"), an inexperienced person.

ambiguous/equivocal

If a person speaks with a forked tongue is he *ambiguous* or *equivocal*?
The speaker may be both, since those words mean "susceptible to two or more interpretations." Yet what they connote distinguishes their usage. An *ambiguous* statement is inadvertent; an *equivocal* one is deceitful. That is the crux of the difference between them. Remember that an *equivocation* is a lie.

> Note: Examples of ambiguous statements are "After the hoodlum robbed Tony, he ran away," which does not make clear who ran away. "The unionist who was welcomed enthusiastically waved hello" may mean "welcomed enthusiastically" or "enthusiastically waved."

among/amid

If you're in it, are you *among* it or *amid* it?
Both *among* and *amid* mean surrounded by or in the middle of. The difference between them lies in their usage. *Among* is employed when the reference is to more than two countable things ("One will see *among* my books three versions of Fowler"). *Amid* is used when what is re-

ferred to is uncountable. The reference is to inseparable things, a mass noun ("Sue is standing *amid* the flowers in the rock garden"; "*Amid* the debris he found his satchel"; "*Amid* all the confusion, Walt remained unperturbed").

> **Note:** At one time *amidst* was a common word, as was *amongst*. Today they are considered literary and old-fashioned. *Amid*, not quite so Victorian as *amidst*, is also a bookish term. Many writers replace it with *in* or *among*.

among/between

1. Is it true that *between* should be used of two persons or things and *among* of three or more?
Yes. The general rule is that *between* is used when the reference is to two persons, objects, or ideas ("This is just *between* Mom and Dad") and *among* when the reference is to three or more countable things ("The dispute *among* the Longs, the Ganers, and the Masons ought to be settled promptly"). An exception to this rule is made when more than two are involved but the items, considered individually rather than collectively, are linked to others. This means that they are being considered in pairs ("The Federal Government is empowered to regulate commerce *between* the states"; "A policy of compliance was reached *between* the five largest companies").

> **Note:** For some unaccountable reason the word *between* leads many speakers and writers to illogical and ungrammatical usages. Perhaps the most glaring solecism is the expression *"between you and I."* Prepositions, of which *between* is one, must be followed by pronouns in the objective case. *I* is a nominative form; *me* is an objective. Therefore, say *"between you and me,"* not *"between you and I."* Another is *between each*, as in *"Between each* inning, he ate a hot dog." *Between* implies two; *each* signifies one. To avoid this contradiction either use a plural noun after *between*, "*Between* the *innings* he ate a hot dog," or say, "*Between* one inning and the next he ate a hot dog." One more caution. The combination *between . . . and* is immutable. When a choice is to be made between two objects the proper connective is *and*, not *or*. Therefore do not say, "*Between* five *to* ten apartments are vacated every year," but "*Between* five *and* ten. . . ." And in "The agent said we could choose *between* Bermuda *or* the Virgin Islands," change the *or* to *and* — "*between* Bermuda *and* the Virgin Islands."

2. Is it not more emphatic, and therefore sometimes preferable, to say, "Nan may choose between this cake or else that one" rather than "between this cake and that one"?
Grammatically, the first example does not set well. Convention has long established that the two objects governed by *between* are to be connected by *and* and not by *or* or *or else*. The second example is worded correctly: "Nan may choose *between* this cake *and* that one."

amount/number

How are the words *amount* and *number* differentiated?
Amount is used of a unified mass (sand, gas); *number*, of countable objects. "Although the *amount* of food left is relatively small, the *number* of apples and oranges is large."

> Note: *Amount* refers to an aggregate—bulk, weight, sums ("Joe is carrying an intolerable *amount* of weight"; "The *amount* of money involved was staggering"). Do not use *amount* of items that can be counted in individual units. Therefore, do not say "The *amount* of people in the room is small." Use *number*. When the article *a* precedes *number* (*a number* of), a plural verb follows ("A number of cats *are* on the front lawn"). The combination *the number* takes a singular verb ("The number of students *is* smaller this year than last year's"). References to time, money, measurement, weight, volume, and fractions that state amount take a singular verb. The phrase "in the amount of" is often replaceable by *for* or *of*. "A draft *in the amount of* one thousand dollars" can be economically written: "A draft *for* one thousand dollars."

ampersand

Is it proper to use an ampersand (&) to replace *and*?
An ampersand, a typographical sign meaning *and*, should be used only where it is part of an established firm name (as indicated on a business letterhead). Otherwise avoid it.

> Note: *Ampersand* is alteration of *and per se and*, literally "& by itself = and."

am presently

present tense ∧   *present tense* ∧

Would a teacher be likely to say, "I am presently teaching at Baylor"?
Not an English teacher. Except when there is a need to express a contrast, using *presently* with a verb in the present tense is redundant. Omit *presently*.

and

1. I see *and* connecting all sorts of odd combinations. What rule governs its proper use?
And should connect wordings of equal rank. For example, not "Joe is well trained (adjective) and of the highest reputation" (phrase), but "Joe is well trained *and* highly reputable" or any other construction of words, phrases, and clauses that are of equal grammatical importance.

2. Is this sentence well written: "We had no hats, no raincoats, no rubbers"?
Omitting *and* before the last *no* makes for emphasis, but that device is not approved in serious writing.

3. May the conjunction *and* replace *not only . . . but also?*
It often may. If emphasis or delayed action is unimportant, prefer simple *and*. Instead of "He not only taught French but also spoke it when possible," say, "He taught French *and* spoke it when possible."

4. I've been told that a sentence should never begin with *and*. Right or wrong?
Wrong. And why shouldn't it? All authorities agree that this rule is a relic of Victorian days. The advice that should govern an introductory *and* is not to overuse and not to follow it with a comma.
  Note: A sentence may begin with *but*, just as one may begin with *and*.

5. Would you criticize this sentence: "Arnold did so well he became a millionaire, and his older brother peddled hot dogs at the stadium"?
The conjunction *and*, which implies addition, is misused. Since the sentence makes a contrast, the conjunction needed is *but*.

and/or

Is there any objection to this construction — *and/or?* It's a word-saver.
Word-saving is not always of paramount importance. Style is to be considered, too. The combination *and/or* is graceless, unsightly, and unnecessary. Rather than "five days in jail *and/or* a fifty dollar fine," prefer "five days in jail *or* a fine of fifty dollars or both."
  Note: Most authorities do not accept *and/or* in general, certainly not in formal, usage. In many instances *or* alone will suffice. The expression is acceptable, however, in legal documents and business transactions, and it is best confined to those writings.

angry

How do you distinguish between the use of *angry with* from *angry at?*
Angry with is applied to people ("I'm *angry with* my roommate"). *Angry at* (sometimes *about*) is used of animals and inanimate objects — a situation, an action, or a thing: "I'm *angry at* that stupid cat because he doesn't know when to come home"; "I'm *angry with* my neighbor and *angry at* his uncalled-for remarks."
  Note: The synonym for *angry* is *mad*, which is now used on almost all levels of English except, perhaps, the most formal. *Mad* is no longer restricted to its traditional meaning of "insane." But those who wish not to skirmish with purists had best avoid that word for *angry*.

ante-/anti-

How do the prefixes *ante-* and *anti-* differ in usage?
Ante- is Latin for "before"; *anti-*, Greek for "against" or "opposite" (*antebellum* means before the war; *antemeridian*, before noon). *Anti-* is

commoner: *antifacist*, one opposed to fascism, *antitoxin*, a drug opposed to the effects of poison.

> **Note:** Write solid all words prefixed by *ante-* or *anti-* unless the second element is capitalized (*anti-German, anti-American*) or begins with an *i* (*anti-industrialization, anti-intellectual*).

antecedent

1. What, if any, objection, is there to "In Lewis's *Babbitt*, he sets a new literary high"?

The pronoun *he* has no noun to refer to. A possessive form (*Lewis's*) may not serve as an antecedent. Correct by saying, "Lewis set a new literary high in his book *Babbitt*" or "When Lewis wrote *Babbitt*, he set a new literary high."

> **Note:** A pronoun must agree with its antecedent (its referent) in number, person, and gender. In "The girls who were selected are leaving," *girls* (plural, third person, feminine) is the antecedent of *who*, hence the plural verb *are leaving*. Remember that the case of the pronoun *who* is nominative, the subject of the verb *are leaving*. The pronoun is determined by the clause in which it stands.
>
> Generally a pronoun should follow its antecedent. It may precede it only when there is no chance for confusion. In "Throughout his school years, Jack never was late even once," *his* precedes with no disturbance in thought.

2. Do you object to "Everyone should watch their step" and, if so, why?

The subject of the sentence is the singular indefinite pronoun *everyone*. Any pronoun that follows the antecedent *everyone* must agree with it in number. Hence *their* should be corrected to *his*.

3. The report read: "The secretary assured Ronald that he would remain as manager if he became the vice president." Is this sentence as confusing to you as it is to me?

It is. The antecedent of a pronoun should be clearly recognizable. A failure to observe this rule can lead to serious misunderstanding. The sentence might be reconstructed as follows: "The secretary assured Ronald that he would remain as manager if he, the secretary, became vice president" or, better yet, "The secretary told Ronald, 'You will remain as manager if I become vice president'."

anticipate

Is it proper to say, "We anticipate a large crowd at today's football game"?

Depends on which usage critic you have faith in. Some would find no fault with the sentence. Others, and perhaps the majority, would say that it is incorrect to use *anticipate* to mean expect, which is certainly the better word for your example. Preferably employ *anticipate* when the sense is to act in advance of, to prevent, to forestall. A person might anticipate an expensive evening by taking along credit cards. Coming back to the example, it would satisfy the most demanding traditionalist if it read: "Because we *anticipated* a large crowd at today's game, we prepared more food than usual."

anxious/eager

Is it linguistically wrong to use *anxious* for *eager*?
It depends on the authority that you consult. *Anxious* implies uneasiness; *eager*, keen desire. One is *eager* or desirous (not *anxious*) to see a football game. In any use of *anxious* a certain amount of worry or concern should be present, as in "In view of the impending snow storm, we're *anxious* to leave."

> **Note:** Although the prevailing opinion favors the use of *anxious* when you would rather avoid something, and *eager* when you want it to happen, some authorities do not agree. They equate *anxious* and *eager*, contending that *anxious* meaning "eager" is now fully established and acceptable on any level of usage. Nevertheless, it is best to restrict *anxious* in this sense to informal language. "We are so *eager* to meet your fiancée" comes across much better than "We are *anxious* to meet your fiancée."

anymore

Should *anymore* be written this way, as one word, or should it be written as two words—*any more*?
Take your pick. Some writers spell it in one word, but most usage authorities prefer two. The trend, however, seems to be toward the single word, possibly on the analogy of *anyway, anywhere, anyone,* and other "any" words. Whichever spelling you choose, the important thing is to use this adverb of time only in an expressed negative sense— "We don't go there *anymore*" (or *any more*); or one that is implied— "Bob *hardly* sees his aunt *anymore*" (or *any more*). In one construction the key word must be spelled as two words: "Since we have five bags of pretzels, we don't need *any more*." In this example the sentence could survive without *any*.

> **Note:** Some authorities condone the use of *anymore* in an interrogative construction—"Will Dad be away *anymore*?" But this use, with its sense of "from now on," might be better expressed by "any longer." Or "Do the Clarks live in Pottstown *any more*?" sounds provincial; more idiomatic is "Do the Clarks still live in Pottstown?" It all boils down to a matter of taste.

anyone/anyone else

Is there an error in the sentence, "Al is more talented than anyone in our boy scout troop"?
If Al is a member of the troop, there is an error—the omission of the word *else*, which should follow *anyone*. The *else* (*anyone else*) is what stamps Al as a member of the group.

> **Note:** The indefinite pronoun *anyone* is a singular form and any accompanying pronouns should agree in number. Therefore, not "If *anyone* is ready, let them strap on their knapsacks," but "let *him* strap on *his* knapsack." To avoid sexism, some critics opt for the plural, as in the example, but it is a faulty use best avoided, certainly in edited writing. *Anyone* is the equivalent of *anybody*, but in formal discourse *anyone* is preferable. When the key word is written as two words (*any one*), it refers to a person or thing in a specific group ("We inspected all the apartments, but we didn't like *any one* of them"). Notice that the stress in *any one* is on *one*. When *anybody* is written as two words, it indicates a corpse ("Although they searched, the firemen did not find *any body* in the charred ruins"). This is an exception to the normal spelling of *anybody* as a solid word. One thing more. In a possessive form involving *anyone* and *else*, add *'s* to *else*, even though logically it should be attached to *anyone*. It is now idiomatic to say *anyone else's*.

anyplace/anywhere

Is it all right to use *anyplace* as here: "We couldn't find it anyplace"?
It is not all right, certainly not in formal prose. Although some dictionaries and other authorities regard *anyplace* as a synonym for *anywhere*, it is preferable not to equate them. When an adverb is needed, use *anywhere*, not *anyplace*, and you will encounter no criticism.

> **Note:** It is best to use *place* as the subject or the object of a verb or preposition, as in "*Any place* will be fine for the reception," "We can't find *any place* to park," and "I would go to *any place* under the sun to cure my arthritis." The adverbial use of *anywhere* rather than *any place* (or *anyplace*) applies to corresponding *where* adverbs: *somewhere* for *some place*, *everywhere* for *every place*, and *nowhere* for *no place*.
>
> Be particularly careful not to pluralize these adverbs. There is no such word as *anywheres*, *somewheres*, and so on. Not "We couldn't find it *anywheres*," but *anywhere*.

anyway/any way

Should I spell *anyway* as one word or as two—*any way*?
It depends on what is meant. The two-word spelling is used in all instances except when the sense is "in any case," "regardless," or "nevertheless." Then it is *anyway*: "*Anyway*, I think we will go." But "We shall dress in *any way* you suggest" (adjective *any* plus noun *way*).

> **Note:** A person who uses *anyways* ("*Anyways*, I think I'll go") is quickly stamped as uneducated. Be sure not to pluralize *anyway*.

apparatus

How is *apparatus* pronounced?
The word has two acceptable pronunciations—ap-pa-RAE-tus and ap-pa-RAT-us (a *ray* or a *rat*).

apparent/evident

The words *apparent* and *evident* have similar connotations, yet their usage is not the same. How should one distinguish between them?
The words are interchangeable in some contexts but distinguishable in others. Both *apparent* and *evident* are defined as being easily seen or understood, but *apparent* has the further definition of appearing as such but not necessarily so. Therefore, because *apparent* connotes contradictory concepts, meaning either seeming or obvious, discriminating speakers and writers use this word cautiously. There are times when *apparent* may be safely used, no matter what it connotes; for example, "Despite his *apparent* love for his country, it is now evident that he has been a spy." *Evident*, since its only meaning is clear to the understanding (or easily understood), is never ambiguous.

> **Note:** The adverb form of *evident*, which is *evidently*, is another story. It may be as dangerous a word to use as the adverb *apparently*, for each may be taken to mean either seemingly or obviously. If a man holding his stomach suddenly leaves a room, and someone says, "*Apparently* he is ill" or "*Evidently* he is sick," did the speaker mean *seemingly* or *undoubtedly*? Safer diction calls for *probably*, if that is what is meant, or *clearly*, if there is no doubt. One more caution. Do not say that a person died of an *apparent* heart attack. An apparent heart attack is not fatal. Say, "He died, *apparently* of a heart attack."

apprehend/comprehend

How are the words *apprehend* and *comprehend* distinguished?
Although both verbs mean to understand, to *apprehend* is to grasp the meaning of something; to *comprehend* is to understand it fully. It may be said that to apprehend is to bite into something; to comprehend, to digest it.

> **Note:** *Apprehend* has two other meanings, to anticipate fearfully and to seize or arrest. The adjective *apprehensive* means feeling alarmed, afraid, worried. It is used oftener than *apprehend*.

apropos

How is the word *apropos* used?
Meaning with respect to something, it is preferably not followed by *to*

(not *apropos to*) but by *of* ("*apropos of* our recent conversation") or by no preposition: "The manager's talk was *apropos* (pertinent) today."

apt/liable/likely

What is the difference in usage between *apt*, *liable*, and *likely*?
Apt suggests a habitual tendency ("Slovenly people are *apt* to litter a sidewalk"). *Liable* implies exposure to something undesirable or unpleasant ("A person is *liable* to lose friends if he doesn't call them once in a while"). *Likely* emphasizes probability. Something likely to happen probably will ("It is *likely* that we'll leave for France this month").

> **Note:** Avoid using *apt* for *liable* (to mean probable) and do not use *liable* for *likely*, as in "Every morning you are *liable* to see Ron fishing." In the correct use of *liable* something disadvantageous is indicated: "If you violate the speed laws, you are *liable* to arrest." *Likely* is an adjective meaning probable ("It is a *likely* result") and an adverb meaning probably. In its adverbial use, convention dictates that *likely*, when used with a verb in the future tense, should be accompanied by a modifier, such as *most*, *quite*, or *very*. Therefore, although "It is *likely* to rain tomorrow" is correctly put (*likely* is an adjective), "It will *likely* rain tomorrow" is not. Correct by adding *most*—"It will *most likely* rain tomorrow." Note the illogicality of that convention, since it does not apply to such adverbs as *probably* or *possibly*. They need no modifying escort.

aren't I

Is it proper for my son to say, "Aren't I a good boy"?
The expression *aren't I* is colloquially acceptable, although grammatically contradictory—*I* is a singular subject, *are*, a plural verb (no one would say "I are not"). Fowler called the expression *aren't I* "colloquially respectable," which has been a justification for many cultivated speakers to use it as a genteelism and thus avoid the culturally unacceptable *ain't*, a low-level word eschewed by anyone who wants to appear educated.

as

1. What pronoun should follow *as* in this sentence: "Bessy likes Harry as much as *I* (or *me*)"?
I is correct if what is meant is "as much as I do"; *me* is correct if Bessy likes Harry and me equally. Clearly, the case of the pronoun that follows the second *as* determines the meaning.

> **Note:** The pronoun following *as* should be in the form it would take if the sentence had been completed: "We say that our relatives are as good as *we*" (not *us*). If completed, the sentence would read "as good as *we are*." "The Blue Jays are as aggressive as *they*"—"as they are"; therefore

not "as aggressive as *them*." The nominative case of the pronoun is used because it is the subject of an understood verb. In "She notified him as well as (she notified) *her*," the pronoun is in the objective case because it is the object of the understood verb *notified*.

Do not employ *as* to introduce an enumeration. Instead use *such as*. Not "I enjoy visiting Midwestern states, *as* Nebraska, Iowa, and Kansas," but "states *such as* Nebraska."

Be alert when employing the correlative conjunctions *as . . . as* not to omit the second *as*. In "Pearl sews as well if not better than her cousin Jean," *as* is required after *well*—"as well *as* if not better than."

2. "Kevin couldn't hear the bell as he was listening to the radio." Something seems wrong. What would you say?
It is best not to use *as* as a conjunction replacing *since* or *because*. Although an equivalent, *as* has a further sense of "while." Preferably use *since* or *because* and avoid ambiguity.

3. In comparison should we use *as . . . as* or *so . . . as*, or doesn't it matter?
It doesn't matter. Both formulas are acceptable but note that many careful writers and speakers prefer *so . . . as* in negative statements ("Jane is not *so* tall *as* Rachel") and *as . . . as* in positive ones ("Rachel is *as* tall *as* Andy").

4. What is your opinion of this sentence: "As the time grew short, the people became fidgety"?
I think it is fuzzy because the word *as* is ambiguous. It may be conveying the idea of time (which needs *when*) or of cause (which needs *because*): "*When* the time grew short, the people became fidgety" or "*Because* the time grew short."

5. I recently heard on television this statement: "Millie said I don't know as I can." Is *as* used correctly?
On a low level, yes. But in better speech or writing the conjunctive use of *as* should not displace *if*, *that*, or *whether* ("Millie said I don't know *if* [*that* or *whether*] I can"). In strict formal prose prefer *whether*.

6. Should we say, "He was appointed dean" or "as dean"?
It is not idiomatic to follow the verb *appointed* with *as*. Say appointed dean. The same ruling would hold if *named* had been used instead of *appointed*.

as far as

The newspaper report said, "As far as the investigative clues that might uncover the reason for the kidnapping, nothing evidentiary has developed." Was *as far as* used correctly?
The expression *as far as* is being used as a conjunction to introduce a clause, but since a clause must contain a verb, the example needs

correcting — a verb following "kidnapping." That verb should be "are concerned."

as good as

1. My son said, "He as good as volunteered." How does that sentence rate?

The wording *as good as* indicates a comparison, but no comparison is being made. More desirable than *as good as* is *practically*. It's shorter and more accurate. ("He *practically* volunteered").

2. We learned from our supervisor that we were as good or better than the other employees. Is there a better way of putting it?

There is. The sentence needs the addition of another *as*: "We learned . . . that we are as good *as* or better than the other employees." The second *as* is essential to complete the comparison.

as how

1. Did my dentist get his teeth into this one correctly: "The professor explained as how bonding was the better process"?

His bite was off. Rather than *as how*, he should have used *that*: "The professor explained *that* bonding was the better process." *As how* should not replace *that*.

2. Is *seeing as how* in "He was leaving early *seeing as how* dark clouds were forming" objectionable phrasing?

The expression is substandard and should be replaced by *because, since,* or *considering that*. *Seeing as how* sounds as if it were cultivated in a rural area.

as if/as though

Is there a preference between *as if* and *as though*? Our group has argued about this for two weeks.

Each of these expressions is acceptable. In a statement contrary to fact, the verb following must be in the subjunctive mood — "It looks *as if* (or *as though*) it *were* about to snow." Formalists prefer *as though* over *as if*.

Note: The subjunctive mood is moribund, although in constructions contrary to fact it exhibits life, especially among the educated. But be not surprised at seeing the indicative used even in those cases. The most common error is using *like* for *as if* or *as though*. Examples: "It looks *like* it's going to snow"; "Beryl is acting *like* he is drunk." Note the conversion to the indicative mood following *like*. With *as if* or *as though*, *is* would be replaced by *were*.

as much as

Is there anything wrong in saying *as much as* in "*As much as* I dislike Arthur, I admire his artistic ability"?
Yes. The first *as* should be omitted. Since a comparison is not being made, the sense is concessive—in effect, "Although I dislike Arthur," which in the example rightly becomes "*Much as* I dislike Arthur. . . ." Drop the first *as*.

> **Note:** The expressions *as much as* or *as good as* meaning practically ("He *as much as* told me"; "Ray *as good as* threatened to quit") are colloquial. *As much as* and *as good as* should compare the quantity or the goodness of two things, which is not so in the examples.

as to

1. Is it true that the phrase *as to* is a poor choice in good writing?
Yes and no. Usually *as to* should be omitted. For example, in "Gary's idea *as to* what to buy was a good one," *as to* should be excised and *about* substituted. But *as to* may begin a sentence to bring a subject to early attention: "*As to* Ferdinand, we're sure he'll play."

2. Is the sentence, "The question as to whether we should adjourn has not been settled," expressed in approved English?
Careful speakers and writers would not use *as to* before *whether*. They would say, "The question *whether* . . . ," presenting the question in direct form.

> **Note:** Avoid using *as to* when a single word will do. For example, rather than "There was some doubt *as to* the speaker's point of view," *about* would do better. In "They adopted rules *as to* conduct," *of* is idiomatic. In "They disagreed *as to* the meaning," *on* is a concise improvement.

as well as

1. What does this sentence mean: "Alice tangos as well as Mickie"?
Out of context, one cannot say. It may mean that Alice's tangoing is as good as Mickie's or that Alice also tangos. The sentence should be recast to indicate the intended sense: "Alice and Mickie tango equally well" or "Both Alice and Mickie tango."

2. Our teacher read us this sentence: "I, as well as she, am going." Is it grammatically correct?
It is—awkward, but correct. Backing up a bit, you would say, "He, as well as she, is going" (*as well as* does not affect the number of the verb, hence *is*). Now using *I,* you would have to say, "I, *as well as* she, am going," *am* being the correct form of verb to accommodate subject *I.* Of course, the sensible thing to do is to reconstruct: "We're both going."

as yet

Is the phrase *as yet* acceptable?
Although *as yet* is invariably inferior to *yet* alone, respected writers have used it. Nevertheless, it is preferable to find a suitable substitute: "up to the present time," "thus far," or an equivalent phrase. But if *as yet* meaning so far begins a sentence ("*As yet* we have not heard"), *yet* needs *as* to escort it.

> **Note:** *As yet* is not used with a simple past tense, as in "*As yet* we did not reply." It regularly takes a perfect tense, as in the foregoing example, "As yet we *have* not replied."

as you (may) know

Is the phrase *as you know* preferred to *as you may know*?
The phrases belong in different contexts. If you know that your hearer knows, you may say *as you know*. But if you aren't sure your hearer knows, prefer *as you may know*.

at about

Is the combination *at about* objectionable?
Using those words in tandem is incongruous. Consider "The Wilkes-Barre bus arrived *at about* 11:15 a.m." *At* indicates a precise time; *about*, an approximation. Omit either *at* or *about* depending on what you mean.

> **Note:** Some critics approve of the use of *at about* if *about* is being used in the sense of "approximately." But who can tell what a speaker has in his mind. Usually the *at* is superfluous, and on that ground alone, it does not belong—"We will meet you *about* (not *at about*) four o'clock."

at/in

How would you distinguish between the uses of *at* and *in*?
I use *in* to mean within ("We live *in* Phoenix") and *at* to designate a local point or a point along a course ("We'll meet *at* Pine Way and Ash Street").

> **Note:** Critics are less than unanimous in deciding on the correct use of *at* and *in*, two of the most widely used prepositions in the English language. A guideline, long followed, was to use *in* for large areas (*in* Wyoming) and *at* for small areas (*at* Birchrunville). But who decides whether a place is large enough to merit *in* or small enough to be denigrated with *at* is an unanswerable question. Idiom usually tells us what is right, which means we are relying on our ear. But we cannot in every case depend on it. For example, when an airplane descends, does it arrive *in* or *at* St. Louis? The consensus is that there is no workable principle that governs. Even your ear won't always help.

A last thought. Do not use *at* as a tag-along when indicating location, a common error in a sentence such as "Where's he at?" *Where* is an adverb; *at* is a preposition helplessly grasping for an object. Omit *at*.

A to Z/A to O

Is it just as well, when the full spectrum or range of something is meant, instead of saying it is the *A to Z* to say it is the *A to O*?
I should not be inclined to use *A to O* because it might not be understood. If you prefer Greek, at least spell out the names of the first and last letters of the Greek alphabet. Say *alpha to omega*. They are more likely to indicate what you mean. However, in general usage the phrase *alpha and omega* (note *and,* not *to*) has come to mean "the first and the last" rather than a broad sequence or range as implied in *A to Z*.

attenuate/extenuate

How can I learn to distinguish *attenuate* from *extenuate*?
Both words basically mean to thin out. An athlete's trim body has been *attenuated* through exercise. *Extenuate,* used in law to suggest circumstances that make a crime less serious or less reprehensible, has within it the sense of *excuse,* but *excuse* should not be equated with it. To *extenuate* is to mitigate, to palliate. Othello's "Nothing extenuate . . ." means not to soften the seriousness of any of his misdeeds, but to tell them as they actually were.

> Note: *Attenuate* means to make slender, fine, or small, but it also means to weaken. The word is often used to suggest a reduction in force, value, or amount. Be careful to see that your context is unambiguous. And be careful to use *extenuate* with reference only to the fault or offense that is made (*extenuating* circumstances), not to the person.

audience

A publisher wrote: "The book will have a wide audience." Is *audience* the proper word?
Audience, from Latin *audire,* means to hear. Readers do not hear; they read—they are a readership. However, with the sanction of most dictionaries, many people use *audience* for all communication recipients— spectators, listeners, readers. In fact, most authorities approve of the application of *audience* to readers.

authored

Is it undesirable to say, "She has authored four books"?
The coinage of verb *authored* from noun *author* has not been accepted

by discriminating writers. Avoid it. Say, "She has *written* (or *is the author of*) four books."

> **Note:** An author is a writer, usually one who earns a living from writing. Converting *author* into a transitive verb is far from uncommon but this practice is not standard English. It is considered falsely economical journalese and offensive to the ear.

authority

What prepositions does *authority* take?
It takes *for* ("The *Times* is our *authority for* the report"); *on* ("Einstein was an *authority on* mathematics"); and *over* ("The chef has *authority over* our daily menus").

awful

May *awful* be used to mean disagreeable, bad, or ugly?
General usage has made those senses acceptable. No longer is "awe inspiring" a widely understood meaning. We say, "The weather is awful"; "My friend feels awful"; "That is an awful-looking dress." Nevertheless, on a formal level, find a more suitable word.

> **Note:** In informal usage the adjective *awful* is often converted into an adverb meaning *very* ("I'm *awful* tired). The adverbial form *awfully* also does duty for *very* ("It is an *awfully* large house").
>
> The dictionary defines *awfully* to mean *dreadfully* and *terribly,* which makes one wonder what is happening to the language when hearing, so frequently, something like "I've had an *awfully* good time because the play was *awfully* good." How can something dreadful or terrible be good?

B

back of/in back of

Are *back of* and *in back of* accepted phrases?
According to some authorities, *back of* and *in back of* are informal phrases, but others accept them as standard. The objection raised by one critic is that they are wordy and stylistically unattractive. That is a good point, since *behind* is more economical and neater while displeasing no one. Prefer it. Change "The field is *back of* (or *in back of*) the red building" to "*behind* the red building."

> Note: *Back of* is a colloquial contraction of *in back of* and on that account has not been welcomed by some authorities. The sister phrase *in front of,* the corresponding opposite of *in back of,* has legitimate standard acceptance. No one questions its propriety. Nevertheless, *before* should be considered a replacement. It is shorter and, if it will do, preferable.

backward/backwards

Does a person look *backward* or *backwards*?
Either adverb may serve when used to mean in reverse order or direction ("Tony is skating *backwards*" or *backward*). The shorter term is preferred. Furthermore, since a person looks *forward,* for the sake of euphony, *backward* is a better choice ("Pop rocked *forward* and *backward*"). *Backward* is also an adjective meaning progressing slowly, bashful, facing the rear (a *backward* boy, a *backward* glance).

bad/badly

1. Is it proper to say, "Horace felt badly about his son's failure"?
Badly is not the word to use. It should be replaced by *bad,* since *feel,* a linking verb, takes adjectives, not adverbs. Adverb *badly* is used when the sense of touch, or feel, is meant. A person whose fingers are numb feels *badly.*

> Note: Verbs of the senses—those that describe conditions, not actions—are properly followed by adjectives. Those verbs are called copulative, or linking, verbs because they tie what follows to the subject and are therefore equivalent to the verb *be,* a form of which can usually replace a linking verb. We say, "Bob *looks* tall," which translates into "Bob *is* tall." "The orange *tastes* sweet," which says that the orange *is* sweet. One more example of a linking verb and adjective versus an action verb and adverb. If we say that the dog smells bad, we mean that the dog needs a bath. Verb *smell* links adjective *bad* to subject *dog.* If we say that the dog smells badly, we mean that the dog has a cold or has a defective smelling

apparatus. In this case adverb *badly* is an adverb of manner modifying *smells*.

Verbs other than those of the senses may be copulative verbs. The most common are *be, appear, become,* and *seem.* Some others are *go, grow, keep, lie, prove, remain, run, sit, stay, turn,* and *wax.* "The cats are *lying dormant*"; "Sheila *stays* (or *remains*) *happy*"; "The trees *grew straight*"; "Alergnon always *waxes elegant.*"

2. May *badly* be used to mean very much?
Many authorities say yes. But it seems more sensible to say, "Your aunt misses you very much" rather than *badly,* and, "The screens are very much (not *badly*) in need of repair."

> **Note:** Personal preference aside, the consensus is that *badly,* meaning very much or greatly, is acceptable on all levels of usage ("*badly* in need of immediate attention"). And saying that a man was badly injured is also approved by critics who equate *badly* with *severely* in this context.

balance/remainder

Why is it better to use the word *remainder* instead of *balance* when talking about the rest of the day?
The word *balance* was derived from a Latin term meaning "two plates," like those on a scale. Hence the sense of *balance* has to do with two matters or items. If you reduce the credit side of your ledger, you affect the debit side, making the balance smaller. But when referring to a part of a day, use *remainder* or *rest.* (And between those two, *rest* is a better choice.) Save *balance* for matters involving your checkbook.

> **Note:** Informally, *balance* is frequently used as a replacement for *rest* or *remainder,* and particularly when applied to the remaining portion of a day. There is nothing wrong with this usage provided it is confined to colloquial speech.

bank on

Is the phrase "bank on," as in "I always bank on my roommate to see me through French," regarded as good English?
It is not. The phrase *bank on* meaning depend on, count on, is colloquial. In standard English we use *rely on* or *have confidence in.*

> **Note:** A sister colloquial expression is *take stock in,* as in "I wouldn't *take stock in* anything he tells me." The sense is to put faith in or rely on.

barely

May a person say, correctly, "I have barely no more left"?
Not correctly. *Barely* carries a negative idea and therefore should not be used with another negative. Change *no more* to *any more* and convert the sentence into an affirmative: "I have *barely* any more left."

Note: *Barely* is followed by clauses introduced by *when*, not by *than* ("*Barely* had the orchestra begun playing *when* [not *than*] a fire broke out"). The sense of *barely* is by the narrowest of margins ("He *barely* missed striking that culvert").

B.C./A.D.

What are the proper placements for B.C. and A.D.?
B.C., although the *B* means before, follows the year ("Cicero was born in 106 B.C."). A.D. precedes the year ("Pompeii was destroyed A.D. 79"). Observe that *in* does not introduce A.D. Latin *anno* means *in the year*. Some stylists, however, approve of the combination *in A.D.*, possibly on the assumption that many people do not know that *in* is included in the word *anno*.

> **Note:** Although a century cannot be in the year of anything, A.D., despite the illogicality, may follow *century* for the sake of brevity and clarity ("Many ancient tombs were discovered in the fourth *century* A.D.").

? because

Does it matter grammatically whether I say, "*Because (since or as)* Sidney was leaving, his wife began to cry"?
Not grammatically. *Because, since,* and *as* all mean for the reason that. But *as* is a poor choice, since it has both a temporal and a causal sense. It could be construed as a reference to time, the equivalent of "*While* Sidney was leaving." If *while* was meant, use it, not *as*. If the cause for the crying was that Sidney was leaving, use either *because* or *since*. Again, not the ambiguous *as*.

begging the question

What is meant by "begging the question"?
First, what *begging the question* is not. It is not a refusal to answer a question directly. It is the assuming as true, in a discussion, of the very point you are trying to prove. For example, if the argument is over whether there is a God, and you contend that of course there is a God because He controls the world, you are assuming the truth of something that you are trying to prove.

begin/start/commence

I was surprised when I was told not to use the word *start* so often for *begin*. I had thought that *start*, a short word, was a good one. Is there anything wrong with it?
At one time *start* was considered a colloquialism for *begin*, but no longer. It is now accepted on every level of usage as the equivalent

of both *begin* and *commence,* although the words are used in different contexts. For example, we start a race; we start a motor; but we begin to grow bald; and we begin to look old. True, *begin* and *commence* are interchangeable, but *commence* is so formal a word that its use is best restricted to formal or ceremonial occasions.

> Note: The beginning implied by the word *start* is quicker, more sudden, than that implied by *begin. Begin* suggests a more gradual, slower, beginning. Jockeys try to get a fast start, but a meal is said to begin.
>
> In negative comparisons *begin to,* with the adverbial sense "in the least," is idiomatic but colloquial. "Bobbie couldn't *begin to* make soup like her mother's" in effect says, "Bobbie couldn't *in the least* (or *at all*) make soup like her mother's."

(in) behalf of/(on) behalf of

In behalf of and on behalf of are so similar that they surely must be synonymous. Are they?
Not at all. *In behalf of* means in the interest of or for the benefit of ("Our company contributed a large sum *in behalf of* homeless boys"); *on behalf of* means on the part of or as the agent of ("A lawyer acts *on behalf of* a client"; "The principal thanked the graduating class for the gift *on behalf of* the teachers").

> Note: Some authorities do not agree that the terms have different significations. They contend that the terms are interchangeable and that no distinctions apply. Which means that a writer has support for whichever tack he decides to take. But undoubtedly many careful writers and speakers look askance at that trend and abide by conventional usage. For them, a person acting *in behalf of* may be acting on his own, independently. He has no authority. But if he acted *on behalf of,* then there would be an agency relationship; an authorization to act would have been granted. In some constructions, either phrase may serve. In those instances neither phrase is exclusive. But think before writing.

being as/being that

Are the expressions being as and being that, as in "Being that it's warm today, we'll go swimming," acceptable English?
The combinations *being as* and *being that* are substandard and therefore should never be used. The English language has many substitutes to replace these unwanted expressions: *as, because, inasmuch as, since,* and so forth. Use the word that is appropriate in the particular context.

> Note: Two sister substandard expressions are *as how* and *seeing as how.* They, too, are vague and wordy and should be replaced by one of the previously suggested words. In *"Being as how* I'm already wet, I may as well wash the dog," change *being as how* to *because.*

belles-lettres

What is *belles-lettres*?
Belles-lettres is defined as the finer form of literature, such as poetry and essays, regarded for its aesthetic value rather than for its instructive or informative content.

> Note: *Belles-lettres* is plural in form but is used with a singular verb. It is pronounced bel-LET-r, with a silent *s*.

beside/besides

Should I say, "Two soldiers sat on the bench *beside* or *besides* me"?
Either *beside* or *besides* is proper in that sentence, depending on the meaning. Preposition *beside* means next to or at the side of, as in "My aunt sat *beside* me at the dinner table." Adverb *besides* means in addition to or over and above, as in "Dick owns two cars *besides* this one"; "*Besides* the lecture there was a concert." When *besides* means except, it is a preposition ("No one loved him *besides* his mother"). Coming back to the example, if what was meant was that two soldiers sat next to you, *beside* would be the word to use there. If what was meant was that two soldiers were sitting on the bench in addition to you, *besides* would convey that thought.

better/best

1. We use *better*, not *best*, when comparing two things. Why, therefore, do we say, "Put your *best* foot forward"?
It does sound silly, or ungrammatical, when you stop to think about it. But the expression is so well established that it is considered idiomatic.

2. Our teacher said, "Tom and Jack have been nominated. Now may the best man win." Did she say it correctly?
When a choice is offered between two persons or things, the one selected is the better one, not the best. The comparative form *better* applies to two; the superlative, to three or more. But some usage critics insist that "the best of two" is now an accepted expression in standard English. Considering its widespread usage, the authorities certainly have numbers on their side.

> Note: *Better* and *best* are both adjectives and adverbs ("Tom's bat is *better* than Randy's"—adjective; "Randy bats *better* than Tom"—adverb; "Audrey was awake the *best* part of the night"—adjective; "Barbara sings *best* as a soloist"—adverb).

better/more

Should we say we like this town better than that one?
Properly, you should say you like this town *more* than that one. *Like* is

a word of quality. To express the degree that you like it, you need a quantitative adverb. *More* is such an adverb, not *better*. Hence, to repeat, you like this town (or that person, or that cocktail) *more* than some other.

> **Note:** The general use of *better* as a replacement for *more* is now widely accepted. It is suggested by authorities, however, that although *better*, in the sense of *more*, is approved for formal writing, the preference for *more* still remains. Indeed, some authorities take a jaundiced view of *better* as a replacement for *more*. They do not agree that "Alex waited the better part of an hour" is acceptable English except as a colloquialism. They would argue that no part of an hour is better than another and would recommend a recasting: "Alex waited the greater part of an hour."

better than

1. Does *better than* mean "more than" or "less than"?
This informal expression could mean either one. In "I stood in line *better than* an hour," the sense is *more than*. In "I made the trip in *better than* an hour," the sense is *less than*.

2. My pastor said his choir sings better than any choir he's heard. Was his statement worded correctly?
It was not. He should have said, *"better than any other* choir." A comparison with other persons or things in the same class requires the word *other* to exclude the one compared.

> **Note:** If the classes are different, *other* would not be applicable: "This choir is the best of any I have heard." No *other*.

between you and I/myself

1. I often hear someone say "between you and myself" or "between my wife and yourself." Has the commonness of this usage given it sanction among authorities?
I don't know of any. You apparently recognize, as should everyone, that *between* is a preposition and must therefore take pronouns in the objective case; hence *between you and me* and *between my wife and you*. Using *myself* and *yourself*, as in the examples, is, in the opinion of some critics, a barbarism.

2. The phrase *between you and I*, or one like it, is very common. What alert is there to avoid this glaring error?
Remember that all prepositions, of which *between* is one, take pronouns in the objective case, not in the nominative. Hence *between you and me*.

> **Note:** It is thought that *I* in *between you and I* is a genteelism adopted by those who think that *me* is as incorrect as it is in "It is me." Not true. The overrefinement is misguided.

biannual/semiannual

What is the difference between *biannual* and *semiannual*?
There is none according to the dictionary. Each term means "twice a year." A distinction, however, has evolved in their usage. *Biannual* refers to two events or happenings that take place at any time during the year. A synonym is *semiyearly*. *Semiannual* is taken to mean a happening that occurs during the midyear—approximately six months after the beginning of a year.

> **Note:** A word involving a period of two years is *biennial*. It means every two years or lasting for two years. In the first sense *biyearly* is a synonym.

big/large/great

Do you approve of "Frank is a big man in his profession"?
A better word than *big* would be *great,* meaning a man of distinction. *Big* refers to physical size; *great* implies mental ability and outstanding qualities. Indeed, Napoleon was a great general but not a big one.

> **Note:** In many instances *big* and *large* are interchangeable in general usage, since each of these terms refers to size, quantity, and extent. We speak of a *big* (or *large*) stadium, a *big* (or *large*) area. But a tuned ear will select one of those words in preference to the other in certain contexts— a *big* talker, not a *large* talker; a man of *large* perspective, not of *big* perspective. The emphasis with *big* is usually on bulk or volume ("A rhinoceros is a *big* animal"; "My violin teacher has a small fiddle and a *big* nose").

bimonthly

If I am to receive a bimonthly check, am I to receive two checks a month or one every other month?
The question cannot be answered precisely because *bimonthly* has two irreconcilable definitions—"occurring every two months" and "occurring twice a month."

> **Note:** This term has been a rich source of confusion. Since a person cannot be certain whether *bimonthly* refers to an occurrence twice a month or every two months, it is safer to spell out what is meant—twice a month or every two months, or consider *semimonthly*. The best advice is not to use the ambiguous term *bimonthly*. A corresponding guideline, of course, applies to *biweekly*. That term also places one in a quandary, since it is defined as happening every two weeks and happening twice a week.

blame

What preposition is used with *blame*?
In standard idiomatic usage, *blame for* is the established phrasing ("The

sheriff *blamed* Tyson *for* the criminal's escape"). More and more, however, some authorities have come to sanction *blame on* ("We *blame* the accident *on* Bronson"), so that no longer need someone be *blamed for* a happening. The happening, according to them, may be assessed with blame.

> Note: Some careful writers are resisting the current trend to accept the combination *blame on* when applied to an inanimate object. Logically, only human beings and their institutions can be held responsible. However, logic is not winning the battle. "Blame on" is making steady headway. Which does not mean that you have to bend in the breeze. It is not yet a strong wind. Shun *blame it on me* for *blame me for it* or *place the blame on me,* and may I assure you, no one will blame you for it.

bloc/block

Is it all right to say, "My neighbor is a blochead"?
I don't know your neighbor, but *bloc* is used in ideological senses; *block,* in all others. The usual expression is *blockhead.*

> Note: A *bloc* is a group united for common action: a political bloc, a union bloc, a bloc of voters. *Block* is a word of many meanings. It is most often used in reference to a section of town bounded by consecutive streets: the *block* where we live.

both

1. Should we say, "We both bought a radio" or "We each bought a radio"?
It depends on how it was bought. Saying, "We *both* bought a radio" implies that the two of you bought a radio jointly—one radio. *Both* means "two considered together." Saying, "We *each* bought a radio" indicates a purchase of two radios, one for each of you. By the same token, it is obviously incorrect to say, "*Both* women wore a straw hat" unless the hat was large enough for both to get under at the same time. Say, "*Each* woman wore a straw hat."

> Note: Since *both* means two, be careful to avoid the redundant use of *both* with such words as *alike* ("They are *both* alike"), *equal* ("Both cousins are *equally* healthy"), or *together* ("The boys *both* swam together"). Omit the italicized words.
>
> The correct combination with *both,* one that is mandated by established idiom, is *both . . . and,* and not *both . . . or* or *both . . . as well as.* Say, "The audience *both* laughed *and* cried," not "The audience *both* laughed *as well as* cried." In "My aunts enjoy *both* marmalade *or* apple butter," *or* should be replaced by *and.*

2. Should one say, "Both of the men enjoy classical music" or "both men"?
One may properly use either construction, but since *of* implies separate

items rather than a single unit, preferably omit *of*.

> **Note:** Avoid such locutions as "Both of the other two books are anthologies" and "Both my uncles live in different cities." Consider carefully any sentence containing the word *both* to be sure that it is required or, to put it in the negative, that it is not redundant.

3. Don't "They both did it" and "Each did it" mean the same thing?
No, because *both* suggests two persons or objects together, whereas *each* points to an individual person or object ("Although *both* sisters were invited, *each* did not respond in the same way").

> **Note:** It is likewise incorrect for a customer, when examining two pitchers, to ask the salesman whether they both cost ten dollars. His reply, "No, each costs ten dollars; both pitchers cost twenty dollars," is grammatically correct. *Each* means individually. Which proves that the customer is not always right.

4. Is this said well: "Both applicants were not accepted"?
It is ambiguous because it contains the word *both* and a negative. Were the two rejected, or was one rejected and the other accepted? Reword affirmatively: "Both applicants were rejected" or "One was rejected; the other was accepted."

5. What do you think of the news report that said, "Both money and support for the community is required"?
It was wrongly worded. Plural subjects *(money and support)* take a plural verb, *are* in this case. Only if the dual subjects have been blended into a oneness ("Ham and cheese *is* my favorite dish"; "The wear and tear *was* more than expected") is a singular verb permitted.

> **Note:** *Both* is defined as relating to two or being two in conjunction. Two, being more than one, requires a plural form, and therefore *both* must take a plural verb. But *both* has its limitations. It is used of only two, which means you may not say that the chess games will be played in both France, Spain, and the Far East. In such a sentence *both* should be deleted. *Both* also is sometimes unnecessarily accompanied by *the*, as in "We saw *the both* of them off." Omit *the*.

both . . . and

What advice would you offer concerning the use of the correlative conjunction *both . . . and*?
Place *both* and *and* immediately before the words they connect so that the elements in the sentence are grammatically parallel. Not "The men *both* are tall *and* strong," but "The men are *both* tall *and* strong."

> **Note:** Do not place *both* before a preposition, as in "Our concern is a matter *both of* finances and personnel," but ". . . is a matter *of both* finances and personnel." For the sake of grammatical parallelism, however, a preposition may follow *both* if another preposition follows *and:* "He did it *both in* the winter *and in* the summer."

bouillon/bullion

Can you imagine a restaurant menu under "soups" listing *bouillon* instead of *bullion*?

I see your point, except that you have your words mixed up. *Bouillon* is a broth, *bullion* is gold or silver.

> **Note:** A homemade mnemonic device is to remember that *bouillon* has an *ou*, just as *soup* has. And note that although *bouillon* has a variant pronunciation of BOOL-yahn or bool-YAHN, the preferred pronunciation is BOOL-yahn.

bowdlerize

What has the word *bowdlerize* to do with Shakespeare?

Dr. Thomas Bowdler decided to remove all "vulgar" expressions from Shakespeare's works to make the plays "fit for perusal by our virtuous females." In 1818 his expurgated version was published. In general usage today, *bowdlerize* means to remove objectionable material arbitrarily from another's work.

> **Note:** Since to *bowdlerize* is to remove offensive passages from written material, if the material is not being censored, it is being deleted, not bowdlerized.

bring/take

The distinction between the verbs *bring* and *take* is elusive. Please help us.

These verbs, when pertaining to movement, are opposites. *Bring* indicates movement toward the speaker ("*Bring* me the *Times*"); *take,* away from the speaker ("*Take* this memo to the boss").

> **Note:** Some authorities exemplify the difference in usage between these verbs by saying *bring* implies come here with (to my place); *take* implies go there with (to another's place). If the direction these verbs imply is confusing, use *carry*. *Carry* has no sense of direction.

Britain

What is the difference between *Great Britain* and the *United Kingdom*?

Great Britain consists of England, Scotland, and Wales. The *United Kingdom* comprises Great Britain and Northern Ireland.

> **Note:** The British Isles is the most inclusive term. It includes the United Kingdom and surrounding islands. However, most people who speak of the British Isles are not thinking of the Orkneys, the Shetlands, or the Isle of Man. They are equating it with the United Kingdom. One caution: *Britain* is spelled as given, with only one *t*.

broach/brooch

Are the words *broach* and *brooch* pronounced alike?
Yes, both are pronounced with an *oh* sound, despite the difference in their spelling. *Broach* is a verb meaning to begin to talk about, to introduce, or to tap a cask. A *brooch,* a noun, is an ornamental breastpin.

broad/wide

Are the words *broad* and *wide* interchangeable?
They often are, since each word indicates horizontal extent (a *broad* or *wide* stream). But be careful to observe established idiom: *wide* mouth, *broad* forehead; *broad* back, *wide* hands; *broad* smile, *wide* eyes.

> **Note:** *Broad* is defined as wide from side to side, which makes it apply particularly to surfaces or areas, as in a *broad* beam, a *broad* field. If the stress is on space (the extent from one side to the other), *wide* is preferable: a room fifteen feet *wide*.

brothers-in-law

What is the plural of brother-in-law?
It is *brothers-in-law,* not *brother-in-laws.* But note that its plural possessive is brothers-in-law's. There you make the first word plural and the last a singular possessive.

> **Note:** Compound nouns are made possessive by adding *'s* to the element nearest the object possessed, which is the last word in the compound. Just as we say, "the attorney general's brief," so we say, "my brother-in-law's radio" and, in the plural, "my brothers-in-law's children."

bulk

Is *bulk,* a favorite word of my uncle's, used correctly in "Angelina did the bulk of the day's work before noon"?
The word *bulk* traditionally applied to a distinct mass or portion of something, a magnitude in three dimensions ("A warehouse of great bulk"). But despite the protests of grammarians, *bulk* has come to mean the necessary portion or the greater part of something. In that sense *bulk* has been elevated from a colloquial level to standard English.

> **Note:** Discriminating writers and speakers do not use *bulk* instead of *majority* where a count is possible. Rather than "The *bulk* of the members voted yes," they would use *majority*. And if dimension is not being considered, they would prefer *most* or *many* to *bulk*. Therefore, returning to the original example, "Angelina did *most* of the day's work before noon" is preferable to "the *bulk* of the day's work."

burgeoning

Was the choice of *burgeoning* a good one in "The population of India is burgeoning beyond belief"?

I think not. *Burgeoning* means budding, sprouting, a sudden emergence, and is correctly used of something just beginning to grow. Its popular sense is to continue to grow, which is not a true or exact meaning. It is best not to use *burgeoning* (the participial form of *burgeon* is the one most often used) when the plain word *growing* is accurate and will do.

> **Note:** Most writing stylists recommend that the word *burgeoning* be avoided because, first, using it to mean continuing to grow is controversial, and second, choosing a pretentious-sounding word shows poor judgment.

burglarize

If a man commits a burglary, what verb do we use to describe what he did?

There is no verb. A robber robs, a thief steals, but a burglar makes an entry to commit a felony. Some writers say the place was *burgled*. Few authorities accept that. Others say it was *burglarized*. More accept that verb, but it is still considered colloquial.

> **Note:** A verb to describe what a burglar does is essential to the English language, if only for the sake of economy. Possibly for that reason, some dictionaries now regard *burglarize* as standard English.

burned up/burned down

Is there a difference in meaning between "His house burned up" and "His house burned down"?

Paradoxical as those sentences seem, they mean the same thing. This is one of the wonders of the English language. And so with "The car slowed *up*" and "The car slowed *down*." In either case, it slowed.

business

Is the word *business* used properly in "You have no business being here"?

Business is being used in the example to mean the right, the word that should have been used: "You have no *right* to be here."

> **Note:** *Business* in the example is one of the many low colloquial, inexact uses of that word. Often we hear such expressions as "Mind your own *business*," meaning stay out of my affairs, and "Let's give him the *business*," meaning a rough time. In none of those uses is *business* employed according to a dictionary definition: the occupation, work, or trade in which one is engaged.

businessman

How is the term *big businessman* properly written?

It depends on what is meant. A *big businessman* is a big person.

A *big-business man* has a big business. The hyphen, or lack of one, distinguishes the meaning. This guideline of course applies to *small* as well.

bust/burst

May one use *bust* to mean *burst?*
Although the words *bust* and *burst* are synonyms, when the sense is a coming apart as by an explosion, use *burst* as the more appropriate word. A balloon *bursts.*

> Note: The principal parts of *burst* are *burst, burst, burst.* Of *bust,* they are *bust, busted, busted.* Dictionaries say that *bust* is the slang form of *burst* in the sense of explode or break out. It is informal in the sense of financial failure ("His business went *bust").* In *busting* a bronco and in *busting* a trust, it is considered standard.

but

1. My question seems simple, but it disturbs me. May *but* begin a sentence?
Yes, it certainly may. And so may *and.* There is no reason why either of those conjunctions should not begin a sentence, even though at one time such use was frowned upon by older teachers. The caveat is to use this device sparingly.

2. Which is correct: "Everyone but (*I* or *me*) will be accepted"?
Technically, *me,* since *but* there is the equivalent of the preposition *except.* Some authorities, nevertheless, would opt for *I,* saying that the pronoun is grammatically attracted to the nominative case *everyone* (*"Everyone* but *I* will . . ."). The combination "me will be accepted" sounds awkward and looks out of kilter.

> Note: A guideline observed by some critics is to treat *but* as a preposition when it precedes a noun or pronoun at the end of a sentence, but to consider it a conjunction when it appears elsewhere. Hence "Everyone noticed the dragging slip *but me (me* is the object of preposition *but),* and "Everyone (subject) *but I* noticed the dragging slip" (*I* following a conjunction takes the same case—nominative—as the pronoun that preceded it).

3. Is it proper to say, "It will take but an hour"?
The phrasing "but an hour" is a commonly accepted colloquial expression. In formal speech, prefer *only* to *but:* "It will take *only* an hour."

> Note: Be careful of this opposite construction: "It won't take *but* an hour." Adverb *but,* meaning only, will not tolerate another related negative in the same sentence. Make that "It *will* (not *won't*) take *but* an hour."

4. Is it correct or incorrect to say, "There is no doubt but that he is guilty"?
The word *but* is unnecessary and should be dropped. "There is no doubt *that* he is guilty" is all you need.

Note: Idiom has established that, where there is a negative assertion of doubt, *that* should stand by itself. Only where *but that* is preceded by a parallel *that* is its use proper ("It is something *that* we should do *but that* we do not relish doing"). *But* in addition to *but that* is a party to other redundancies. For example, "We didn't know *but what* he went" needs *but what* excised and *that* put in its place, and "The coach has *but only* one more game before retirement" is correctly phrased if either *but* or *only* is deleted.

5. Do you agree with me that in "But nevertheless it should be done with no delay," the introductory words make for emphasis and are therefore good English?

I would use either *but* or *nevertheless,* not both. When these words are used next to each other, they are redundant. Repeating the same idea with other words is frowned upon by all usage authorities, and *but nevertheless* does not make an idea more emphatic.

Note: A somewhat similar question is sometimes raised with the combination *but however,* as in "He didn't pitch a good game yesterday, *but however* we know he's good." The questioned phrase, too, is redundant. Either word would do.

C

callous/callus

Are the terms *callous* and *callus* merely variant spellings?
No. *Callous* is an adjective (a *callous* attitude); *callus* is a noun (a *callus* on the foot). Both words refer to hardened skin, but the adjective in figurative language may also mean emotionally hardened or unfeeling.

> **Note:** Be careful with the spelling of these words, particularly the noun, which is often misspelled *callous* (*callus* and *callous* are pronounced alike). Correct "John had a large *callous* on his right hand" to "a large *callus*." Its plural form is *calluses*. These words can become even more confusing. Both are verbs and, as such, mean to form a hard skin. Applied figuratively, they mean to desensitize: "Crimes in our cities have *calloused* us all."

cancel

1. How should I spell *cancel* words when the suffix *-ed* or *-ing* is appended? Shall I use two *l*'s or one?
Spell it with one *l*. The American rule is that a final consonant preceded by a single vowel is not doubled before a suffix beginning with a vowel, provided the last syllable of the base word is not stressed. Therefore, *cancel, canceled, canceling*. But be aware of the double *ll* in *cancellation*.

> **Note:** The British prefer the double *ll* (*cancelled, cancelling, travelled, travelling*), using it with nouns as well (*traveller, jewellry, jeweller*).

2. Is it all right to use the phrase *cancel out*?
It is not. Omit *out;* it adds nothing useful. *Cancel* means to cross out or delete, which says it all: "Under the terms of the contract, the rain *cancels* (not *cancels out*) all obligations."

can/may

1. Since almost everyone says something like "Can I go out and play, Mom?" instead of "May I?" is *may* now an obsolete form in this kind of sentence?
May is still very much alive and kicking, even though often ignored in general speech. For the example to be grammatically correct, *may* must be used instead of *can*.

> **Note:** The functions of the auxiliary verbs *can* and *may* are different. *Can* expresses mental or physical ability. A person who is able to do various things — sing, recite poetry, play badminton, lift a piano — can do so. *May*

implies permission. A pupil may leave a classroom if the teacher approves. Although *can* is the darling of informal speech to indicate permission instead of *may*, in edited writing these words should not be confused.

Some authorities, it should be noted, say that *can* is now interchangeable with *may*. If that trend continues,the battle to maintain the distinction between these words will be lost. But until the white flag has been raised, it is best, certainly in formal writing, to conform to tradition.

Many grammarians accept the use of *can* when permission is sought in interrogative sentences involving a negative because such use sounds natural. We say, "Why is it that I *can't* be allowed to leave early?" Saying, "Why *mayn't* I be allowed to leave early?" even though technically correct, sounds awkward. The response, nevertheless, should be "You *may not*," not "You *cannot*."

2. Should I say, "I can do it" or "I am able to do it"?
Conciseness is a linguistic virtue. Prefer *can*, even though you must use *able* when speaking of the future, since *can* has no future tense ("I *will be* able to"). But avoid its present tense: "I *am* able to." Say, "I *can*."

cannot

1. What do you think of the phrase "cannot and will not"?
Not much. If you cannot do something, there's no point in saying "and will not." In fact, adding "and will not" makes for an absurdity. On the other hand, if you can but are not agreeable, you may say, "I will not," omitting *cannot*.

2. Which is the correct spelling: *can not* or *cannot*?
Either spelling is correct. The one word — *cannot* — is the predominant spelling, but *can not* — two words — is sometimes used when the intent is to emphasize *not*.

can't keep from/help but

1. My son insists that he can't keep from humming while in class. Is *can't keep from* the way to say it?
The expression *can't keep from* is a colloquialism that enjoys widespread usage. In better, certainly in formal, English the proper expression is "refrain from."

2. Is *cannot help but* acceptable in such a sentence as "We cannot help but wonder why he takes so long"?
The phrase contains a double negative and is therefore unacceptable. Omit *but* and use a gerund: "We cannot help *wondering* why he takes so long."

Note: Some writers accept the double negative *cannot but* (without *help*) in such a sentence as "The secretary gloomily remarked that we *cannot* *but* regret such a foolish decision." Of course, a recasting might be an improvement: "We can *only* regret such a foolish decision."

canvas/canvass

Do the sound-alikes *canvas* and *canvass* have the same meaning?
No, they do not. Noun *canvas* is a heavy, coarse fabric, the kind used to make sails and tents. Verb *canvas* is seldom seen; it simply means to cover or line with canvas. On the other hand, verb *canvass* (with two *s*'s) is used more often than its corresponding noun. To *canvass* is to go through a city or district soliciting votes or donations ("The incumbent mayor *canvassed* most of the wards"). Noun *canvass* denotes either a solicitation, as for votes or sales, or a public opinion survey.

> **Note:** Word historians have theorized that because flour was sifted in bags made of canvas, a polling of voters' and buyers' preferences was a sifting of their opinions, hence *canvass,* but with two *s*'s, perhaps to distinguish it from the cloth.

capitalization

1. When do we capitalize a direction or a section of the country, such as the word *west*?
When it refers specifically to western states or the general area. "The *West* was won." "Oregon is in the *Far West*." But "Iron was discovered in *western* Michigan."

> **Note:** Although a generic term accompanying a proper noun is usually capitalized (Missouri *River*), it is not when it follows two proper nouns (the Ohio and Mississippi *rivers*).

2. What words in a title should be capitalized?
Capitalize all principal words but not articles, conjunctions, or prepositions unless they begin or end the title ("Stop the Train; We Will Get Off"). Many stylists capitalize prepositions of five or more letters: *Before, Except, Between.*

3. Should the seasons of the year be capitalized?
Stylebooks recommend that seasons of the year, unless personified ("Beautiful Spring is dancing in our garden"), should be written in lower case. Promoters and advertisers usually capitalize the seasons to make them more outstanding.

> **Note:** Academic years are treated like the seasons. They are written in lower case (*freshman, sophomore, junior, senior*). But the names of the classes themselves are treated differently; they are capitalized ("Audrey is a member of the Senior Class"). Also best set out in lower case is the number of a century (the *twentieth* century). With points of the compass — *north, south, east, west* — lower case is mandated by all stylists.

carat/caret/karat

What difference is there between the words *carat, caret,* and *karat*?
The first and last terms — *carat, karat* — are used by the jewelry industry. A *carat* is a unit of weight employed to measure gem stones ("The ruby weighed three *carats*"). A *karat* is a unit of fineness employed when measuring the purity of gold ("The bracelet was made of 18 *karat* gold"). A *caret* (∧) is an editor's mark to indicate where missing material is to be inserted.

> Note: The pronunciation of *carat, karat,* and *caret* is the same. The word *caret,* from Latin *carere,* means "there is lacking," hence a symbol for the insertion of a missing letter or word.

cardinal/ordinal

1. Are cardinal numbers and ordinal numbers used in the same way?
No, they are not. Cardinal numbers answer the question how many, which indicates quantity but not order: 1, 4, 9, and so on. They are the numbers themselves. Ordinal numbers — adjectival forms — refer to numerical order: first, second, third, and so on.

> Note: Days of the month may be expressed by cardinal or ordinal numbers. A cardinal number follows the month: December 12, 1912. An ordinal number precedes the month and is spelled out: the twelfth of December. A sign listing activities should say, for example, "the meeting will be on June 1" (not "on June 1st") and the picnic "on July 10" (not "on July 10th").

2. When an ordinal and a cardinal number are used next to each other, which comes first?
The *ordinal.* "The *first ten* men were picked," not the *ten first* men. Ten men can't be first. And if during a race you refer to the two first runners, it must have been a dead heat.

careen/career

I don't understand the newspaper reporter who said the car careered down the highway until stopped by the police. Didn't he mean *careened*?
He could have used *careened,* but he was not wrong with *careered.* *Careen,* originally used of boats that were tilted to allow barnacles to be scraped off the bottom, has taken on the meaning to sway from side to side, to move rapidly in an uncontrolled manner, swerving. But *career* is a synonym. It means to move forward at top speed, to go headlong, or to move erratically. Regarding the movement of automobiles, the word *career* is seldom used and would probably not be understood by many people to describe a wildly driven car. Although the reporter was accurate in using *careered,* he would have been better understood had he used *careened.*

careless

What prepositions does *careless* take?
It may take *about, in, of,* or *with.* A man is *careless about* his dress, *in* the way he ties his shoelaces, *of* the feelings of others, *with* his belongings.
   Note: Adjective *careful* may take those same prepositions.

Caribbean

What is the correct pronunciation of *Caribbean*?
It has two acceptable pronunciations — KAR-a-BE-an and ka-RIB-e-an. The former has a slight preference because the sea was named for the Caribs, South American Indians. The stress in their name is on the first syllable.

carry/convey

May the words *carry* and *convey* be interchanged?
Usually, but they receive different idiomatic treatment. You may *carry* a message *back* to your uncle, but you do not *convey* a message *back.* You simply *convey* a message.

catchup/ketchup

Which is correct, *catchup* or *ketchup*?
Both are correct. Some cookbooks spell it one way and some the other. The entries of dictionaries simply mirror these preferences.There's another established spelling: *catsup.* Take your pick and pour.
   Note: *Ketchup* is derived from a Chinese word that looks like it (ke-tsiap), and that is, perhaps, a good reason to prefer that spelling.

cause of

1. Why is it wrong to say, "The cause of the accident was due to a defective steering wheel"? Isn't the sentence clear?
The meaning is clear, but the sentence is unnecessarily wordy. It says the same thing twice — *cause* and *due to.* Economize and make it either "The *cause* of the accident *was* a defective steering wheel" or "The accident *was due to* a defective steering wheel," not both *cause* and *due to.*

2. My shoe clerk came to work late and said, "The cause of my lateness is on account of the unexpected snow storm." What do you think of him?
Of him, I can't say. He may be an excellent clerk. But his use of the English language is less than excellent. He spoke redundantly. He should have said, "The *cause* of my lateness *was* the unexpected snow

storm" or "My lateness *was due to.* . . ." Time is valuable. Don't waste it on redundancies.

celebrant/celebrator

Should I call a balloon-popper at a New Year's party a *celebrant* or a *celebrator?*
Although in informal speech the words are used synonymously, prefer *celebrator* to represent one who's celebrating, making merry, having a good time, and *celebrant* to mean a person peforming a religious rite or a participant in a religious ceremony.

cement/concrete

May one correctly call a *sidewalk* a *cement* sidewalk?
Technically, no. Cement, a binding element, is an ingredient used in the making of concrete. A sidewalk is formed by pouring concrete into a mold. When set, the result is a concrete, not a cement, sidewalk. But the term *cement sidewalk* has become standard.

center around/center on

Does it matter whether one says, "His major activity centered around the tennis court" or "His major activity centered on the tennis court"? I have heard it said both ways.
It does matter if correct usage is desired. *Center around,* although frequently heard, is a misusage because it suggests a physical impossibility. A center — a point — may have something *center in* or *on* it, or even *center at* it, but it cannot have something center around it.
> **Note:** If *around* is so important a word, try a verb with which it will work comfortably, such as *revolve* or *cluster*. But be alert to the fact that some authoritative sources do not disapprove of *center around.*

ceremonial/ceremonious

How is the word *ceremonial* distinguished from *ceremonious?*
Ceremonial is applied to occasions, costumes, and so on, referring to that which is formally suitable for a ceremony (a *ceremonial* headdress). *Ceremonious* means formal and may refer to an elaborately polite person or to someone who is pompous ("A person who makes a *ceremonious* entrance is ostentatious"). Adjective *ceremonial* is applicable only to things; *ceremonious* may be used of persons or things.

chaise longue

Should we give up on *chaise longue* and call that chair a *chaise lounge?*
Don't do it unless you want to seem uneducated. True, a long chair to

lounge on might understandably be called a *chaise lounge*. But *chaise longue*, carried over from France, is the proper wording. Some Americans simply pronounce it incorrectly.

> **Note:** By all means, do not corrupt the word more by calling it a *chaise*. Use its full name and pronounce it shez-lounhg.

chaos

May I assume that the phrase *complete chaos*, which is often heard, is in good standing?

You may not. *Chaos* is complete disorder. *Complete chaos* is grammatical disorder. Drop *complete* and avoid a redundancy.

> **Note:** The original definition of *chaos*, according to the dictionaries, is "the infinite space in which formless matter was thought to have existed before the universe came into existence." When spelled *Chaos*, with a capital letter, it refers to the ancient Greek god who personified the formless state before the universe existed.

character/reputation

How do you distinguish between character and reputation?

Character is what a man is; *reputation* is what others think he is.

> **Note:** Beware of the fuzzy use of *character* in some contexts. Not "activities of civic-motivated *character*," but "civic-motivated activities"; not "effects of an intermittent *character*," but "intermittent effects"; not "an incident of this character," but "an incident of this kind." It is best to restrict the use of *character* to people rather than things or events.

chauvinist

I have often heard the expression "a male chauvinist pig." What is the word *chauvinist* doing there?

A *chauvinist* is a person possessing an unreasoning loyalty to a cause, hence an undue attachment to a particular group. The word stems from the name of Nicholas Chauvin, a much-wounded, excessively enthusiastic patriot in the army of Napoleon Bonaparte. Chauvin was so fanatically devoted to Napoleon that he came to be an object of ridicule. Hence the present sense of blind patriotism or extravagant loyalty.

chic

How is the word *chic* pronounced?

This French word is pronounced sheek ("What a *chic* outfit"), just the way the word *sheik*, an Arab leader, is pronounced.

> **Note:** Although many people pronounce the word for a leader of an

Arab family or village sheek, remembering the old movie and song, "The Sheik of Araby," in which the word was so pronounced, others say the proper pronunciation is shake.

childish/childlike

Is a senile person *childish* or *childlike*?
The behavior of a senile person may be called *childish,* certainly not *childlike*.

> Note: *Childish* and *childlike* point to behavior manifested by some children. The former suggests the less admirable qualities found in a child — temper tantrums, selfishness, silliness; the latter, the more appealing qualities — trust, love, endearing innocence. When these terms are applied to adults, *childlike* is a favorable word, whereas *childish* is invariably pejorative except if applied to a senile person, whose behavior must be sympathetically understood.

chutzpah

What does the Yiddish word *chutzpah* mean?
The word, now in popular usage, means unmitigated gall. The classic example is the boy who killed his parents and then told the judge he was entitled to mercy because he was an orphan.

cities/citys

Two cities are named Kansas. Do we say there are two *Kansas Cities* or *Kansas Citys*?
Although common nouns ending in *y* preceded by a consonant change *y* to *i* to make a plural (*library, libraries; city, cities*), with proper nouns, simply add an *s* to the singular form. Hence *Kansas Citys*.

claim

Is there any objection to equating *claim* with *declare* or *mention*?
Yes, because *claim* is not an acceptable substitute for those words. Use *claim* when a personal claim is put forth. It may be the assertion of a right ("Sandy *claimed* he had an easement on the property") or the demanding of one's due ("The customer *claimed* she was entitled to a refund"). *Claim* is often erroneously used to mean *assert* or *state*, as well as *declare* or *mention*. Tread lightly when using this word.

> Note: Some authorities would not agree that *claim* is erroneously employed to mean *assert* or *maintain*. They argue, and their argument deserves to be weighed, that usage has established the extended sense of *claim* and that it no longer is to be confined behind its traditional barrier. So they claim.

clause of purpose

What might you say about this sentence: "Bob made sure he talked all the time, so no one could argue with him"?
A clause of purpose should not be introduced by *so* but by *so that* ("Bob made sure he talked all the time *so that* no one . . ."), and it should not be preceded with a comma because the clause is essential to the main thought. Incidentally, an infinitive could have served: "Bob talked all the time *to keep* anybody from arguing with him."

> **Note:** A *so that* clause of result, unlike a clause of purpose, is preceded with a comma: "The dog was dead, *so that* there was nothing further she could do."

clichés

The word cliché frequently surfaces in columns and elsewhere. How do you define it?
A *cliché* is defined in dictionaries as a trite phrase, a hackneyed expression. It is so worn out by long use ("Father Time," "white as snow," "busy as a beaver") that it has lost its sparkle and is now devoid of freshness and appeal. But be careful not to take all clichés to task, since many make for conciseness, and some are the best way to make a point. Further, everyone does not agree that a phrase is so hackneyed as to be labeled *cliché*. One thing more. When speaking, we cannot easily avoid clichés because they come quickly to mind and our tongues spit them out as quickly. But in writing, considering the moments of pause and the opportunity to edit, clichés are less excusable.

climatic/climactic

What relationship does *climatic* have to *climactic*?
Climactic is the adjective form of *climax,* the culmination of a series of events. *Climatic* is the adjective form of the noun *climate*. It refers to weather conditions.

> **Note:** A word that sounds like the key words but is not related is *climacteric* (stress the second syllable — *mac*). It means a crucial period of a person's life when physiological changes occur, such as menopause.

climax

I have read that a *climax* is an upward progression, and I have also heard it called the peak. Which is it?
Technically, a *climax* (Greek *klimax,* "ladder") is an ascending series. The top, or peak, is its acme. But in today's usage *climax* is the equivalent of peak or summit, the high point of intensity in a progression of events. It is, it might be said, the *culmination,* which is now a synonym for *climax*.

coincidence

Is it proper to say, "His arrival at my house was a pleasant coincidence"?

The word *coincidence*, to be used correctly, must refer to a chance, simultaneous occurrence of two or more things in such a way as to seem remarkable. It may not refer to a single event. Unexpectedly meeting your roommate and your college professor while standing on the corner is a coincidence.

collective nouns

When I use such words as *family*, *jury*, and *committee* followed by a plural verb (regarding the individuals separately), I feel uncomfortable, and here and there I notice a questioning eye. How can I best resolve this matter?

It is true that many collective nouns (nouns that name a group or aggregate) have become so deeply ingrained as singulars that when a plural verb follows, the sentence seems awkward, even though a plural idea is being conveyed. The remedy is to precede the collective noun with a plural noun in such cases; for example, "The members of the *jury are* disagreeing among themselves" rather than "The *jury are* disagreeing among themselves," even though the second example is as proper as the first.

Note: The governing rule is to treat the noun as a singular if totality is implied but as a plural if individual items or persons are emphasized. "The Republican majority *is* from the Midwest" (totality). "The majority of Republicans *were* angered by the poor reception" (collection of individuals).

Some collective nouns—money, weight, distance, and the like—are always considered singular. We say, "Tony paid a bill of fourteen dollars, of which four dollars *was* for his father." The dollars are regarded as a unit, not as individual dollars. "Twelve pounds *was* (not *were*) all it weighed." "Thirteen miles *is* (not *are*) all he could run cross-country." Businesses and other organizations are denominated by nouns regarded as singular—*firm, company, corporation, society*. The caveat is to make referents agree with the singular subject. Not "Sears is expanding their suburban store," but "Sears is expanding *its* suburban store."

Some words are plural in form but express a singular idea. These words are not collective nouns; for example, "*Taps is* being blown"; "*Politics is* my life's blood."

collision

Is it correct to say the truck collided with a pole?

Strictly speaking, a *collision* is a coming together of two moving objects, which excludes a striking of something stationary. To be precise, you might say the truck crashed or ran into a pole. But *collided,* as so used in the example, is now idiomatic. In edited writing, nevertheless, prefer using *collided* and *collision* in their traditional sense.

> **Note:** If the example had said a truck collided with a car, instead of a pole, the implication might be that the truck driver was at fault. The phrase "collided with" imputes, or may seem to impute, negligence. Saying, "A truck and a car *collided"* will sidestep the problem.

colon

When would a writer who does not write for publication be most likely to use a colon?

1. After a quotation ("John stated the rules: Do not . . .").
2. After such words as *such as these* or *as follows* ("The referee's rules will be *followed:* . . ." or "*These* rules will be *followed:* . . ." or "The procedure will be *as follows:* . . .").
3. To separate numerals in times of day (3:30 p.m.).

comma

1. Is a comma placed before *and the like, and so on, etc.?*
Yes, usually before *and,* and except when it ends a sentence, after the expression because it is parenthetical.

2. Newspapers do not use a comma before *and* in a series of three or more. Why is this so?
It is universal journalistic style to omit a comma before *and* or *or* in a series. Probably the saving of space was a consideration. In other writings, the serial comma (red, white, and blue) is desirable as an aid to clarity.

3. Should the comma have been used in this sentence: "During the morning hours, we stroll in the park"?
The comma is preferably omitted. Introductory prepositional phrases, unless seven or more words in length, need not be followed by a comma. Remember that today's trend is to use as few commas as possible.

4. Are the commas surrounding these *like* phrases proper: "Learning a new alphabet, *like all learning,* requires much study"; "Men, *like Adlai Stevenson,* make Americans proud"?
The first example is properly punctuated, since *like* introduces a parenthetical phrase, which must be set off. But not the second, since all sense without the *like* phrase would be destroyed. It is not that "Men make Americans proud," but that certain men, those like Adlai Stevenson, do. The phrase is therefore restrictive; that is, it is essential to the meaning of the sentence.

5. Do I write "I went with my wife Susan" or "I went with my wife, Susan"?

The first example, without the comma, stamps you as a bigamist, Susan being one of your wives. The second is correctly punctuated, Susan being used as an appositive. Take an example of a mother with two daughters. If she writes about her daughter Janet, that means that this daughter is named Janet and that she has at least one more. If she refers to her daughter, Janet, it would mean that Janet is her only daughter, as the comma before Janet indicates.

6. Would you use the commas, as I did, in this sentence: "He, himself, did it promptly"?

I would not. The word *himself* is a reflexive pronoun, and such pronouns are not set off.

commonly/generally

Is there any distinction in usage between the words *commonly* and *generally*?

There is. What is *commonly* done is common to all or to almost all. What is *generally* so or done is true of the larger number.

comparatively/relatively

When is it proper to use the word *comparatively* in a sentence?

The answer is that when a stated comparison is being made, *comparatively* is an appropriate term. "Following his strikeout record of ten men a game, McDowell struck out *comparatively* few today." To state it in reverse, if there is nothing to be compared to, the term *comparatively* does not belong.

> **Note:** The same caution concerning the unnecessary use of *comparatively* applies to *relatively*. To justify its use, the sentence must indicate that there is something that can be related to.

compare

How *compare to* and *compare with* are used is confusing. An explanation would be appreciated.

The combination *compare to* is used to liken things, to show a resemblance between two persons or objects. The likeness, however, is not real. It is figurative, a simile, as is comparing a swimmer's antics to those of a dolphin, a person's voice to thunder, an electric light to the sun, or the world to a stage. When an actual comparison is made — when comparing two similar things — the established idiom is *compare with* ("The mayor *compared* his city *with* the city of his birth"; "We will *compare* the statements of this year *with* last year's"). The stress when *compared with* is used lies in the differences. An example involving Shakespeare is often made to exemplify the distinction in use between *compare to* and *compare with*. It is said that if a poet *compares* himself *with* Shakespeare, he will learn how poorly he measures up. If he *compares* himself *to* Shakespeare, he had better consult a psychiatrist.

> **Note:** When employing *compare to,* be sure that a comparison is being made of comparable things. One cannot say, at least not correctly, "He *compared* that man's ears *to* a donkey." It should be *to a donkey's* or *to the ears of a donkey.* And neither is it correct to say, "He *compared* Holmes's opinion *with* his contemporaries." The correction needed there is *with his contemporaries'* or *with the opinions of his contemporaries,* so that *opinions* and *opinions* are being compared, not *opinions* and *contemporaries.*

comparisons

1. May I say, correctly, "My brother plays the piano better than my sister," or must I say, "better than my sister does"?

You need not add the word *does,* even in formal discourse. The omission of a word readily inferable is permitted. This omission is called *ellipsis.*

2. The ad said, "This is a more stimulating coffee." My question is, "More stimulating than what?"

Your question cannot be answered because a specific or implied standard is lacking. This type of comparison is known as a suspended comparison, and it is, of course, grammatically unsatisfactory.

3. I see the forms *commoner* and *commonest* in print, but I thought adjectives of two or more syllables take *more* and *most.* Is this not true?

It is not. The choice is the writer's. A disyllable may take *more* or *most* or *-er* or *-est.* This means that *commoner* and *commonest* are acceptable forms.

4. One often hears something like "I enjoy August more than any month of the year." Is that sentence worded correctly?

No, its comparison is illogical. August, a month of the year, is being included when it should be excluded. Correctly put: "I like August more than any *other* month of the year."

5. My husband and I never agree on the case that follows *as* in such a sentence as "I like custard as much as he/him." Please save our marriage.

The sentence you present contains an elliptical clause of comparison. The case of the pronoun following *as (he/him)* is the one required if the sentence were written out fully. This means that "I like custard as much as *he*" (*likes custard* understood) is correctly put. It compares my likes with his likes. In "I like custard as much as *him,*" the objective case is called for because the comparison is between *custard* and *him,* the sentence saying that I like custard as much as I like him. The question to be answered in your example is, What is the intended meaning?

6. What do you think of this sentence: "Ronald is brighter than any senior in our school"?
The bright Ronald would probably have corrected the sentence to read *any other,* so that it would be clear that he is a senior at that school. It's the *other* that brings him into the group. The rule is that *other* is required when comparing one thing with members of the group of which it is a member.

7. What, if anything, is wrong with "Anne is a most intelligent person"?
The comparison is incomplete, since we don't know with whom Anne is being compared. Although general English accepts this false comparison, formal writing prefers *very* for *most.*

8. When recommending a lawyer, my friend said, "He is the best lawyer of any I know." Is what he said possible?
It is not, because the recommended lawyer is among those whom your friend knows. The problem here is that *any* includes the thing being compared, whereas that thing or person should be excluded. Correct by dropping *of any:* "He is the best lawyer (no *of any*) I know."

compendium

The controller said the surveys were a compendium of his department's practices. Was *compendium* used correctly?
No, *compendium* does not mean all-inclusive or exhaustive. Coming from Latin *compendiosus,* "a shortening," it is not a large, thorough work but a brief compilation, a summary, or outline.

complected

I have been told that the word *complected* is dialectal, but since I hear it so often, I wonder whether its use is now justified?
It is not, and it is disapproved of by almost all current authorities. *Complected,* despite its widespread usage, is a nonstandard substitute for *complexioned.* If Ralph has dark skin, do not say "Ralph is dark complected." Make it *dark complexioned* or *of dark complexion.*
> **Note:** The word *complected* that appears in dictionaries is unrelated to a person's complexion. It is a verb meaning "joined by weaving or twining together."

compliment/complement

How can I keep straight the words *compliment* and *complement*?

A *compliment* is an expression of praise or approval ("Successful writers receive *compliments*"). A *complement* is something that completes ("Her earrings *complemented* her coiffure"). Note that both *complete* and *complement* have two *e*'s and that only *compliment* has an *i* because (as a mnemonic) "*I* like *compliments*." *Complement* is the usual misspelling culprit. Seldom is *compliment* misspelled.

> **Note:** In grammar, a *complement* is the word or words following the verb that completes the meaning of the sentence. A *complement* may be a direct or indirect object, but most often it is taken to mean the noun or adjective that completes the meaning of a linking verb and that modifies the subject ("Andy is *tall*"; "Ronald became the new *principal*").

comprise

Someone told me that one of these sentences was not worded correctly: "The committee was comprised of people from all races"; "The Armac Company, an international organization composed of diverse interests, met yesterday in Paris." I ask, Which one and why?

The first sentence is substandard. The second is written in approved formal English. The difference between them is the combination *comprised of* versus *composed of*. Since the whole comprises the parts and the parts compose or make up the whole, the passive form *comprised of* is unacceptable. The transitive verb *comprise* must be followed by a direct object: "The orchestra *comprises* two violinists, a pianist, a saxophone player, and a drummer"; "The United States *comprises* fifty states." Or, if you wish to circumvent *comprise*, you may say, "The United States *is composed of* (or *consists of* or *is made up of*) fifty states," but not *is comprised of*.

> **Note:** The words *comprise* and *include* are not synonyms. Whereas *comprise* suggests the totality of the constituent parts, *include* suggests that some component parts are missing. "The exhibit *includes* artifacts from China and Japan" means that artifacts from other countries are also on exhibition. If the artifacts on display were from China and Japan only, the sentence would read "The exhibit *comprises* artifacts from China and Japan."

condign

May *condign* be used to mean "severe"? We see it used that way.

I do, too. Even though many people seem to think so, *condign* does not mean severe; it means deserved. Although the word is used today only where severity is an important element, as in condign criticism or condign punishment, the result or outcome must be deserved, the key point.

Note: It is best to replace *condign*, a bookish term, with a simpler, every-day word, one readily understood by anyone. Incidentally, before usage associated the sense of *condign* with punishment, it was used, generally, to mean well merited. An award may have been a condign award. Praise may have been condign. But no longer is this so.

conniver/conspirator

If a man convicted of a crime had someone connive with him, wouldn't that person be equally guilty?
Avoiding legal possibilities, a *conniver* is not a *conspirator*. The second person did not plan the misdeed with the culprit. By looking the other way, what he did was not to interfere with the commission of the crime. "Leary was accused of *conniving* at embezzlement" (usually conniving is *at* something). Leary did not scheme, conspire, or plot. He figuratively shut his eyes so that he would not see what was happening.

    Note: *Connive* comes from a Latin word meaning "shut the eyes." *Conspire* (from Latin *con*, "with," and *spirare*, "to breathe") is to breathe together; that is, to plot. The ancestors clearly indicate that *connive* implies a toleration of wrongdoing, a looking the other way, not an active participation, whereas *conspire* suggests a scheming or plotting together with others.

conscious/aware

Are the senses of *conscious* and *aware* different?
They are. *Conscious* refers to what we feel within ourselves—a pain in the toe, a fear of the dark. To be *aware* is to know or realize something by perception or through information ("He was *aware* of the smell of smoke"; "She was *conscious* of the sun's warmth on her shoulders").

    Note: Usually *conscious* is applied to a physical condition. *Aware* requires the preposition *of* and an object. Not "He was *aware* the kind of man his neighbor was," but "He was aware *of* the kind of man his neighbor was."

consensus

A columnist criticized the phrase *consensus of opinion*. Was he justified in doing so?
He was, even though some good writers condone that usage. The origin of *consensus* is found in Latin *con*, "with," and *sentire*, "to think." A *consensus*, therefore, is a thinking with others, a thinking together, or a collective opinion. A dictionary definition is "the opinion of all or most of the people consulted." Which means that, to avoid being redundant, one should not speak of a *consensus of opinion*. Omit *of opinion*. "The *consensus* of the delegates was to adjourn at five."

    Note: Most authorities frown on the expression *general consensus* as much as they do *consensus of opinion*, since the idea of general is found in *consensus*. But no one has voiced an objection to *a broad consensus*. If the word *consensus* cannot go it alone, consider *broad* as its escort.

Be careful not to misspell the key word *consensus*. There's no *census* in *consensus*. Note that the word has three *s*'s.

consider

1. May *consider* be followed by *as*?

No, when meaning regard ("I *consider* him [no *as*] a good man"); yes, when meaning discussed or examined ("We *considered* him *as* teacher and then *as* provost").

Note: Idiomatically, *consider* is followed by a direct object when its sense is to regard as. This means, that unlike *regard*, *as* may not follow it ("We *regard* it *as* a fracas"; "We *consider* it [no *as*] a fracas").

2. Please criticize "The teacher considers the student's homework is unacceptable."

The verb *is* should have been omitted—"*considers* the student's homework (no *is*) unacceptable." A clause may not be the object of *consider*.

Note: Just as *is* does not belong, so also any form of the verb *to be*, including *to be* itself. Therefore, not "Everyone *considered* the mayor to be a thief," but "Everyone *considered* the mayor (no *to be*) a thief."

contact

Is it good English to ask someone to *contact* you?

The verb *contact* in the sense of get in touch with has not yet been elected into full membership in standard English. But since it says so much and usually saves words, most of us do not hesitate to use it.

Note: It is best to regard the verb *contact* as informal and to avoid it in formal writing, in which *telephone, write, interview, look up,* or any other appropriate term would be preferred.

contemptible/contemptuous

How does one discriminate between the words *contemptible* and *contemptuous*?

A *contemptuous* person is disdainful, one who feels or shows contempt, perhaps by a scornful look or by merely ignoring someone's presence ("He is *contemptuous* of whatever she does"). A *contemptible* person is despicable, one deserving of scorn ("A person who defrauds the government is *contemptible*").

continue on

Does the phrase *continue on*, as in "We must continue on till we're finished," merit approval?

It does not. Since *continue* means to go on or to keep on, the *on* after *continue* is unnecessary and should be dropped.

continuous/continual

I am *continuously,* or is it *continually,* confusing these words. Please clarify them for me.
Continuous means continuing without interruption, the way water runs from a tap. *Continual* means continuing with interruptions, the way a telephone rings.

> **Note:** Some dictionaries regard these terms as synonyms. Equating their meaning, however, raises a barrier to effective communication. If the words are confusing, and you don't know which to use, think of intermittent (which means "continual") and uninterrupted (which means "continuous"). Simply use those easily handled and quickly understood words instead, or say, "very frequent" for the first and "unbroken" for the second. Afterthought: Although *continuous* is usually applied to an unbroken occurrence while it continues (a *continuous* rain for four hours, a *continuous* surveillance), it also is used of unbroken extent or space (a *continuous* expanse of savannah, a *continuous* slope).

contrast

How is the word *contrast* constructed?
Used as a verb, it is followed by *with* ("We would like to *contrast* this setting *with* the one in the other room"). Used as a noun, it takes *to, between,* or *with* ("There is a noticeable *contrast between* the condition of their lawn and ours"; "Allen's lifestyle is remarkable *in contrast to* [or *with*] his brother's"). Remember that *contrast* is not followed by *from.*

> **Note:** *Contrast* and *compare* are not equivalent. To *compare* is to examine similarities and differences, but primarily to observe similarities. To *contrast* is to set in opposition in order to show or emphasize differences. Verb *contrast* is stressed on the second syllable—kahn-TRAHST; noun *contrast,* on the first—KAHN-trast.

contributing factor

Does the phrase *contributing factor* make sense?
Not really. A *factor* is a cause contributing to a result; hence the word *contributing* is unnecessary. If you wish to use the vogue word *factor,* say, for example, "His father's wealth was a *factor* in the son's business success" rather than a *contributing factor.*

convince/persuade

1. I am not sure that I know the difference in meaning and usage between *convince* and *persuade.* Please set them out.

Convince means to cause someone to believe; *persuade* means to cause someone to act. A father may convince his son that the car needs washing but be unable to persuade him to wash it. To put it in other words, to *convince* is to satisfy by argument or evidence; to *persuade* is to win over by reasoning or inducement to a course of action.

2. What structural applications apply to *convince* and *persuade*?
Persuade may be followed by a *to* infinitive ("Ralph *persuaded* Joe *to run* for office"); *convince* may not be (not "Ralph *convinced* Joe *to run*"). Idiomatically *convince* takes either *that* ("Ralph *convinced* Joe *that* he should run") or an *of* clause (". . . *of* the need to run"). The thing to bear in mind is that, although a person may be *persuaded to*, he may not be *convinced to*.

cope

Is it permissible to say, "He could not cope"?
The intransitive verb *cope* should be followed by *with* to indicate what is being coped with. That person or thing is the object of the preposition *with;* for example, "He could not *cope* with office problems." Careful writers do not end a sentence with *cope*, although such usage is not uncommon in popular speech. To repeat, do not use *cope* unless followed by *with*.

> **Note:** Constant usage by people establishes idiom. A trend today is to use *cope* to mean the ability to get along despite obstacles. Hence we hear something like "He had serious problems at work, but now he is able to *cope*." It may well be that such phraseology, now decried by almost all authorities, will, with time, become idiomatically acceptable.

correspond

What preposition follows the verb *correspond*?
When the sense is to write letters, *correspond with* is the correct combination. When its meaning is to be like, to fit, to be in harmony with, *correspond* takes *to* or *with* ("Ralph's thoughts *corresponded* closely *with* Ted's"; "This figure does not *correspond to* that one").

correspondent/corespondent

Why are the words *correspondent* and *corespondent* so frequently misused, one for the other?
Probably because of carelessness. Clearly one who corresponds — exchanges letters with another — is a *correspondent* (two *r*'s). One charged as the paramour in a divorce action is the *corespondent* (one *r*). Think of the defendant as the respondent and the person involved with the defendant as the *co-respondent*. The conclusion here is that it is better

to write letters and be a correspondent than to be accused of adultery and be a corespondent.

could of/have

What accounts for the frequent use of *of* for *have* in a sentence such as "My sister could of gone to the dance if she weren't sick"?
Grammatical thoughtlessness. I am sure that educated people who use *of* where *have* is required do so out of sheer negligence. They know better. But many, unfortunately, write the way they speak—sloppily. Clearly, "The score might *of* been worse" and "I should *of* told you sooner" are the product of lazy speech habits.

> **Note:** In speech, *could've* (which is indistinguishable from *could of*), *would've*, *should've*, and so forth, are assumed to be contractions of *could have*, *would have*, and so on, even though no one stops to wonder whether the speaker meant *of* or *have*. Grammatically, *of* could not have been intended because *of* is not a verb.

coup de grâce

How is *coup de grâce* pronounced?
The word for putting one out of his misery (the telling blow, that is) is pronounced KOO-(no p)-DE-GRAHSS.

couple

May the word *couple* by itself precede a noun or must *of* come between them? For example, is it correct to say, "I took a couple books" or must it be "I took a couple *of* books"?
The answer is that the preposition *of* must connect the nouns *couple* and *books*—"We took a couple *of* books home with us." Only when a word such as *more*, an adjective of degree, is inserted between *couple* and the noun is *of* dropped ("We want a *couple more* pretzels, Mom"). Returning to the first example, *couple* is properly used when it refers to two persons or things joined or related in some way. We speak of a married couple or a couple of matched horses. To be accurate, we should therefore say, "We took two books home with us," not *a couple*. However, idiom, which ignores logic, recognizes *couple* on an informal level as the equivalent of *several* or *few*. The man who says he jogged a couple of miles today, although not speaking in the best English, is acceptably idiomatic.

> **Note:** You will have no trouble with the agreement of subject and verb if you treat *couple*, a collective noun, as a plural noun (the *couple are*), although a singular verb may be used in those cases where two are regarded as one ("The *couple* in the farthest corner *is* the one we're looking for"). The guideline that should be strictly adhered to, however, is to be

consistent, whichever way you go; that is, if you treat *couple* as a singular, use singular referents. Saying "The newlywed *couple* is spending *their* honeymoon in southern Italy" is substandard. Say, "spending *its* honeymoon." Or make it all plural: "The newlywed *couple are* spending *their* honeymoon in southern Italy." Generally using a plural construction is preferable. Think of two—the two *are;* the couple *are.*

credible/credulous/creditable

1. *Credible, credulous,* and *creditable* are three words that should be given careful thought, considering how often they are misused by prominent speakers and newspaper reporters. Would you write something to impress the distinction on their minds?

A newspaper report may be *credible;* that is, plausible, worthy of belief. If well written, the report is *creditable;* that is, deserving commendation, praiseworthy. Those who immediately believe what they read, without evaluating it, may be said to be *credulous;* that is, gullible, quick to believe on slight evidence.

> Note: The antonym of *credible* is *incredible.* The antonym of *creditable* is not *incredible* but *discreditable.*

2. The question is whether *credibly* is the right word in "His actions reflected *credibly* on the image of the school board."

No, it is not the right word. The word required is *creditably,* which means in a commendable or praiseworthy manner, and not *credibly,* which means in a believable manner. The key words—*credibly* and *creditably*—are the adverb forms of *credible* and *creditable.*

> Note: *Credibly* is frequently misused for *creditably,* perhaps because some people cannot get that middle syllable out—*ta.* Be particularly alert to this one.

creek

How is the word *creek* pronounced?

The word meaning a brook is pronounced kreek, not krihk. The latter pronunciation is for *crick,* a muscle spasm.

criterion

"Our agenda has not yet dealt with this criteria for promotions." Is something wrong with that sentence?

Very much so. Although *agenda,* a Latin plural, is treated as an English singular and is used correctly in the example, this is not so with *criteria.* It was a plural form and has remained so. Therefore, *this criteria* is a misusage for *these criteria* or, if put in the singular, *this criterion.*

> Note: It is not uncommon to see *criteria* treated as a singular. But such expressions as *a criteria, one criteria,* or *this criteria* are not accepted in

better English. Be careful, and safe, and treat *criteria* as plural.

Some authorities approve of *criterions* as a plural of *criterion,* along with *criteria.* Others object to the anglicized version. Undoubtedly, *criteria* is the generally preferred form and one sure to avoid any criticism.

cupfuls/handfuls

Is there not a choice in forming the plural of *cupful*—either *cupsful* or *cupfuls*?

All linguists agree that the solid compounds *cupfuls, handfuls,* and so forth—those with no hyphen—are made plural by adding a final *s: cupfuls, handfuls, spoonfuls, bucketfuls.* No choice. There are no such words as *cupsful, handsful,* and so on.

> **Note:** A person who has had two cupfuls of coffee has had his cup filled twice. A person who has two cups full of coffee is drinking from two cups.

cured

What preposition does verb *cured* take?

It takes *of.* A person is cured *of* a disease.

> **Note:** The common error is to use the preposition *from.* A person is not cured *from* but *of.*

D

dais/podium/lectern

How do you distinguish between the words *dais, podium,* and *lectern*?
A *dais* is a speaker's platform that accommodates a number of people.
A *podium,* from which lecturers speak, is a platform that sits on a dais.
A *lectern* is a slanted table on which speakers place their notes. Pronounce *dais* DAY-ihs.

dangling participles

Dangling participles are perhaps the most worrisome error a writer can make. How can they be avoided?
The easiest way to avoid a dangling participle is to remember that every participle must have a noun or pronoun to modify, and it should be the first word after the modifying phrase or clause, or to state it differently, the participle must modify the subject of the independent clause that follows. A typical example of a dangling participle is "Running through the woods, spruce trees were spotted on a knoll." Of course the spruce trees were not running. We were. Correct by saying, "Running through the woods, *we* spotted spruce trees on a knoll." Take another: "Being made of silk, the salesman handled the dress gingerly." Clearly the dress was made of silk, not the salesman. Amend: "Being made of silk, the *dress* was handled gingerly by the salesman."
> **Note:** A present participle is a verbal, a verb that functions as an adjective. It ends in *-ing,* just as a gerund does, but the gerund, also a verbal, functions as a noun. In "The teacher was happy that the student's *researching* bore fruit," what was meant was the student's works: reports, surveys, and diagrams. *Researching* is a gerund. But in "The teacher liked to see the student *researching*," what was meant was the *activity* of working—the process, not the product. Here, *researching* is a present participle.

dashes

1. What objection, if any, is there to the use of dashes?
None unless overused. Some writers who prefer the effect of dashes to that of commas or parentheses tend to use dashes excessively. Remember that dashes make prominent by separation ("We have agreed to close down—that is our decision—because the customers we cater to have moved away"). The recommendation is to consider using commas before using dashes. If the commas suit, avoid the dashes.

2. When are dashes preferable to commas?

An appositive or parenthetical expression that has several commas within it is best set off by dashes for the sake of clarity. Furthermore, the dashes remove two commas and reduce monotony. For example, "A crate full of fruit—oranges, apples, grapefruit—was delivered today" rather than "A crate full of fruit, oranges, apples, grapefruit, was delivered today."

3. May a dash be used with another mark of punctuation?

No. Although a dash following a comma in a salutation (Dear Al,—) is frequently seen, it should not be. And neither should the combination of a dash followed by a semicolon.

> Note: Dashes are like hyphens, only twice as long. They are written on the typewriter with two hyphens, with no space before, between, or after. Dashes are useful marks of punctuation to indicate an interruption of thought, a breaking off of a sentence, or a sudden change ("I would like to tell you about Victoria—but I see that everyone is half asleep").
>
> In addition to the uses of the dash already given, a dash may serve as a light colon before a summarizing or explanatory statement ("Travel, a country club, three houses—these are what bankrupted me") or a dramatic conclusion ("I suddenly realized—my best friend was gone").

data/agenda

We say the *agenda is* short. Why do we not say the *data is* insufficient?
Data, meaning facts given, is an English plural noun, and it therefore takes a plural verb (its singular Latin form, rarely used, is *datum*). The sister word *agenda,* meaning things to be done, unlike *data,* is an English singular noun. It evolved, for whatever reason (its Latin singular form is *agendum),* into a singular. Hence, despite the illogicality, in standard English we must treat *agenda* as a singular and *data* as a plural. Since *agenda* is universally regarded as a singular, an anglicized plural evolved—*agendas.*

> Note: The singular form of *data, datum,* is so unfamiliar that it is best not used. Prefer *fact* or *figure* to *datum.* It should also be noted that a growing tendency among some wordsmiths is to consider *data* a collective unit, especially when it refers to information in a general sense, thus taking a singular verb: "The available *data is* unexpectedly helpful." The plural form *paraphernalia* is following suit: "The *paraphernalia is* more than we can cope with." But many writers do not follow suit. They say, "the *data are,*" just as they would say, "the *criteria are,*" as well as "the *paraphernalia are.*"

dates from

May I rightly say, "The professor's tenure dates back to 1967"?
You should say, to be correct, "dates from 1967." A span of time beginning with a particular year *dates from.*

daughter-in-law

What are the plural and possessive forms of daughter-in-law?

If you have two married sons, you have two *daughters*-in-law, not daughter-in-*laws*. The pluralizing is on *daughter,* the primary word. If you visit the house of your daughter-in-law, you are then visiting your daughter-in-*law's* house. The last element is made possessive.

> **Note:** Be careful of the possessive plural. It's tricky. When you speak of, say, the homes of the wives of your two sons, they are your *daughters-in-law's* homes. Here you use both the plural and the possessive. The rule being applied is the one that governs the formation of possessive compound nouns: The last element in the noun is made possessive.

deal

1. Do educated people use the word *deal,* as in "We made a good deal today"?

Yes, but primarily only in colloquial speech. In more cultivated language, they would probably prefer *bargain* or *transaction.*

2. Is the phrase *deal with* an accepted part of our language?

It is not a desirable construction, since it is a vague phrasal verb for which a specific substitute is preferable. Rather than *dealt with,* say, "I *negotiated with* the bankers today" and "I will *comply with* the bankers' demands." In "The lecturers will *deal with* the movement of newly discovered stars," prefer "The lecturers will *discuss* the movement. . . ."

debt

Why is *debt* pronounced with a silent *b*?

Originally *debt* was spelled "det" but under French influence became "dette," which was its spelling in Chaucer's *Canterbury Tales.* The *b* was added later by medieval scholars who thought they were paying a debt to the classics by making the word conform with its Latin ancestor, *debitum.*

debut

Would you accept this sentence: "Chrysler's new model will debut today"?

Yes, but not happily. Converting *debut* into a verb, whether intransitive ("My son *debuts* as a professional today") or transitive ("Rommel *debuts* its new cosmetic line on Friday"), is not desirable. It sounds slangy and is unnecessary to boot. Prefer "Chrysler's new model will make its debut today." It is best to use *debut* only as a noun.

> **Note:** The widespread use of *debut* as a verb will probably, in time, give

it literary credentials. That time may not be far away. For centuries nouns have been converted into verbs, and the process certainly will continue, and to the benefit of our evolving language. But when a functional change becomes justified is a difficult question to answer. The reason that seems most plausible is the linguistic need for the change. If there is a need for the conversion, it will be welcomed. If not, it will die, as most vogue words do.

decimate/annihilate

Are the words *decimate* and *annihilate* synonyms?
The ancestor of *decimate* is Latin *decimare*, "to take a tenth." *Decimate* now means to destroy much or to kill a large part of. *Annihilate* comes from Latin *ad*, "to," plus *nihil*, "nothing." It means to destroy completely, to wipe out of existence.

> **Note:** The current meaning of decimate, to destroy or kill a large part of, to cause great loss of life, is an extension of its historical meaning, the killing of every tenth person. In the light of its present meaning, all authorities agree that it is illogical to combine *decimate* with a percentage or a fraction and that it should not be equated with obliteration. *Decimate,* therefore, should not be modified by either *totally* or *completely*. Some newspaper reporters consider *decimate* the equivalent of *destroy* ("The bomb *decimated* the building and a nearby car"). But if you mean destroy, say "destroy."
>
> To *annihilate* is to reduce to nothing. Inherent in the word is total destruction, which means, as with *decimate*, that neither *totally* nor *completely* should modify it.

deduce/deduct

Why do people have trouble using the verbs *deduce* and *deduct* properly?
Possibly because both verbs have the same noun form—*deduction*. To *deduce* is to reach a conclusion by reasoning. To *deduct* is to take away a quantity from another, to subtract. "Holmes *deduced* that the knife had been thrown from the upper window." "Jack's withdrawals will be *deducted* from his wages." The result of Holmes's inference and Jack's withdrawal was a *deduction*, but each of a different kind.

> **Note:** A more technical name for *deduction*, one used in logic, is *a priori* from a Latin word meaning something previous. Reasoning that goes from cause to effect, from a general to a particular, is *a priori*. Philosophers use this method of reasoning. Its opposite number is *a posteriori* (also from Latin, meaning from the later). This reasoning, used by scientists, is induction, from effect to cause, from particular cases to a general rule.

delusion/illusion/allusion

How are the terms *delusion, illusion,* and *allusion* distinguished?
A *delusion* is a mistaken belief that is fixed in the mind. Such self-deception suggests a mental disorder. A scarecrow, for example, creates an illusion of a real person, but whoever thinks it is alive suffers from a delusion. An *illusion* is a false perception. ("Shimmering sunlight can create an optical *illusion*"). An *allusion* is an unspecific reference ("The speaker made an *allusion* to the author of the first English dictionary").

> Note: Illusions and delusions have something in common — false belief. An illusion may be a freakish phenomenon of nature, like a mirage on a desert, or it may be a contrived false impression, the result of a magician's trick. Delusions may be of all kinds — of grandeur, of poverty, of power. A poet who fancies himself a Shakespeare is deluding himself.

demean

The word *demean* has gone through various stages of meaning. What is its present meaning?
Demean has two unrelated meanings. One, its traditional sense, is to conduct or behave oneself in a particular manner ("He *demeaned* himself like a gentleman"); the other, its popular sense, is to debase in dignity or stature ("Laura *demeans* everything I say"). *Demean* also means to humble oneself. The first sense is seldom used anymore. It is obsolescent, but if it is used, it should be accompanied by a reflexive pronoun (*demean yourself, demean themselves*).

> Note: Historically *demean* meant only "to behave," "to comport oneself." Although this use is practically dead, its noun form — *demeanor* — still enjoys literary grace. A later development attributed another definition to *demean* — to disparage, to debase, or to degrade. It is believed these meanings resulted from confusion with the adjective *mean*. Some critics are fearful that *demean* in the sense of to behave oneself would be misunderstood every time. The public assumes that "I wouldn't *demean* myself" means "I wouldn't lower myself," not "I wouldn't behave myself."

demise

Is not *demise* a good synonym for death?
It is a fancy synonym. Originally associated with the transfer of title to real estate as a consequence of death, *demise* has come to be equated with *death* when used of royalty or when used humorously of others. Use it sparingly, if at all.

> Note: The verb *demise* has several meanings used in legal terminology; for example, to convey by will and to pass by descent.

denotation/connotation

What is the difference between *denotation* and *connotation*?
A word's denotation is its explicit, literal meaning, the one given in a dictionary. A word's connotation is its overtone, its suggestions, and the emotional responses it evokes. *Home* is defined as a residence. That is its denotation. But *home*, because of pleasant associations, connotes warmth, love, and security. When people say they're going *home*, they expect to be welcomed — and safe. It is their haven. A home is therefore more than a residence; it is where the heart is.

> Note: The connotation of words may differ with every person. What a word connotes — suggests or implies — to readers or hearers depends on their experience and level of education. A classic example of dissimilar connotations would be the word *camp*. To an American child, *camp* means a happy summer vacation. To the survivors of the Holocaust, *camp* has an entirely different connotation.

depends

"Are we going?" I asked my brother. He said, "It depends whether it rains." Does his English need correcting?
When *depends* indicates condition or contingency, it needs to be followed by *on* or *upon* ("It *depends on* whether it rains"; "Whether you like heavy drama *depends upon* your background and taste"). Do not leave intransitive *depends* hanging in the air. Anchor it to *on* or *upon*.

deprecate/depreciate

These look-alikes and sound-alikes are confusing. Would you clarify them?
To *deprecate* is to express strong disapproval of ("Pacifists *deprecate* war"). To *depreciate*, transitively, is to play down, belittle, or disparage ("My brother *depreciates* everything I say"). When used intransitively, its sense is to lessen in value, as of securities or investments. Hence people who belittle themselves make less of themselves or are self-depreciatory. But that is not the way it is in common usage. Most often, if you belittle yourself, you're said to be *self-deprecating* or *self-deprecatory*. We say, "She *deprecated* her contributions to the art museum"; "The minister has a *self-deprecating* (or a *deprecatory*) manner."

> Note: Etymologically *depreciate* and *deprecate* are unrelated. The confusion in their usage, therefore is not because of their ancestry, but because they look and sound so much alike. The use of *deprecate* (in *self-deprecatory* and *self-deprecating* to mean *self-belittlement*) as a replacement for *depreciate* is so deeply embedded in the language that many authorities now find it acceptable and consider it reputable usage. Which places some writers and speakers in a quandary. The only thing anyone can do is make up his or her own mind on how to handle these ambiguous words.

de rigueur

What is the native sense of *de rigueur*?
In French, *de rigueur* means obligatory, referring to any custom required by strict etiquette. Note the spelling *ueur*—two *u*'s. *De rigueur* has been anglicized and its French sense has been continued in English.

despite/in spite of the fact that

Which is preferable—*despite the fact that* or *in spite of the fact that*?
Writing stylists are not kindly disposed toward either one. They would prefer simple *although*. Between *despite* and *in spite of* (forgetting "the fact that"), the preference is for *despite* because of its compactness.

desserts/deserts

Does a convicted killer get his just *desserts* or his just *deserts*?
The word *dessert*, with two *s*'s, is a course of sweets at the end of a meal. This word comes from French *desservir*, meaning "to clear the table," therefore the last course. The word *deserts* means "something deserved," that which is due; for example, life imprisonment for a convicted killer. Commonly we say, "He got his just deserts," but the phrase actually is redundant. *Just* means "something merited," and so does *deserts*.
> **Note:** The plural of the word denoting an arid region, *deserts*, is not being considered here. It has a pronunciation of its own: DEH-serts.

deus ex machina

How does *deus ex machina* translate into usable language?
Literally, "god from a machine," it is now used of anything or anyone appearing unexpectedly to resolve a seemingly unresolvable situation.
> **Note:** Originally the device called *deus ex machina* was employed in theaters during ancient times to terminate a play that had no logical ending. A god (*deus*) descended onto the stage by a machine (*ex machina*) and promptly ended the play.

devil's advocate

We have been saying that our cousin Clyde, who always supports the wrong causes, is a devil's advocate. Have we been using the term correctly?
In popular usage, yes; technically, no. A devil's advocate was someone appointed to ferret out derogatory history of a person being consid-

ered for canonization. Today such an advocate is taken to be an up-holder of the wrong side, an espouser of an unpopular cause.

dexterous/dextrous

Which is the correct form—*dexterous* or *dextrous*?
Both forms are correct; both are in use; and both mean a person hav-ing skill with the hands. Pick the one you want.

> **Note:** Although dictionaries equate adjectives *dexterous* and *dextrous*, they list only one corresponding adverb and noun; *dexterously* and *dexterousness*.

diagnose

What might be said about this sentence: "Fred was diagnosed as suf-fering from leukemia"?
The word *diagnosed* is being misused. It is the ailment that is diagnosed, not the patient. A simpler and more economical rewording of the ex-ample might be: "Fred is suffering from leukemia."

> **Note:** A *diagnosis* is the act or process of finding out by examination what disease a person or animal has. After physicians have made a diagnosis, they usually follow it with a *prognosis*, a forecast of the probable course of the disease, a prediction of the outcome of the illness.

die is cast

When Caesar crossed over the Rubicon, what did he actually say?
Speaking in Latin, he said "Jacta alea est!" the English translation of which is "the die is cast."

> **Note:** A *die* is a small cube—made of bone, ivory, or plastic—used in games of chance. Its plural form, a common word, is *dice*. Rarely would anyone ask for a die (one of a pair), although it would be accurate. More likely, the request would be for one of those *dice*. Caesar was referring to the gambling cube. And note, not "a dye."

dies

Was the report worded correctly that said the patient died from an aneurism?
According to traditional English, a person dies *of* a disease or ailment. If death results from the effects of an inward agent—disease, old age, thirst—*of* is the correct preposition to use, not *from*. A person dies *from* the effects of an outward agent—from a gunshot wound, from suffocation. In general usage, however, and as seen more and more in the works of respected writers, *from* is replacing *of*. If the medical profession switches to *from*, we may all have to follow suit. Until that time, it is best to use *of* as previously indicated.

differ

1. Since idiomatically *different* takes *from*, is the same true with *differ*?

One may always follow *differ* with *from* ("Boys *differ from* girls in many ways"). But *differ*, in addition to its sense of dissimilarity, may indicate disagreement. When that is so, *differ* may take *with* or *from* ("My neighbor's son always *differs with* me"). In this construction, *with* is more common than *from*.

2. The word *differ* takes various prepositions in different constructions. What are they, and when are they used?

Differ may take preposition *with, in,* or *from.* "Agnes *differs with* her aunt all the time" means that she disagrees with her constantly. "Agnes and her aunt *differ in* their political views" means that they have different political ideas. "In many ways Agnes and her aunt *differ from* each other" suggests dissimilarity.

different

1. Should one say, "It is different *from* (or *than*) anything I've ever seen"?

Prefer *from.* Idiomatic *different from* is firmly established because *different* implies distinction or separation (denoted by *from*). The argument advanced against the use of *than* is that adjectives in the comparative degree take *than* (*more elegant than, more sturdy than*). *Different* is an adjective in the positive degree.

2. I have read that there are times when *different than* is acceptable. What times?

The combination *different than* is usually acceptable when part of an elliptical construction: "Today's style of dancing is different *than* it was in Grandma's day" rather than ". . . different *from that which* it was in Grandma's day." In this construction *different than* is tight; *different from* is wordy. Brevity is on the side of *than;* convention on the side of *from.* In all but the most formal writing, *than* would be preferable in this situation.

3. Why do some people say something like "I have four different friends visiting me" or "I have three different reasons to advance"?

Probably they think the word *different* intensifies. Of course it is being used unnecessarily. Clearly the four friends are not the same person. And, as clearly, if the reasons were the same, there would be only one. *Different* can often be omitted without loss.

> **Note:** Use *different from,* and not *different than,* when *different* precedes a noun or pronoun ("My slacks are *different from* yours"). But when what follows *different* is a clause, *than* may replace *from,* although that need not be. Normally *than* follows a comparative adjective (which *different* is

not). Hence *larger than, warmer than,* but *different from.*

Different to is strictly British, and it is strictly avoided in American English. Be careful when using *other than* not to toss in a superfluous *different.* In "Placing a *different* value on the property, other than the value of the appraisers, is questionable," *different* should be excised.

dilapidated

May I say without fear of contradiction that my rundown wooden shack is dilapidated?
Yes, but bear in mind that many people know that the Latin word for stone is *lapis* (hence *lapidary,* "an expert in precious stones," *lapis lazuli,* "a semiprecious azure blue stone"). A deteriorated stone construction was said to be dilapidated. But today the term *dilapidated* has taken on a more extensive meaning; it may refer to any rundown building ready to fall to pieces or on the verge of decay, whether made of wood, brick, or stone. The dictionary definition of *dilapidate* is to bring or fall into a state of disrepair, decay, or ruin. Although the term is applied chiefly to buildings, the dictionary does not so limit it. Which means it may refer to an automobile or to some other object, and most certainly to a wooden shack.

dilemma

Does my mother have a dilemma on July 4 because she is not sure whether to invite her uncle for dinner?
A *dilemma* is not merely a choice or a predicament. It applies to a situation in which a choice must be made between two undesirable things, bad alternatives, like having to choose between communism and fascism.

> Note: The full expression is "to be on the horns of a dilemma," and being gored by either one would be painful. And so the traditional sense is that if both alternatives from which one must choose are unpleasant, the situation is rightly called a dilemma. But by the same token if of the two choices one is thought to be good and the other bad, *dilemma* will not fit. Bear in mind that the practice of using *dilemma* to signify any difficulty, problem, or predicament is widespread and therefore not to be scorned. But since such usage weakens the word, it need not be approved or adopted either.

directly

If a note tells me to go *directly,* what should I do?
Out of context, one cannot say. Adverb *directly* may mean either at once or in a straight course. Which means that you have been instructed to leave immediately or to go in a direct line or way. Adverb *direct,* which

is as much an adverb as *directly,* but has only one sense of "without detours," should be considered where it will serve. It might avoid ambiguity. Both adverbs, *direct* and *directly,* are interchangeable when they mean in a straight line (went *direct,* or *directly,* to school) or without anyone intervening (*direct* or *directly* from teacher to principal).

> **Note:** The dictionary definition of *directly* is immediately, at once, and in a little while. With those imprecise, even contradictory meanings, one can see why not only foreigners but also native-born Americans have trouble with English.

disclose/reveal

Are not the words *disclose* and *reveal* synonyms?
Yes, but they are used in different contexts. To *disclose* is to make known or to expose to view. To *reveal* is to disclose suddenly, strikingly, or unexpectedly, as though a magician lifted a curtain.

> **Note:** Avoid these words in reference to commonplace happenings. They may be used when the disclosure or revelation is of something decidedly important. Which, of course, means that neither word is apt when applied to a mundane activity or event, as in "He *disclosed* to all his family that he had bought a new pair of shoes" or " 'My corns are hurting terribly,' he *revealed*." The proper word there is *said,* and whenever *said* is suitable, the chances are that neither *disclose* nor *reveal* would be appropriate.

discussed

Is it objectionable to say, "This is a proposal as was discussed last night"?
Yes. The verb *discussed,* a transitive verb, is being misused as an intransitive. You might say, and properly so, "We *discussed* this proposal last night." Simple, economical, and correct.

> **Note:** The commonest misusage of *discuss* as an intransitive verb similar to the one in the example is in "As *we discussed* at the meeting, I. . . ." The point is that *discuss* must have a direct object.

discreet/discrete

Homophones always cause trouble, and *discreet* and *discrete* are not exceptions, especially since they come from the same Latin ancestor. Please distinguish between them.
The words do have the same Latin forebear, *discernere,* meaning "to distinguish," "to separate." Currently, *discreet* means prudent and judicious. A discreet person exercises sound judgment. *Discrete* means separate, unattached, or unrelated ("Light is made up of *discrete* particles").

Note: *Discreet* applies only to people. *Discrete* is used only of things. The misapplication of these words is usually of *discrete* for *discreet,* probably a misspelling ("The memo was *discretely* distributed only among the supervisors" —*discreetly*). An objection to *discrete* is that it sounds bookish. Avoid it.

discriminate/distinguish

How should we discriminate between the words *discriminate* and *distinguish* or, to put it another way, how are the uses of these words distinguished?
The sense of both words is to recognize that something is distinct. But to *distinguish* is to recognize qualities or features of a thing that make it different from the others (the horn of a rhinoceros). It generally has reference to external qualities. To *discriminate* is to perceive differences and then to evaluate them. It refers to distinctions influenced by emotional or intellectual judgments ("Casper could *distinguish* roses from carnations and other flowers, but he could not *discriminate* between poor floral arrangements and good ones").

disgust

What prepositions does *disgust* take?
It may take *at, by,* or *with,* but there is no complete consensus as to their applications. In general, we are disgusted *with* a person; *at* or *with* a sight, fact, object, or occurrence; *by* a quality, action, or behavior. We are disgusted *with* Andy's peculiar hairstyle; we are disgusted *by* Selma's rudeness.
> Note: Noun *disgust* may take *for* ("We feel disgust *for* people who litter the highway").

disinterested/uninterested

What should we do about the words *disinterested* and *uninterested*? Shall we follow the crowd and regard them as synonyms or fight to maintain their distinctions?
Stand firm. Communication is not aided by blurring the senses of two words that have distinctive meanings. *Disinterested* means impartial, unbiased, having no self-interest, the way a judge or an umpire should be. *Uninterested* means bored, unconcerned, not interested. A person who knows no chemistry would probably lack interest in seeing chemical formulas.
> Note: If you fear that *disinterested* might be assumed to mean uninterested, bypass the problem by using a synonym instead: *impartial, unbiased, neutral,* or say "not personally involved." Some dictionaries apparently are not fearful. In fact they regard *disinterested* for *uninterested* as

standard English. Although the battle to maintain the distinctions between these words is wavering, no flag of surrender appears on the horizon. Many concerned speakers and writers remain stalwarts, and they may yet turn the tide, dictionaries or no.

dissociate/disassociate

Is there a preference between *dissociate* and *disassociate*?
Both forms, meaning to disunite, have legitimate standings and therefore any preference is personal. Some authorities recommend *disassociate* because it is commoner, sounds more emphatic, and pairs with *associate*. This view runs counter to the trend to prefer the shorter word, which most wordsmiths would choose on the theory that what is simpler is preferable.

Note: When a preposition is required, *dissociate* takes *from*.

dived/dove

Is it better to say the school champion *dived* or *dove* off the fifteen-foot board?
On a formal level, *dived* is preferable, even though *dove* is regarded in some dictionaries as a variant spelling. Sports announcers use, and will no doubt continue to use, *dove*. Most formalists will continue to use *dived*.

Note: Judged by the preferences of authorities, anyone should feel free to use either *dived* or *dove* as the past tense of the verb *dive*, for just about as many critics choose *dived* as choose *dove*. Using *dived*, of course, will subject one to no criticism from either camp. It is therefore the safer course to follow. Although the past tense of *dive* is *dived* or *dove*, depending on preference, the past participle is *dived*. No one has a choice there. One should not say, "After he *had dove* from the pier, the police came to the water's edge," but "After he *had dived* from the pier. . . ."

divers/diverse

Is the word *divers* used correctly in "Paul had *divers* interests"? Or should it have been diverse?
It depends on the meaning. *Divers* means various or sundry. *Diverse* means unlike or of a different kind. Therefore, if the thought to be conveyed was unlike in kind or distinctive, the word that should have been used was *diverse*. Be careful of *divers*. It sounds literary.

Note: The word *divers* is seldom used today. It is more of a curiosity than an active adjective. Rather than *divers* ("There were *divers* objects on the chief's desk"), use *several, various*, or *more than one*.

do

**I am concerned about the use of *do* and its various forms. Is it prefera-
ble to say, "I believe you" or "I do believe you"?**
There is no preference. Whether to use the emphatic *do* is a writer's
choice. The only caution is not to overuse it.

> **Note:** Some other uses of *do*, strictly speaking, are not grammatically
> acceptable. For example, when *have* indicates possession, it needs no
> support. Yet idiomatically *do*, or a form of it, is often used with *have* in
> questions—perhaps to get the speaker started. We hear *"Do* you *have*
> the right change?" rather than *"Have* you the right change?" Or *"Did*
> Jack *have* approval?" for *"Had* Jack approval?" *"Does* he *have* the tickets?"
> for *"Has* he the tickets?"
>
> Notice that when either *did* or *have* appears alone in a question, each
> connotes a different time frame. Be careful. *Did* implies past action; *have*,
> an action continuing to the present. *"Did* they call you?" means at any
> past time—yesterday, last week. *"Have* they called you" means at any
> time up to the present moment. Note further that it is incorrect to say,
> *"Did* they approve yet?" for *"Have* they approved yet?" Likewise, instead
> of *"Did* they go already?" say, *"Have* they gone already?" *Have* keeps the
> question current.

2. Is it better to say, "He intends to go" or "He does intend to go"?
The sentences are equally acceptable and their meanings are the same.
The difference between them is one of emphasis. The auxiliary verb
do emphasizes the main verb.

> **Note:** *Do* is regularly used as an auxiliary verb to avoid repeating an-
> other verb ("My uncle played baseball every Sunday, as *did* his son years
> later"; "Lou rode his bicycle past my store, as he *did* every morning"; "I
> know that Harriet didn't wait. I'm wondering who *did*").
>
> Except in the most formal writing, *do* is accepted in the sense of to
> treat or deal with. It is therefore correct to tell your daughter to *do her
> homework* and to tell your husband to *do the dishes.* A newcomer in infor-
> mal speech is "Let's *do* lunch next week."

done

**Almost everyone uses *done* as in "The manuscript is about done." Do
usage critics approve?**
There is no unanimity among the authorities. Some say yea and some
say nay. In formal writing, rather than *done*, say *completed* or *finished*.

> **Note:** In the example *done* is an adjective, its sense being *completed* or
> *finished;* it is not serving as a form of the verb *do*. Used in those senses,
> *done* may be a source of confusion. Consider this sentence: "The renova-
> tion will be *done* next July." Does this mean that it will be completed in
> July or begun and completed in July? For the sake of clarity, make it
> "The renovation will be completed in July" or "will begin and end in
> July."

don't think/don't let's

1. Is it wrong to say, "I don't think we'll win"?
Not at all. The argument that if you don't think there's nothing to talk about doesn't hold water here. Adverb *not* embedded in "don't" negates the entire thought, not merely *think*.

2. When I said, "Dad will be home soon," my son said, "Don't let's count on it." Was his reply couched in proper English?
It was not. His expression is dialectal or unwittingly jocular. No educated person would write that way. And it doesn't belong in conversation either. It is just as easy to say it correctly: "Let's not count on it."

double entendre

What does *double entendre* mean?
It means that an expression has two meanings, one of which is indecent or risqué. Interestingly, *double entendre* is not a French spelling. The French used *double entente*. But the English changed it to its present, and now thoroughly accepted, form.

doubt/doubtful

1. Is it permissible to say, "There's no doubt but that he'll say yes"?
It is not grammatically permissible. Since *but that* connotes a negative quality, it is redundant when used with a negative that is already expressed. Say, "There's no doubt *that* he'll say yes."

> **Note:** In the positive statement "I doubt that he will come," *doubt that* is idiomatic to express unbelief. When uncertainty is expressed, the formula to follow is *whether* or *if,* preferably *whether* ("The economist *doubts whether* a rise in interest rates is imminent"). When *doubt* is used in a question, it should be followed by *that* ("Do you *doubt that* my father will win?").

2. Is there a preference between *whether* and *if* in "I doubt if I'll go"?
Yes. Prefer *whether,* even though some accomplished writers feel that *if* and *whether* are interchangeable. But they would bend if alternatives are expressed or implied and use *whether* rather than *if.* All this leaves a writer wondering what to do. There is no easy answer because opinion is almost evenly divided. Although *if* is commoner in general usage than *whether,* the safer course to take is to use *whether.* No one will fault you.

> **Note:** The problem when deciding what conjunction should follow *doubt* to introduce a clause is the same with adjective *doubtful. Whether* is required when the clause begins a sentence *("Whether* it snows or not, it is doubtful that we will leave") or follows a form of the verb *be* ("The question is whether to go or to stay").

dozen

Is it correct to say, "Several *dozen* eggs have been eaten"?
Idiom calls for *dozens of;* therefore, "Several *dozens of* eggs. . . ." Only if a number precedes *dozen* is *of* unnecessary *("Two dozen* eggs have been eaten").

> Note: When *dozen* is used with reference to a larger quantity, *of* must follow: "We want a *dozen of* those tangerines." Be careful not to use plural *dozens* following a plural number. Not "Three *dozens* bottles were on the steps," but "Three *dozen* bottles."

drowned

A question sometimes raised is whether, when death occurs by drowning, should it be reported that the deceased *drowned* or *was drowned*?
There is no set opinion on this wording, but most grammarians would say that those expressions suggest different meanings. Saying a person drowned is merely to report an unfortunate accident. Nothing else is indicated by what was said. Saying a person was drowned, however, is to report more than a death by drowning. The implication is that a murder was committed. A person who was drowned had to be drowned by someone, and that suggests a homicide. Safer wording is not to use the passive voice — *was drowned* — unless a crime is indicated. Or to put it in another way, do not use the passive voice if the drowning was accidental.

> Note: *Drowned* is the only correct form in both the active and passive voices. There is no such word as *drownded*.

due to

1. I have been criticized for writing sentences like this one: "Due to the snow, our trip was postponed." The objection was the use of *due to*. Do you agree with the critics?
Yes, the criticism was merited. Although many people use *due to* to function adverbially as you did, grammatically the sentence needs a prepositional phrase like *because of* or *owing to* ("Because of the snow"). *Due* is an adjective and must have a noun to modify — for example, "His *absence* is *due to* his illness."

> Note: Some grammarians disagree with the traditional requirements imposed upon *due to* and consider it a prepositional phrase as much as *because of, owing to,* or *on account of.* To be sure not to offend anyone's grammatical sense, however, the safeguard is not to begin a sentence with *due to* (in that position it rarely serves as an adjective) and to precede *due to* with a form of the verb *be* (in that position it is invariably used correctly as a predicate adjective). In "The change in weather *is* due to an unexpected low-pressure system" and in "His success *was* due to

consistent effort," *due* adjectivally modifies *change* and *success,* respectively. Strictly speaking, *due to* means caused by or attributable to. If either of those expressions fits, *due to* is being used properly.

2. What do you think of the phrase "due to the fact that"?
It is wordy for *because* or *since* and should be avoided. Certainly careful writers and speakers avoid it.

dumb/dumfound

1. If people's mental apparatus is slow, may they rightly be called dumb?
Such people are dull, dense, or possibly stupid, but not speechless, which is what *dumb* means. Substituting *dumb* for any of those adjectives is not recommended on any level of speech or writing.

2. *Dumbbell* is spelled as given. Why is it that I see *dumbfound* sometimes spelled with no *b*?
It's a matter of choice. *Dumfound* is the usual spelling, but *dumbfound,* a variant, is still very much in use. Frankly, it should be the prevalent spelling, since *dumbfound* is a blend of *dumb* and *confound.* But *dumfound* is commoner.

> **Note:** The word *numskull,* which indicates a numbness or dullness in the brain, is another word that has dropped its *b* (*numb* plus *skull*). Here again, you will occasionally see its variant spelling — *numbskull.*

during

What should be said about these popular phrases of my supervisor: "during the course of" and "during the time that"?
They are verbose and should be shunned. Use *during* for the first and *while* for the second. Your supervisor shouldn't waste time on unnecessary words.

> **Note:** A cousin phrase is "during such time as." It is almost always verbose for *while.*

E

each

1. Should one say, "Has *each* of the companies (referring to many) filed *its* report?" Or should it be "*their* reports"?

The correct formulation is *its report*. *Each*, a noun, the subject of the sentence, is singular and invariably takes a singular verb and a singular pronoun, even though followed by *of* and a plural noun or pronoun. And so we say, "*Each* of the architects *has* to decide on the plan *himself*," not "*have* to decide on the plan *themselves*." Likewise, when *each* modifies the subject, there too it is singular ("*Each* soldier gets *his* due").

> **Note:** When *each* follows a plural subject, with which it is in apposition, it does not govern the verb, which must be plural ("The dentists *each are* trying to reduce X-ray radiation"). If adjective *each* preceded the word it modified, the subsequent verb would be singular ("*Each* dentist *is* trying to reduce X-ray radiation").

2. Is *each* always followed by a singular verb?

No. As the subject of the sentence, yes. Since pronoun *each* serving as the subject of a sentence is singular, the verb it controls must be singular, too. But observe that in "Alfred and Mitchell each *are* subject to immediate dismissal," *each* is not the subject. The compound subject is plural, and so is its verb.

3. Is *each and every* a recommended phrase in "Each and every one of you must vote for me"?

It is not. If *and every* were omitted, the sense would be the same, since *each* means every. The loss would be two useless words; the gain would be a more forceful sentence — and a cliché avoided.

> **Note:** If you use the phrase *each and every*, remember that it is the equivalent of *each* (*and every* is ignored) and that it therefore takes a singular verb ("Each and every man *has* to shoulder his responsibilities").

4. My supervisor said, "I wish each and every one of you a good day." What do you think of that?

Very little. Mountebank's jargon for "each of you" or "every one of you." Useless words serve no purpose.

each other/one another

1. Are the traditional distinctions between *each other* and *one another* still observed?

Yes, at least in standard English. Careful writers use *each other* with regard to two persons or things and *one another* with regard to more

85

than two ("My twins love *each other*"; "The five of us will see *one another* at the next meeting").

> **Note:** The rule just stated is traditionally correct. But many writers refuse to conform to convention and, for reasons that are hard to understand, insist on interchanging these expressions, using *each other* for more than two and *one another* for only two. One may ask, what is gained by ignoring a simple principle, with centuries of approval behind it? The answer is that nothing is gained. Confusing these phrases is of no benefit to the English language.

2. Does the possessive form of *each other* and *one another* require distinctive handling?

The possessive case is formed by adding *'s* (*each other's, one another's*) followed by a plural noun ("We liked *each other's* hairstyles"; "The pirates were cutting *one another's* throats"). With an abstract noun, a singular form is needed so as not to convey an unintended meaning ("Let us not waste *each other's* time"; "Fred and Jean did not ask for *each other's* opinion"). And be careful with the possessive plural of *other*. It is *others'*, not *other's*.

effete

1. Spiro Agnew used the word *effete*, which sent us all to the dictionary. What does it mean?

It means worn out, barren, like a painter who has lost his touch because of age or overwork. It does not mean, as frequently seen or heard in common usage, effeminate, affectedly intellectual, sophisticated, or snobbish.

> **Note:** Some dictionaries define *effete* as marked by self-indulgence, decadence, or weakness. All these extended senses have captured the public fancy, and so more and more we see *effete* used in one of those popular ways. In fact, seldom is *effete* used to mean exhausted or unable to reproduce, its conventional meaning.

either

1. I have seen *either* followed by a singular verb ("*Either* of these apples *is* edible"), and I have also seen it followed by a plural verb ("*Either* of his ideas *are* bound to be accepted"). May *either* be used either way?

When *either* is the subject of a clause, it takes a singular verb even when followed by *of* and a plural noun or pronoun. Using a plural verb is a gross error. *Either* means one of two, and there is only the one way to use it.

> **Note:** Since *either* suggests two ("*Either* this or that"), it should not be used when more than two persons or things are being considered. Instead of "*Either* of the three encyclopedias will do," say, "Any one of the

three . . ." When *either* is used as an element in a correlative conjunction—*either . . . or*—the number of the verb following *or* depends on the number of the preceding nouns. If both are singular (*"Either* the teacher *or* the principal looks the class over daily"), the verb is singular. If both are plural (*"Either* the legislators *or* their constituents *have* to be consulted"), the verb follows suit. But when one noun is singular and one plural, the verb takes the number of the nearer noun (*"Either* the furniture *or* the *draperies are* to be selected first"; *"Either* the draperies or the *furniture is* to be selected first").

2. Something about this sentence bothers me, but I'm not sure what. Can you diagnose my trouble? "The painting *either* was genuine or a good copy."
What you are experiencing is akin to walking on a tilted floor. Stabilize the sentence by switching the position of *either*: "The painting was *either* genuine or a good copy."
> Note: In an *either . . . or* construction, the elements should be couched in similar grammatical form. A balanced pattern facilitates reading by clearly connecting the elements of equal rank. Each member of this group must be followed by the same part of speech. It matters not where the elements *either . . . or* are placed in the sentence provided they are in a grammatically parallel position. For example, you may write *"Either* the painting was genuine *or* it was a good copy," "The painting *either* was genuine *or* was a good copy," or as was said at the beginning, "The painting was *either* genuine *or* a good copy."

3. I am confused by the use of *either*. It seems to mean one thing at one time and something else at another. I could use some help.
You are probably, and understandably, referring to two meanings of *either* that seem contradictory. You may say, *"Either* you eat or drink," which means one or the other (but not both). You may also say, "Pictures hung on *either* side of the hall," which means on both sides. *Either* has two opposite meanings.

elapse

Is it proper to say, "After the *elapse* of five years, we met"?
It is not improper to use noun *elapse*, but it is archaic. The accepted noun form today is *lapse*. Use *elapse* as a verb: "After five years *had elapsed*, we met again."
> Note: Some dictionaries contend that noun *elapse* is standard, but popular as well as formal usage refutes it.

elected/appointed

1. Of what should one be careful when using the words *elected* and *appointed*?
Be sure not to follow these verbs with *as* in such sentences as "Rachel

was *elected* house mother" and "Roslyn was *appointed* counsel" — not *elected as*, not *appointed as*, because *as* is unidiomatic after words of designation such as *elected*, *appointed*, and *named*.

2. Does the word *elect* take a hyphen?
As a suffix referring to a person elected but not yet installed in office, *elect* is always hyphenated. Not "Lauren Rose is the *president elect*," but the "president-elect."

elicit/illicit/extract

Please straighten out the confusion between the words *elicit* and *illicit*.
The confusion caused by these words can be attributed to their almost identical sounds. *Elicit* means to bring out, to draw forth, as one draws out a confession ("They tried to *elicit* more information"). *Illicit* means unlawful or prohibited ("Our neighbor admitted that he had had an *illicit* love affair").

> Note: One might think that it is impossible to mistake these terms for each other, especially since *elicit* is a verb and *illicit* is an adjective. But these mistakes do occur.
>
> *Elicit* and *extract* are synonyms but not exact synonyms. Inherent in *extract* is a sense of force — that is, something has been forcefully removed (possibly the way a tooth is extracted), but it is also used figuratively of threats and intimidation. The word *extort* comes into comparison with *elicit* and *extract*, for it suggests wringing something from a person who does not want to give it up.

ellipsis

What is meant by an *ellipsis* and how does it function?
An *ellipsis* is an omission of one or more words needed to complete a grammatical construction of a sentence. If what is omitted does not alter grammatical construction, the ellipsis is satisfactory, a true ellipsis. In "Steve is tall, his brother short," the missing *is* after *brother* is mentally supplied. And since *is*, the carried over word, is the correct one for that place, the ellipsis is true. But in "The teammates either have or will unite for victory," the ellipsis is false because *united* belongs after *have* ("The teammates either have *united* or will *unite* . . .").

> Note: A form of ellipsis often found in formal writing appears in a compound sentence in which the elements are separated by a semicolon but a verb from the first element is carried over in the mind to the second. To indicate a missing word (the carried-over verb), a comma is inserted ("The employer contributed 70 percent; the employees, 30 percent").
>
> *Ellipses* are marks used to indicate an omission of a word or words from a sentence by the insertion of three dots or periods, or they may be asterisks ("And he then said he wanted to go and . . ."). If the ellipsis

takes place at the end of the sentence, as shown, four dots are needed if a period would ordinarily follow the sentence, the fourth being the final period.

else

May it be my choice whether to follow *else* with *but* or *than* in a sentence such as "Nothing else *but* (or *than*) this will do"?
To follow *else* with *but* is impermissible. However, you may combine *else* with *than* ("Nothing *else than* this will do") or if you wish, drop *else* ("Nothing *but* this will do").

> **Note:** When a person or thing is compared with others in its own category, that person or thing must be excluded. It would make no sense to say, "My stockbroker is more knowledgeable than anyone in his office," but it is proper to say, "My stockbroker is more knowledgeable than anyone *else* in his office." Bear in mind that *else* is primarily an adverb, not a conjunction. Therefore, rather than "We have to leave now, *else* we'll be late," say *or else*, or simply *or*. One thing more. When *else* follows an indefinite pronoun — *anyone, everyone, someone* — it takes the sign of possession. No longer, although it is still technically correct, is the indefinite pronoun made into a possessive. Not *anyone's else*, but *anyone else's*. And be sure not to write *whose else's*. The possessive form of *who else* is either *who else's*, followed by a noun ("*Who else's* hat might it be?") or *whose else* ("*Whose else* could it be?").

emigrate/immigrate

My grandfather migrated from Russia to the United States. I understand that he emigrated and immigrated. How did that come about?
Your grandfather emigrated from Russia and immigrated to the United States. To *emigrate* is to leave; to *immigrate* is to enter. Your grandfather left one country and then entered another, to settle there.

> **Note:** Verbs *emigrate* and *immigrate* are followed by different prepositions. A person *emigrates from* and *immigrates to*. Be alert to the spelling of *emigrate* and *immigrate* — *immigrate* has two *m*'s. A sister word, *migrate*, with no sense of direction implied, enjoys a latitude with prepositions. It may be followed by *from* or *to*. "Alex *migrated from* France to Switzerland. After staying for a while, he *migrated to* Italy."

enamored

Is it proper to use the phrase *enamored about* to mean in love with or very fond of?
It is not. Idiom allows *enamored of* or *with*. "Sally is *enamored of* her boss." "Bob is *enamored with* Renaissance art." *Enamored* takes *of* with a person and *with* with impersonal things.

> **Note:** Although almost all authorities agree that *enamored* may take only

of or *with*, occasionally *by* seems appropriate: "She was enamored *by* her own mirrored image." The British spell *enamored* with *-our* (*enamoured*).

endorse

Why say *endorse on the back*? Does anybody endorse anywhere else?
Etymologically the expression is redundant because *endorse* comes from Latin *dorsum*, "the back." But since *endorse* is often equated with *sign*, the phrase *endorse on the back* has come to be widely used for definiteness, its sense being sign, preferably on the back, but not necessarily.

> **Note:** One may endorse a bill by signing anywhere on it. It need not be on the back. *Indorse* is a variant spelling, but *endorse* is by far the more accepted form. These words, figuratively, mean to support or approve ("Will you *endorse* my campaign?").

end result

Is the phrase *end result* objectionable?
Yes, because it's redundant. Omit *end*. Only where there are intermediate results may *end result* rightly serve. And such instances are rarities.

> **Note:** A cousin to *end result* is the phrase *as the result of,* as in "*As the result of* the automobile accident, Andrew had double vision for three days." The accident undoubtedly was the cause of many results—damage to the vehicle, other personal injuries, for example. The proper expression, therefore, is as *a* result of ("As *a* result of the automobile accident, Andrew had double vision for three days").

ennui

How should *ennui* be pronounced?
Ennui, which means boredom, has two syllables and is pronounced ahn-wee. The syllables are evenly stressed. The word, borrowed directly from the French, is still pronounced in Gallic fashion.

enormity/enormousness

What should one say about this sentence: "The *enormity* of the stadium thrilled us"?
The word *enormity* is being misused. The word called for is *enormousness.* *Enormity* means excessive wickedness or outrageousness (the *enormity* of his crimes); it does not refer to size. *Enormousness* does. Synonyms are hugeness and vastness.

> **Note:** The frequent misuse of *enormity* for *enormousness* does not alter the course of the English language. Even the misuse of these words by President Bush is no justification for anyone to follow suit. Nor is the fact that some dictionaries equate the terms. True, the noun form of

enormous, which is *enormousness*, is clumsy and some people stumble over its pronunciation. But the English language is filled with words that cause similar problems. Confusing meanings of words will not clarify them or make for precise communication. Hold fast to this one!

enthuse

I hear the word *enthuse* used so frequently that I wonder whether it has achieved literary status?
Not at all. In formal discourse *enthuse* has not been welcomed. It remains an unacceptable back formation from the noun *enthusiasm*. It is correct to say, "I am *enthusiastic* about my son's prospects," but not "I am *enthused.* . . ."

> **Note:** Many verbs evolve from nouns and are warmly received into standard English. In each case it was felt that a need existed for the verb or that the verb had a flavor of its own. For example, *donate*, from *donation*, has been adopted with no travail. It has taken its place alongside *diagnose, drowse, orate*, and others. But verbs so formed are at first resisted, perhaps to test their mettle in the literary cauldron. They usually undergo a long trial period before full acceptance.

entrust

How is the word *entrust* properly constructed and used?
Idiomatically a person *entrusts* something *to* someone ("He *entrusted* all the information *to* his partner"), but *entrusts* someone *with* something ("He *entrusted* his partner *with* all the documents").

> **Note:** To *entrust* is not merely to trust or to place trust in. It is to give into the charge of, or to place in charge of something.

enumeration

Which is preferable in an enumeration —*first, second, third; first, secondly, thirdly;* or *firstly, secondly, thirdly?*
The first form, since it is the shortest. The third is seldom if ever used. *Firstly* is an abomination. The second form has many followers —"*First,* I believe he is right. *Secondly,* I think we should agree with him." But style is a matter of personal taste. Choose the one you want.

> **Note:** *First, second,* and *third,* although they have no -*ly* ending and are adjective forms, may serve as adverbs as much as *firstly, secondly, thirdly.* Consistency in practice should lead one not to write *first* and then follow it with *secondly.*
>
> Good writers would not condone the phrases *first of all, second of all,* and so forth. The *of all* is unnecessary. Avoid it.

epigraph/epitaph

On a recent trip our guide talked about *epigraphs* and *epitaphs*. I was confused. Would you please clarify?

According to the dictionary an *epigraph* is an inscription, as on a statue or building or on a tomb, and an *epitaph* an inscription on a tombstone or monument in memory of a dead person.

> Note: The confusion caused by these sound-alikes comes from the same meaning ascribed to each word—an inscription on a tomb. It would be better if the use of *epigraph* were restricted to an inscription on a building, especially since *epitaph* may not be so applied. Then only *epitaph*, which in Greek literally means on a tomb, would refer to a writing in memory of someone buried, whether the inscription was on a statue or a tomb.
>
> A monument erected to honor a dead person whose remains are elsewhere is called a *cenotaph*. That word comes from two Greek words that mean empty tomb.
>
> Addendum: An *epigraph* is also a quotation at the beginning of a book to indicate the leading idea or theme.

epithet

Is an *epithet* an abusive word?

Yes. In general usage an *epithet* is regarded as an abusive or contemptuous term ("Sam the Shifty"). But primarily an *epithet* is a term to characterize a person (Honest Abe) or to serve as a descriptive substitute for a name or title (Richard the Lion-Hearted). The epithets are "Honest" and "Lion-Hearted."

> Note: Be careful with this word *epithet*, since it has two disparate meanings. It may be better, if derogatory remarks are referred to, to speak of "words of contempt," for example, instead of saying a person spoke with epithets, even though more people would take *epithet* to mean abusive words or phrases rather than its primary meaning, a descriptive term.

epitome

Is *epitome* used correctly in "As a danseuse, Charlotte is the epitome of grace"?

Dictionaries give two unrelated meanings to *epitome*. In its primary sense an *epitome* is a summary, an abstract, as of a book or article. The Greek forebear of *epitome* meant to cut short. And that is what an epitome does. It offers a short statement that typifies the whole. But it has also come to mean an ideal or representative example. In this latter sense Charlotte, figuratively, is the epitome of grace.

> Note: The error that is sometimes made with *epitome* is to regard it as the equivalent of acme, the high point. *Epitome* does not mean that.

equal

Is it permissible to say *more equal* or *most equal*?
Not grammatically. *Equal* is an "absolute" term and is therefore not capable of comparison. Something cannot be *more equal* than something else or the *most equal* of all. The latitude allowed is in the expression *more nearly* equal. That extension is acceptable on all levels of English.

> **Note:** A number of "absolute" terms are discussed in this book. They are all subject to the same restrictions; that is, they may not be compared because they are absolute unto themselves. Hence *more dead, most complete, more round, most square* are poorly constructed. The saving grace, as previously pointed out, is to use the modifier *more nearly.* But be aware that some dictionaries approve a comparison of *equal* (as in "a *more equal* distribution of funds"), which gives one authoritative approval to do likewise. It is wiser, nevertheless, not to go along. The importance of precision in language cannot be stressed enough. One might just as well speak of "a *more nearly equal* distribution" or "a *more equitable* distribution" and have no qualms about correct usage.

equally as

How should these kinds of sentences be handled: "Vivian is equally as bright as her sister" and "Frank continued equally as adamant on all announced policies"?
In the first example, adverb *equally* is unnecessary. Drop it ("Vivian is as bright as her sister"). In the second example, drop *as*, since *equally as* is redundant ("Frank continued *equally* adamant on all announced policies").

> **Note:** In an *as . . . as* comparison, as in the example, *equally* does not belong, since *as* means to the same extent or degree, which is equally. Therefore, these words in tandem are redundant. Whether to keep *equally* and drop *as*, or vice versa, is a matter of emphasis. *Equally* makes the comparison more emphatic. Another remedy is to drop *equally* for *just as.* Instead of "Brussel sprouts are *equally as* healthful as spinach," say, " . . . *just as* healthful as spinach." Of course, neither *just* nor *equally* is necessary. The sentence reads as well without either one: "Brussel sprouts are *as* healthful *as* spinach."

-er/-or

How do I know when to choose the *-er* or the *-or* ending of a noun?
You can't. You must be taught or you must consult a dictionary (*teacher, fighter, writer; actor, creditor, protector*). Each ending denotes a doer, one who does something.

> **Note:** Selecting the proper spelling of these *-er* and *-or* nouns is particularly vexatious because no rule governs. As a general proposition, but

shot through with exceptions, words derived from Latin take -*or* and those of Anglo-Saxon origin take -*er*.

A sister problem, but one not so serious, is determining whether a word should end in -*er* or -*re*. Words borrowed from the French were imported with -*re* spellings. Most of these words, with time, were converted into -*er* endings; a few (*acre, massacre, mediocre*) retained their original ending. The British favor -*re* and so do those Americans who think the ending gives the noun a touch of class; hence *theatre, centre, sceptre*.

erstwhile

Is *erstwhile* an acceptable substitute for *former*?
It is an archaic synonym. It sounds pretentious and is best used only when humor is intended. Rather than saying, "Barney is an *erstwhile* bartender," prefer "a former bartender."

escape

Where did the word *escape* come from?
The word is a combination of Italian *ex* (out of) and *cappa* (cape). In former times when an attacker grasped a man's cape (a customary garment for men), the victim would squirm out of it, leaving the attacker holding the bag—or in this case, the cape. Breaking loose and fleeing was a leaving "out of the cape," *ex cappa,* or as anglicized, an *escape.*

> **Note:** Some authorities have pointed out that in recent times one who escapes is called an *escaper*. And some dictionaries go along, listing both an *escapee* and an *escaper* as one who has escaped. Accordingly, you may choose either word to describe someone who has fled captivity.
>
> Verb *escape* is both transitive and intransitive. As a transitive verb, it takes a direct object and is not followed by a preposition ("He *escaped* boredom by leaving for India"). As an intransitive verb, meaning to get free, to get out and away, *escape* takes preposition *from* ("Paul *escaped from* his confining cell," not "Paul *escaped* his confining cell").

especially/specially

Should we say, "This car is built *especially* (or *specially*) for large families"?
Choose *especially*, which means particularly, more than others, to a marked degree ("Roger is an *especially* capable negotiator"). *Specially* means for a specific purpose or for a designated reason ("The house was *specially* planned for an invalid"; "Those students were *specially* selected for their artistic talents").

> **Note:** In many cases these words are interchangeable with no loss in sense. But be aware of the distinctive meanings of each word. "Rose Mary is *especially* (particularly) fond of chopped liver, which her favorite

chef makes *specially* for her." Usually *specially* modifies a verb form such as *planned* or *selected* rather than an adjective such as *fond*. In "We ought to make a party for Mom, *especially* now," *specially* could be substituted without affecting the meaning. This is a case in which those words may be interchanged. However, *especially* has more force there than *specially*.

et al./etc.

1. The chairman announced, "At the board meeting we discussed policy, implementation, personnel, et al." I didn't think *et al.* belonged.

You're right. The abbreviation *et al.* is from Latin *et alii*, meaning "and others." To be accurate, therefore, it may be used only of people, not things. For "other things" *etc.* is called for. Hence on two counts *et al.* should not have been used in the example.

> Note: The abbreviations *et al.* and *etc.* are inappropriate in formal writing. They belong in technical writing, footnotes, or legal compositions. Observe that *et* and *al.* are separate words. Since *et* is not an abbreviation, it takes no period. But *al.*, an abbreviation for *alii*, does.

2. The abbreviation *etc.* looks ugly to me. And I find it generates errors in usage. If you agree would you discuss this matter?

True, *etc.* does not belong in literary prose. Where *etc.* serves a useful purpose (usually in footnotes), it is not spelled out, not *et cetera*. Only the abbreviated form, *etc.*, is used. And since *et* means "and," it is wrong to say "and etc." *Etc.* is best preceded by a comma or a semicolon.

> Note: *Etc.* can be avoided in formal writing by introducing an enumeration with *for example* or *such as* or by replacing it with *and so forth*.

eternal/everlasting

Is there a difference in meaning between *eternal* and *everlasting*?

Although often interchanged, the words are to an extent distinguishable. *Eternal* refers to that which is without beginning or end; it is unceasing ("Religionists think of God as the *eternal* father"). *Everlasting* refers to that which goes on without end; in other words, lasting forever ("The beauty of this park is *everlasting*").

> Note: *Eternal* is defined as everlasting, which from a layman's position, makes the words synonymous; hence frequently interchanged. The words are regarded as "absolute" terms and therefore should not be compared, which means that neither word may properly be modified by *more* or *less*.

etymology/entomology

What is the distinction between *etymology* and *entomology*?

Etymology is the study of the origin and history of words. *Entomology* is the study of insects. Be sure not to confuse these terms.

> Note: *Etymology* comes from Greek *etymon,* "the original sense of a word," from *etymos,* "true," "real." *Entomology* comes from Greek *entomon,* "insect."

euphemisms

Is the use of *euphemisms* objectionable?

Euphemisms (Greek, "words that speak well") are properly used when they relieve pain, reduce coarseness, or avoid offensiveness. There's nothing wrong with saying you're going to the lavatory when you're really looking for a toilet. Explicit terms are shocking to some people and may be censurable in print. Substituting softer and gentler names for an offensive one is the purpose of euphemism.

> Note: There is nothing wrong with removing the distasteful from printed matter so long as we don't cater to the squeamish. Selected wording walks a thin line. What will satisfy everyone or even most people are unanswerable questions. A writer must use good judgment, which is simply the best judgment he has.
>
> A word that looks and sounds somewhat like *euphemism* is *euphuism.* It is an uncommon word but appears occasionally in literary works. *Euphuism* is an affected literary style, characterized by extended comparisons, alliteration, and elaborate antitheses. It was an invention of John Lyly, a sixteenth-century novelist, who wrote *Euphues, or the Anatomy of Wit.*

even

What warning should one heed when using the word *even?*

Remember to place it immediately before the word it modifies. Its placement can affect the meaning of the sentence; for example, "*Even* Roger did not speak to me today"; "Roger did not speak *even* to me today"; or "Roger did not speak to me *even* today." Each of those sentences has a meaning quite different from the others.

> Note: Such limiting adverbs as *ever, exactly, just, nearly,* and *only* join *even* regarding proper placement. According to convention, they should stand before the word they modify so as not to spoil the meaning of the sentence.

ever

1. "Do you *ever* think there will be free medical services?" is a kind of sentence frequently heard. What is your opinion of it?

The sentence would improve if *ever* were repositioned—"Do you think there will *ever* be free medical services?" Modifiers should be kept close to words they modify.

> Note: *Ever* appears in some accepted expressions, as in *ever so often,* meaning very often or repeatedly. It comes into contrast with the idiom

every so often, which means at different times or now and then. Sometimes misconstructed are the phrases *rarely if ever* and *seldom if ever*. They mean infrequently, if at all. The caveat is not to omit *if*. Saying, "He *rarely ever* visits New York" or "He *seldom ever* eats Italian food" is substandard. *Ever* means at all times; *rarely* and *seldom*, occasionally or infrequently. Which means that the words, without *if*, are in conflict with each other. Say, "He *rarely if ever* visits New York."

2. When should the word *ever* be followed by a hyphen?

When it attributively accompanies a modifier before a noun: *ever*-increasing costs. But not when it comes after a verb: "The costs are *ever* increasing." Always hyphenate *ever-faithful* and *ever-ready*, regardless of position. *Everlasting* and *evergreen* take no hyphen.

3. How does one know whether to write *who ever* or *whoever*, *what ever* or *whatever*?

Opinion among authorities is split on whether *-ever* words should be written as one or two words. The best approach is to write *-ever* words solid if generalizing ("*Whomever* I see first I will appoint") but open if part of a question ("*Who ever* would say that?" "*What ever* could have been in his mind?" "*When ever* will it come to pass?" "*Where ever* have you been?").

> Note: In each case *-ever* serves as an intensifier, giving greater emphasis to the question. But its presence is unnecessary as far as the sense of the sentence is concerned. Rhythm and euphony, however, play a part in the decision. In those regards, the *-ever* words may be useful.

every

1. Would you criticize this sentence: "Every one of the delegates who voted *were* given a plaque"?

Yes. The error in that sentence lies in the number of the verb. *Every one* (adjective plus pronoun) is singular and, of course, requires a singular verb. The verb *were* should therefore be changed to *was*.

2. Why is it that we say, "Every boy and girl in our class *has* been given a diploma"?

It is simply a matter of idiom. *Every* connotes a plural sense, but idiom is not concerned with sense. Furthermore, your sentence has a compound subject. Certainly in most cases a plural verb is required when two nouns or pronouns are joined by *and*. But not if preceded by *every*. A compound subject modified by *every* requires a singular verb because in this construction *every* means each person individually.

> Note: The idiom *no . . . and no* is treated in the same way. It takes a singular verb even though the subject elements are joined by *and* ("*No* man *and no* woman belonging to the opposite party *is* allowed to enter").

every day/everyday

When I mean daily, should I write *every day* or *everyday*, or doesn't it matter?

It does, very much so. Those words are unrelated in meaning and serve different functions. *Every day* (adjective plus noun) is an adverbial phrase of time, meaning each day in succession ("My father goes to work *every day*"). The compound word *everyday* is an adjective meaning common or not unusual (an *everyday* occurrence, an *everyday* dress).

> **Note:** If the word wanted is employed as a modifier, it must be *everyday* ("This is my *everyday* coat"). *Every day* serves differently: "He visited his aunt *every day*" or "*Every day* he visited his aunt."

everyone/every one

How does one know when to spell *everyone* as one word and *every one* as two?

Always use two words (*every one*) unless *everybody* is meant. Then use *everyone*. For example, "Since *everyone* is here, we will catalogue *every one* of those books." But because you cannot substitute *everybody* for *everyone* in "*Every one* of the boy scouts is doing his duty" or in "*Every one* of those books belongs to the library," *every one* is required. In those last two examples the meaning is of every single one, and the stress is on *one*.

> **Note:** *Everyone* and *everybody* are interchangeable pronouns, but *everyone* is thought to be more euphonious and therefore predominates in formal writing. These pronouns, as subjects, although they seem to have a plural sense, are singular and take singular verbs and singular referents: "*Everyone has* to be seated before *he* may address the chair." To avoid the awkwardness of such sentences, as "If *everyone* is hungry, let *him* come to the dining room," recast by employing plural elements: "The dining room is open for *all* who are hungry." And so with the example before the last: ("*Every* person must be seated before *anyone* may address the chair").

everywheres

Is it correct to say, when thinking of many places, "We looked every-wheres but could find nothing"?

Everywheres is substandard and not an acceptable replacement for *everywhere*. The *s* at the end does not belong. This advice applies equally to *anywheres* and *somewheres*.

> **Note:** In informal discourse *everyplace* is often used adverbially for *everywhere:* "We searched *everyplace* (or *every place*) but could not find Dad's watch." Many authorities frown on this usage, even for casual speech. It is best to employ *every place* (two words) as an adjective and a noun ("We drilled in *every place* suggested by the geologist") and *everywhere*, which

is invariably written as one word, as an adverb ("We searched *everywhere* for Dad's watch").

evidence/testimony

Is testimony considered evidence?
Yes. *Evidence,* information that contributes to the discovery of truth, may take various forms — fingerprints, business records, photographs, or testimony. It includes all means by which a matter at issue is established or disproved. *Testimony* is a form of evidence, a subcategory. It consists of only one form: statements of witnesses, which incidentally, may be false or baseless.

except

1. Should I say, "Everyone *except* (or *excepting*) me was included"?
Take your pick. Either preposition (*except* or *excepting*) may be used correctly in the example. The preference is for *except.*
   Note: In negative constructions *excepting* is the preposition to use: "All day students, not *excepting* the athletes, must attend chapel services."

2. This sentence bugs me: "The United States and Canada are alike except for the fact that Canada has no tropical zones." Does it bug you, too?
It is bothersome. The verbose phrase *except for the fact that* is reducible to *but,* a saving of four words. Unnecessary words lower the quality of writing and tire the reader.

3. Was my cousin right when she said, "Everyone was there except you and I"?
She was not. *Except* is a preposition. The noun or pronoun following a preposition is its object and must accordingly be in the objective case. *I* is a nominative-case form; *me* is an objective-case form. Therefore, *except you and me.*

exceptional

My son sometimes confuses the words *exceptional* and *exceptionable.* How can I help him keep those words straight?
Tell him that *exceptional* means unusual and *exceptionable* means objectionable. Let him note that *exceptionable* and *objectionable* not only mean the same but end the same — with *-able.*

exigency

May *exigency* be stressed on the second syllable?
This noun, meaning an urgent need, is preferably stressed on the first

syllable, EHK-sih-jehn-sih, rather than ek-SIJ-en-sih. And the first syllable should be pronounced ek, not eg.

expect

Is it correct to say, "I expect it is so" or "I expect it was so"?
Expect is a verb that looks to the future, to the probable occurrence of something. It does not look to the present or at the past. Therefore, the examples are out of focus. You may properly say, "I *expect* to leave tomorrow." The examples would not be subject to criticism if *think, believe,* or *suppose* replaced *expect.*

Note: Although critics have different ideas about the acceptability of *expect* as a synonym for *presume* or *believe,* the predominant thought is that in formal discourse the meanings of those words are not to be equated. The synonyms are characteristic of informal speech, and on that level should not be criticized.

Occasionally you might hear someone say, "I *suspect* it will happen." What was meant, and what should have been said, was "I *expect* it will happen." *Suspect* means to distrust, to be suspicious of, to imagine someone to be guilty of something. It is not a synonym of *expect.*

expletive

What is an expletive?
The word *it* or *there* when serving as anticipating subjects is an expletive, as in "*It* is a pleasure to be here" or "*There* are two matters to discuss." An *expletive* is also a sudden exclamation or oath, especially one that is profane. Nixon's tapes, when transcribed, contained the warning "*expletives deleted,*" meaning that Nixon's obscene remarks were being withheld.

Note: In grammar, an *expletive* serves as a filler word to introduce intransitive verbs: "*It is* time for us to leave"; "*There are* more books here than we need." The expletive *there* takes a singular or a plural verb, depending on the number of the deferred subject: "*There is* a big cat on the front lawn"; "*There are* five trees to be trimmed."

Be careful that the inversion occasioned by an expletive does not lead to an incorrect number of the verb. In "There remains for consideration those problems we discussed yesterday," *remains* should be changed to *remain.* But it is a writer's choice to use *is* or *are* or *was* or *were* in a series of nouns when the first one is a singular. Although technically a plural (*are, were*) is required, the attraction of the initial singular noun may justify a singular verb: "There *is* a book, a pen, two pencils, and a ruler on the desk."

One more thought. Expletive *there* delays the true subject. "There are many patients waiting" needs only "Many patients are waiting."

And note that an expletive (pronounce it EHKS-plih-tihv) that is an exclamation or oath may be any word or phrase uttered simply for emphasis or to vent feelings. It need not be a curse word. For example, *Good gracious! O darn! Golly!* are all expletives.

ex post facto

What does *ex post facto* mean?
Literally "from what is done afterwards," its dictionary definition is "made or done after something but applying to it." In law, it applies to actions done before the law was passed. An *ex post facto* construction contains an impossible attribute made after an event: "The chief had warned the dead policeman to wear a bulletproof vest." (The chief couldn't warn a dead man.)

F

fact

1. Would you criticize this sentence: "If we had been told of the fact that a terrorist was loose, we would have barred our doors"?

The sentence would improve if the useless phrase *of the fact* were omitted. "If we had been told that a terrorist was loose, we would have barred our doors" is all that is necessary.

> **Note:** It is a fact that the word *fact* sometimes intrudes into a sentence where it is not needed. A person who begins by saying, "I appreciate the fact that," is already guilty of verbiage. "I appreciate your coming" is simple and direct; "I appreciate the fact that you came" is uneconomical. Also unnecessary is *the fact* in such a sentence as "The candidate mentioned *the fact* that he was a war veteran." His candidacy will not suffer if *the fact* is omitted. And neither would the sentence. In fact it would improve. What perhaps is more to be deplored is the redundant *true facts*. A fact by definition is true. And one should be particularly careful not to use the word *fact* if no fact is being presented. Saying, "I wish to make a point of the *fact* that I intend to change things" is wrongly put because an intention is not a fact. Say instead, "I wish to make a point of my intention to change things."

2. My partner frequently begins a sentence with "The fact is." Is that phraseology recommended?

It is not. That there is a fact should not be telegraphed in advance. It should simply be given.

> **Note:** Saying, "We *acknowledge the fact that* (or *admit the fact that*) the contract was not fully complied with" could just as well be given "We *acknowledge* (or *admit*) *that* the contract was not fully complied with."

failed

1. Does one say, properly, "He failed to notice that he had left his umbrella"?

The word *fail* is not a satisfactory equivalent of "not." *Fail* implies a conscious effort, which means that to fail one must have tried. There is no notion of "trying" implicit in the example. Therefore, say, "He did *not* notice that he had left his umbrella."

> **Note:** Be careful not to use *fail* in a strictly negative sense. Newspaper reporters frequently note that someone failed to make any comments yesterday or failed to confirm an appointment or a story. To put it precisely, the reporters should have said that "no comments were made yesterday," "that an appointment was not made," and "that so and so did not confirm the story."

Fail is often misused concerning a student's failure in a course in school. One hears "The teacher *failed* Billy because Billy *failed* his last exam." This should preferably be restated: "Billy *failed* to pass the course because he *failed* in an examination." In the sense "to be unsuccessful in an examination," *fail* is both an intransitive and a transitive verb ("Billy *failed* his examination").

2. My son Bobbie said he flunked English. Was that a proper way of saying it?
Colloquially *flunk* is used synonymously with failed. But in the best English, the word to use is the verb *failed* ("Bobbie *failed in* English," and not "Bobbie *flunked* English").

famous/notorious

Is it wrong to say, "He was famous for his misdeeds"?
Famous in that context is a poor choice. True, a person who has received widespread attention is said to be famous, but that word carries a favorable connotation. A suitable word, since you are talking about misdeeds, is *notorious*. Both *famous* and *notorious* develop their sense through the same means, except that the latter word is nurtured by unfavorable publicity.

> **Note:** The notorious may become famous after their death. John Dillinger was a notorious criminal during his lifetime, but we now speak of him as a famous bandit. And quite oppositely, the famous can become notorious. John Wilkes Booth was a famous actor who became, after his heinous crime, a notorious criminal. From famous he became infamous.

farther/further

Some writers frequently use *further* for *farther* ("We have a little *further* to travel"). Is this trend, that ignores the distinction between these words, encouraged by authorities?
Not by many. The prevailing opinion is that *farther* suggests physical distance and *further* metaphorical distance, which is any distance that cannot be measured. People who have not reached their destination must continue *farther*. But a discussion is continued *further*.

> **Note:** *Farther* is the comparative degree of *far*, which makes a strong case for using *farther* when distance is being referred to. This leaves a wide field open for *further*. It may properly be used in most other cases. In each instance, meaning additional or to a greater extent, the sense of *more* can be felt. It is the word to use to indicate continuation, time, quantity, or degree. "Let's talk a bit *further*." "You will receive no *further* contribution from me." "His thoughts are *further* from reality than one might imagine." *Further* also means moreover.
>
> Be careful with the superlative forms of these words. They are not *fartherest* and *furtherest,* but *farthest* and *furthest.* Interestingly enough,

although *further* is often used for *farther,* one seldom if ever sees *furthest* used for *farthest.*

favors

Is *favors* in "She *favors* her aunt" a generally accepted word?
It has wide colloquial usage. In formal prose prefer *looks like* or, better still, *resembles.*

Note: Some respected writers use *favors* meaning to resemble in features. They consider the expression standard and not colloquial, a trend gaining momentum.

faze

How is the word *faze* regarded by word-usage authorities?
Meaning to disturb, to disconcert, to agitate, *faze* is considered a colloquialism. It is usually used with a negative ("What she says doesn't *faze* me"). *Faze* should not be confused with *phase.* The moon has *phases,* not *fazes.*

Note: Webster equates *phase* with *faze,* but other dictionaries do not follow along. They maintain the distinction between these words.

Phase refers to one of the changing states or stages of development of a person or thing ("A *phase* of childhood is complete dependence on parents"). As a verb, *phase* is often used with *in* or *out.* To *phase in* is to integrate into; to *phase out* is to discontinue or eliminate. And then there is *phase down:* to reduce gradually.

feature

I find the word *feature* tiresome and sometimes used imprecisely. Do others have this feeling?
Be assured that you are not alone; others think as you do. *Feature* is a journalist's counter word, and it should be replaced, at least occasionally, by an equivalent noun *(trait, characteristic, attribute, mark, sign, main item)* or by a more suitable verb or verb phrase *(set apart, make a special point of).* There is no doubt that some of these suggestions more exactly convey the meaning that the writer had in mind.

Note: At one time *feature* was considered a colloquial expression and was frowned upon by literary writers. But time has passed, and now *feature* has become an accepted, perhaps even an indispensable, word. The thing to guard against is its too frequent use and, as pointed out, its use when a more suitable term is available.

The feature film is the main film in a cinema. The word, as so used, implies a number of films, the feature film being the most important. One should be careful, therefore, not to introduce a person as the featured speaker of the evening if there is only one speaker.

feminine endings

1. Are the words *authoress* and *poetess* in current usage?
No. An author or a poet is a person of either sex. Words to distinguish the sex of writers have long since disappeared. You'll find them in a linguistic museum.

> **Note:** Through the centuries it has been established that the masculine pronoun *he* refers to both sexes. Using *he* does not elevate a man to a higher position than that held by a woman. It equates them. And the word *man* has, in one sense, referred to mankind, not to one sex. The fact is that there is a *man* in *woman*, and no feminist has decried that word. But the trend is to remove feminine endings where possible: *server* rather than *waitress*, airline *attendant* rather than *stewardess*, and so forth. A few words have, however, withstood the onslaught and have retained their feminine endings: *hostess, actress, heroine, seamstress.*

2. Was the movement to eliminate feminine nouns of occupation successful?
It was in many respects. For example, *sculptor* and *editor* have become appropriate to refer to either sex. Even in law, an *executor* of an estate may be a man or a woman, the term *executrix* (a woman executor) being moribund. *Testatrix* is now seldom heard. The term *testator* is used of both sexes.

> **Note:** The best advice is to avoid sexist words where possible. But this is not a recommendation to resort to ugly or awkward terms or constructions to achieve that result. A writer today must walk a thin line if he or she wishes not to offend persons sensitive to sexist language. Unfortunately, there are no ironclad rules to restrain us in all instances. We must be our own judge.

few

1. The word *few* intrigues me. It is used in so many ways. It could mean a great deal or a short supply. Your comments would be appreciated.
The sense of *few* changes, almost reverses itself, depending on how it is used. The opposite of *few* is *many*. Therefore, if you say few people were there, you mean not many. But if you say quite a few were there, you mean a good many, possibly more than you expected. If you say only a few were there, clearly the attendance was disappointing.

> **Note:** Avoid the combination *few in number.* Drop *in number.*

2. Why do we say, "A few *are* here," but "A little *is* sufficient"?
It's a matter of idiom. *Few* refers to numbered units and is invariably plural ("A few men *are* here"). *Little,* referring to quantity, is invariably singular ("A *little* sand *is* in the bucket").

3. Isn't it contradictory to say *a few,* as in "A few people were there"?

So it seems. But *a few* is correct idiomatic English, even though *a* has a singular sense and *few* a plural.

4. Does *few* take a singular or a plural verb?
As an indefinite pronoun, it may take either a singular or a plural verb, depending upon the way it is used. We say, "A few *is* all I want" and "Many are called, but few *are* chosen."

fewer/less

I struggle with the words *fewer* and *less* is some usages. For example, should I say, "*Fewer* (or *less*) than four persons showed up"?
You should say "fewer than four." *Fewer* refers to numbers; *less* refers to amounts. Or, to put it differently, *fewer* is used of countable items; *less*, of collective quantity. "If we eat *fewer* calories, we'll have *less* fat."

Note: *Fewer*, not *less*, should be used before plural nouns because a smaller number is always possible. "Because the construction was completed, we now have *fewer* delays on the Expressway." This means a smaller number of delays. *Less* is used with singular nouns. "We are experiencing *less* delay than before" means that each delay is shorter in time.

Remember that saying *fewer in number* is redundant, but saying *a lesser number* is idiomatic. Be aware of units of time, money, weight, and distance. They take *less*, not *fewer*, since they express a unitary measure. "The price was *less* than five dollars." "He attended *less* than three weeks." "We walked *less* than four miles." "My wife weighs *less* than 160 pounds." The dollars, the pounds, and so on, are considered a total sum, not individual units. And also be careful of the phrase *no less than*. Although we often hear something like "There were *no less than* five bonds offered," what should have been said is "no *fewer* than five bonds." However, *no less than* seems to be on its way to idiomatic acceptance.

finalize

The word *finalize*, as in "If we work hard, we will finalize the project by next week," has suffered much linguistic battering. Should one use it?
Preferably not. Use instead *complete, conclude, finish, end,* or *make final*.

Note: *Finalize* may find its way into standard English someday. It is even now recognized by some authorities as an acceptable addition to the language. But many careful writers and speakers frown upon it, think it inept, and express themselves differently. The objection to this *-ize* coinage is that it is unnecessary and, what put a final stamp of disapproval on it, it sounds like a word from a bureaucrat's glossary. President Kennedy used *finalize* twice in a speech that was edited by Harvard professors. Which does not necessarily give it a badge of literary respectability. It is a calculated risk to use *finalize*, since so many writers and editors deride the word and think it an example of "jargonese."

final result

Does *final* in *final result* make the sense more forceful?
Final should be omitted unless the result is being compared to an intermediate result, which is rare.

> **Note:** A fellow redundancy is *final culmination,* as in "The last big drive for funds was the *final culmination* of our efforts." *Final* is unnecessary and should be dropped.

finish/complete

Are the words *finish* and *complete* synonymous?
Sometimes, but the sense of *finish* is to end; to *complete,* to arrive at a point where there's nothing more to do. Although the painters said they were *finished,* they hadn't *completed* the job. Students may throw down their books and say they're finished for the day, but that doesn't mean they have completed their homework.

> **Note:** In the sense used here, *complete* means to attain the limit of development. It is therefore an absolute term, and subject to no comparison. Something cannot be more complete than something else. If less than complete, it can properly be said to be *most nearly complete.*

first

1. How is *first rate* used correctly?
When it is used adjectivally, not adverbially. You may say, "He's a *first-rate* singer," but not "He sings *first rate.*"

2. Is the commonly heard introductory phrase *first of all* recommended? And how about *first and foremost*?
Both phrases contain verbiage. In the first, *of all* should be dropped. And so should *and foremost* in the second. Be alert to unnecessary words. They do not make a thought stronger; they weaken.

3. Should we say, "The three *first* applicants in line will be chosen" or "the *first* three applicants"?
The adjective *first* (and *last,* too) invariably precedes the numeral in such expressions as in the example. Although some authorities say the placement of *first* is unimportant, others disagree. The argument, a cogent one, is that there cannot be three who are first. Therefore, put *first* first.

flammable/inflammable

Since *flammable* means burnable, *inflammable* should mean not burnable. Why is that not so?
The *in* in *inflammable,* from Latin *in,* meaning "in," should not be confused with the Latin word *in* that means "not." *Inflammable* and *flamma-*

ble mean the same thing—burnable. The words, therefore, are inter-changeable. They are, in fact, exact synonyms. The terms for not burnable are *nonburnable* and *nonflammable*.

> Note: The traditional word that means something capable of burning is *inflammable*. For fear, however, that *inflammable* might be taken to mean nonflammable, not burnable, the word *flammable* was coined to disabuse that idea. *Flammable* is a good word to serve as a warning on oil trucks or on labels.

flaunt/flout

On several occasions I have heard political figures inveighing against their opponents for flaunting the law. What causes such a gross misusage?

Probably a mouth that moves faster than the mind. *Flaunting,* of course, is boasting. A man who bedecks his wife with jewelry and furs is flaunting his wealth. *Flouting* is ignoring. In the 1920s the women who "bobbed" their hair flouted convention. The opponents in the example should have been accused of *flouting* the law.

> Note: Even though it is clear that to *flaunt* means to show off, to display ostentatiously, to boast and that to *flout* means to mock, to scorn or scoff at, to treat with contempt, the U.S. Supreme Court in one case used *flaunt* twice where *flout* belonged. Nevertheless, that decision did not alter the meanings of those words. Perhaps like so many others, the Court was confused and thought that *flaunt* was a telescoped version of *flout* and *taunt.* Jimmy Carter once said, "The Government of Iran must realize that it cannot *flaunt. . .* the will and law of the world."

flounder/founder

If a boat couldn't make it, did it *flounder* or *founder?*

Both *flounder* and *founder* signal failure. To *flounder* is to struggle about clumsily, to thrash about helplessly, as in a mire. To *founder* is to sink. A boat may flounder if it loses its rudder, but if it hits bottom, it foundered.

> Note: Since *founder* means to fill with water and sink, saying the ship foundered and sank is redundant. Both *flounder* and *founder* may be used figuratively. A speaker who is unprepared or confused may *flounder* in trying to address a group. A project is said to *founder* if its goals are far from being met.

fly

1. Was the commentator wrong when describing an escape with the words, "The jailbird flew from the prison"?

If a jailbird was really a bird, *flew,* the past tense of *fly,* was correct.

But if the jailbird was an inmate, then *fled,* the past tense of *flee,* was required.

2. Is it correct to say, "Fly for your life"?
No. Instead of *fly,* the word to use is *flee,* which means to run away.

3. What do you say to this: "Three blue jays were spotted in the deep South after they flew from the far North"?
An auxiliary verb is missing. To show that the flying occurred before the birds were seen, make it "after they *had* flown from the far North."

> Note: Both verbs, *fly* and *flee,* are irregular verbs. The principal parts of *fly* are *fly* (present tense), *flew* (past tense), and *flown* (past participle). Of *flee,* they are *flee* (present tense), *fled* (past tense), and *fled* (past participle).

foible/forte

What do *foible* and *forte* mean and where did the words come from?
The words originated as fencing terms, *foible* being the flexible part of a sword, the pointed half, which is the weaker part, and *forte,* the upper part, the stronger part. In general usage a person's foibles are his shortcomings; fortes are strong points, the things the person does well.

> Note: *Forte* is pronounced with one syllable, fort. When it is used as a musical term, meaning very loud, it has two syllables, FOR-tay. Incidentally, *forte* was once spelled *fort,* but an *e* was added to analogize it with *locale, morale,* and other words with silent *e*'s. Fowler decried the addition, but it stayed.

following

Was the headline "Following the shoot-out, the police searched everyone" worded correctly?
No. *Following* is not a preposition. What should have been used is *after:* "*After* the shoot-out. . . ." Another caution: Avoid the redundant *follow after,* as in "The dinner will *follow after* the reception." Say, "The dinner will *follow* the reception."

> Note: In a sentence such as *"Following* the outbreak of war, a curfew was imposed," *following* is justified because it implies a consequence of a momentous event. But *"Following* the dinner, we will hear from Tom Smythe," needs only *after.*

for

1. The bank's slogan is "For all the things a bank is needed for." Was it proper to repeat the preposition *for*?
The combination *needed for* has a distinct meaning, which depends on the combination of both words. The second *for* in the example is not

a preposition but an adverb that has been acquired by, or merged with, *needed*.

> Note: *For*, like *because, as,* or *since,* may be used as a conjunction to introduce a subordinate clause that states the reason for the action in the main clause. Most often *because* is the most appropriate word, but *for*, which lends itself best in formal contexts, may serve as well.

2. Is there any serious objection to such phrases as *for the purpose of* and *for the reason that*?

Serious? They do not offend rules of grammar. But they are undesirable because each phrase is guilty of verbiage. "The course was given *for the purpose* of teaching tax reforms" is reducible to "The course was given *to teach* tax reforms." "For the reason that" may be replaced by *because* or *since.*

3. The *for* phrase that bothers me most is *for free*, as in "At the movies everyone got a pretzel for free." Am I foolishly bothered?

You are not. The slang phrase *for free* is illogical, since something given as a gift is free of obligation (if you get it free, you get it for nothing). Moreover, the phrase is ungrammatical. *Free* is an adjective and an adverb, not a noun. Preposition *for* cannot have an adjective or an adverb as its object. Incidentally, the expression *free pass* is just as illogical as your example *pretzel for free.*

4. My little boy has learned from his friends to say, "I want for you to go with me." Shall I overlook this colloquialism, or should I make efforts to correct him?

First, I would call the expression "for you to" a provincialism. Second, I would try to correct him by encouraging him to drop *for:* "I want you (no *for*) to go with me."

> Note: The phrase *for you to* is not inherently wrong. True, it should not follow a verb, as in the above example, but it may properly follow a noun ("I would like the opportunity *for you to* display your wares") or an adjective ("I would be happy *for you to* come early").

forbear/forebear

Is an ancestor a *forbear* or a *forebear*?

We can't choose an ancestor but we can choose the name to designate one—either *forbear* or *forebear*. Dictionaries enter them as variant spellings. But since *forbear* is also a verb (meaning to refrain or desist from) as well as a noun (meaning an ancestor), it is wiser to choose *forebear* to mean an ancestor. *Ancestor* is its only meaning.

> Note: When using the verb *forbear*, stress the second syllable. The stress in *forbear* or *forebear*, a noun, is on the first syllable. The principal parts of *forbear* are *forbear* (present tense), *forbore* (past tense), and *forborne* (past participle).

forbid/prohibit

What prepositions do the synonyms *forbid* and *prohibit* take?
Forbid is used with a *to* infinitive or a gerund. It never takes *from* ("We *forbid* him to leave"; "We *forbid* his leaving"). *Prohibit* takes *from* or an object noun ("We *prohibit* a person *from* doing something"; "The law *prohibits* the erection of houses over four stories tall").

> **Note:** Both *forbid* and *prohibit* have similar meanings. A person forbidden to do something or prohibited from doing something is simply not allowed to do it. The only difference of any consequence between them is the preposition each takes. The past tense of *forbid* is either *forbade* or *forbad*.

forceful/forcible

Is it permissible to say, "The habitual use of the active voice makes for forcible writing"? Would *forceful* have been a better word?
Today most authorities would prefer *forceful,* meaning vigorous and effective. They use *forcible* when there is physical force, such as a forcible entry into a burning building.

> **Note:** The words are synonyms. They mean possessing force. *Forceful* is a common word, frequently used (a *forceful* argument, a *forceful* personality). *Forcible* is an uncommon word, now used to refer only to what is accomplished by force (a *forcible* entry, a *forcible* ejection).

forego/forgo

If *forgo* may be spelled *forego,* how can we tell which to use?
Good question. *Forgo* means to abstain from, to relinquish, to give up ("To lose weight, you must *forgo* deserts"). To *forego* means to go before, to precede. But dictionaries do list *forego* as another spelling of *forgo*. The best approach to avoid confusion is to use only *forgo* when to do without is meant. This will confine the use of *forego* to its primary meaning of to precede.

> **Note:** Verb *forego* is seldom seen except in the participle *foregoing*. Its past tense, even more rarely seen, is *forewent*.

forehead

How should *forehead* be pronounced?
Preferably with a silent *h* (FAWR-ehd). You may rhyme *forehead* with *horrid*. Remember the nursery rhyme of the girl with a curl on her forehead who when "she was bad she was horrid."

> **Note:** Notice the word "preferably" in the first sentence. An accepted variant pronunciation is FOR-hehd.

forever/for ever

Does it matter whether the term meaning "for always" is written *for ever* or *forever*?
Not really. Use the form that pleases you. The term originally was written as two words *(for ever)*, but the single word now predominates *(forever)*.

> **Note:** Compounds made with *-ever* — *however, whatever, whenever* — are written solid. Adverbial phrases with *-ever* are written as two words — *how ever, what ever, when ever*. They are used with interrogatives and to express wonderment. *"How ever* did you get him to go along?" "We all wonder *how* you *ever* succeeded in convincing Milton." *"What ever* made you do that?" Notice that *ever* could be omitted from these examples without affecting the sense. It merely serves to emphasize.

former/latter

Is a writer who, when referring to two persons, repeatedly uses *former* and *latter* being slovenly?
Slovenly? No. Preferably the writer should repeat the names or sometimes use pronouns to save the reader from having to retrace steps to see "who is who." But occasional use of those words, to avoid an awkward repetition of names, has merit and is a device employed by many good writers.

> **Note:** The signposts *former* and *latter* may be used to direct attention to two items, but never more. When there are more than two, reference should be made to the *first* or *first-named* and to the *last* or *last-named*. *Former*, of course, refers to the first of two; *latter*, to the second. They should be avoided, however, if they interrupt the clarity of the sentence, or if the sentence is too intricate to tolerate them. Dr. Samuel Johnson deplored their use. He said, "As long as you have the use of your pen, never be reduced to that shift." Modern writers do not take so stringent a view. One thing more about the word *former*. When referring to a person who had held a position, a banker, for example, do not call him a *former ex-banker*. It is redundant to use both terms, since both *former* and *ex-* refer to the past. Say he is a *former* or an *ex-banker*.

fortuitous/fortunate

If something is fortuitous, is it not fortunate? Certainly meeting my college roommate in Macy's was fortuitous, and fortunate.
In part you have answered your own question. *Fortunate* pertains to good fortune, something pleasing. *Fortuitous* refers to a happening by chance or by accident, which may turn out to be fortunate or quite the opposite. In your case, both words are apt. If you had been an escaped convict and met your warden in Macy's fortuitously, that is, accidentally, the result might not have been fortunate — for you.

Note: *Fortuitous* is so frequently misused in the sense of fortunate that its correct use is being herewith reinforced. *Fortuitous* means unplanned; it has nothing to do with the nature of the occurrence. This means that a *fortuity* may be advantageous or disadvantageous. If it is advantageous, it is fortunate; if not, then it is unfortunate.

Frankenstein

Is it proper to refer to a situation that destroys its creator as a *Frankenstein*?
Theoretically, no. *Frankenstein* was the doctor who fashioned the monster, which ultimately destroyed him. But since almost everyone speaks of the disaster itself as being a Frankenstein or a Frankenstein monster, it may be so used in general speech.
   Note: Mary Wollstonecraft Shelley, the wife of the poet Percy Shelley, together with her husband and his friend Lord Byron, was spending time during a rainy day in Switzerland. To keep themselves amused, they decided to tell ghost stories. Mrs. Shelley's story was of a medical student, Victor Frankenstein, who infused life into bones stolen from a charnel house. What was created turned out to be a monster, who eventually killed Frankenstein's wife, his brother, and his best friend. Frankenstein's efforts to destroy the monster failed, and he himself was killed. The monster finally disappeared into the Arctic. When a reference is made to the monster as frankenstein, that name should be put in lower case.

friend/acquaintance

1. Are the word *friend* and *acquaintance* synonymous?
Not exactly. A *friend* is an acquaintance for whom a certain affection has developed, a person admitted to terms of intimacy. An *acquaintance* is merely a person whom one knows.

2. What is the adverb form of *friend*?
The adverb form of *friend* most commonly used is *friendly* ("She acted friendly toward me"). Another standard form, but one seldom seen or heard, is *friendlily*. Notice that *friendly* is also an adjective ("Pete is a *friendly* boy"). When referring to a member of the Society of Quakers spell *Friend* this way, with a capital *F*.

3. My daughter always alludes to a neighbor as a personal friend. Is that a good descriptive?
A friend is a friend. Unless distinguishing one from, say, a business friend, do not accompany *friend* with *personal*. Even worse is saying "a personal friend of mine." That phraseology is pointless and redundant.

from

1. What do you think of this sentence: "The company earned *from* $400,000 to $500,000 last year"?
The construction is redundant. Make it "The company earned $400,000 to $500,000 last year." Avoid the unnecessary *from.*

2. In our chancellor's biography, may we say that he served from 1979-1985?
Not properly. Since 1979-1985 is a period, it may not be introduced by *from.* You may phrase it "The chancellor served *in* 1979-1985," or use *from,* as in "*from* 1979 *to* 1985," in which *from* one year to another is indicated.

3. The story said, "He traveled to Essex, and from thence to Shropshire." Is *from thence* a correct usage?
It is not proper phrasing. *Thence* means from there or from that place. The preposition *from* is already built in. *From,* therefore, is redundant.
> **Note:** The expressions *from hence* (*hence* means from here, from this place) and *from whence* (*whence* means from where, from which place) should be given the same treatment — an excision of *from.*

4. If I am to be paid wages from June 1 to June 15, should I be paid for fourteen or for fifteen days?
You are to be paid for fourteen days, a two-week period. The last day is not included in the computation unless the wording says "from June 1 through June 15" or "from June 1 to and including June 15."

fulsome

Why is it that so many speakers — even prominent ones — fail to understand the meaning of *fulsome?* Have you not heard the expression *fulsome praise* time and again when an official was lauding somebody?
Possibly speakers are led into this error because of the misbelief that the "ful" in *fulsome* must denote full, abundant, or lavish. But it is not so. Instead of being complimentary, fulsome praise is insincere and overblown. Can you imagine how chagrined the person introducing the guest of honor would be upon looking up *fulsome* in a dictionary?

fungus/fungous

Which is right, "His *fungus* (or his *fungous*) needed a salve"?
Use *fungus.* Nouns end in *us*; adjectives end in *ous* (a *fungous* growth). Note *callus, callous; mucus, mucous.*

funny

May the word *funny* be used to mean odd?

Not on a formal level. It's colloquial to say, "It's *funny* he didn't call me." Use *odd, strange,* or *peculiar,* restricting *funny* to its basic meaning: humorous or comical. "A *funny* thing happened to me on the way to the Forum. My toga fell off."

> **Note:** Educated people often use *funny* to mean "I don't understand" ("It's *funny* that he hasn't arrived yet"). *Funny* is also used colloquially to suggest a foolish impropriety ("Horace tried to get *funny* with me").

G

gender

1. The *gender* of a noun or pronoun — masculine, feminine, neuter, common — connotes the sexual relationship. What's the difference between the last two?

The neuter gender implies no sex: chair, table, radio. The common gender pertains to people or animals, which of course have sex: baby, child, cat, student, but without any indication of a specific sex.

2. Feminists frequently refer to gender to mean *sex*. Is this approved style?

It is not in the opinion of most authorities. *Gender* is a grammatical term, and its use should be so confined. It is not a synonym for *sex*. Saying, for example, that gender is not a determinative for this job should be restated using *sex* for *gender*.

general

When a plural is needed, how is the word *general* handled?

It depends. As a military term, the noun *general* is pluralized by adding *s: generals*. As an adjective in a compound title, it is let alone; its accompanying noun is pluralized: *postmasters general*.

> **Note:** A compound term is one that applies to two or more words used as a single word. The compound might be written together: businessman *(businessmen)*, joined by a hyphen: soldier-statesman *(soldier-statesmen)*, or written separately: editor in chief *(editors in chief)*. It is a compound because it expresses a single idea. In general, a compound term is pluralized by adding *s* to the most important word, the one that tells what the principal is; *aides*-de-camp, deputy *chiefs* of staff, *notaries* public.

general public

Is it desirable to speak of the *general public*?

Preferably not. The phrase *general public* is redundant for *public* unless a contrast is being made with a particular segment of the public. And such a distinction is seldom necessary.

> **Note:** *Public* is a collective noun. Unlike many collective nouns that may take a singular or a plural verb, depending upon whether the members of the group are acting separately or as a whole, *public* usually takes a singular verb ("The public *is* all wrong"). In British English, *public* is regarded as a plural noun and thus takes a plural verb.

geographical names

How do we know not to capitalize a word derived from a geographical name?

Words used in a sense distinct from their original source, having lost their original importance, are written in lower case (*anglicize, arabic, bohemian, morocco, manila*).

gerund

1. Our teacher chided me for writing, "I dislike Rachel always trying to avoid kitchen duties." Do you agree with her?

Your teacher was justified in criticizing the construction of the sentence. What you should have said was *Rachel's always trying*. A noun or pronoun that is the subject of a gerund is in the possessive case.

> **Note:** Gerunds and participles look alike. They both end in *-ing*. The distinction between them is the way they're used. Gerunds are verbals that serve as nouns ("*Swimming* is Mike's best sport"–the gerund is the subject of the sentence; "Mike prefers *swimming* to any other sport" – the gerund is serving as the direct object of *prefers*; "Mike is tired of *wading*" – the gerund is the object of the preposition *of*). The thing to remember is that a noun or pronoun immediately before the gerund should be in the possessive case ("The *Inquirer's publishing* the story came as a big surprise"; "*His running* away was unexpected").

2. The judge of elections said, "Robertson's obligation for the paying of the bills will be passed on to Talmadge." Shall we judge the Judge to be a good grammarian?

Not on that example. The sentence would be counted a good one if *the* and *of* were omitted. The sentence would then read, "Robertson's obligation for (no *the*) paying (no *of*) the bills will be . . ." in which *bills* is the object of the gerund. Gerunds need not be set off by an article and a preposition.

3. The phrase *dangling participle* is common. Can a gerund dangle?

Yes. A gerund, like a participle, is a verbal, and it too dangles if it has no noun or pronoun to modify, as, "After considering the matter, a vote was taken" (the vote didn't consider the matter – the committee did). Correct as follows: "After considering the matter, the *committee* voted."

4. What do you think of this sentence: "The report should be synopsized before attempting to write it"?

The problem here is that the subject – the author – is not doing the acting. If the passive voice is converted into the active, the sentence, with a little recasting, would be acceptable: "Before attempting to write the report, the author should synopsize it."

5. I know that both a gerund and a participle end in *-ing*. Please give

us an example of each to show their distinctive use.
"Jogging is his chief pastime." *Jogging,* the subject of the sentence, is serving as a noun. It therefore is a gerund. In "We saw him *jogging* yesterday," *jogging* is a participle serving as an adjective, describing the pronoun *him.*

gibe/jibe

If I sneer at something or someone, do I spell it *gibe* or *jibe*?
Many dictionaries and other authorities say that the spelling of these words, which express a sense of mocking or sneering, is interchangeable. But others prefer *jibe* alone when taunting or heckling is meant and *gibe* when the sense is to match, to correspond, to be in agreement with.

> **Note:** *Gibe* and *jibe* are pronounced alike and rhyme with "tribe." The nautical sense of *jibe,* not being considered here, is "to swing from side to side when running before the wind."

gobbledygook

What is *gobbledygook*?
It is stuffy, pretentious, wordy, roundabout language. Coined by the Honorable Maury Maverick to imitate the cries of a turkey, *gobbledygook (gobbledegook)* is a forceful but informal term.

goes without saying

When I said, "It goes without saying," I was stopped dead in my tracks by someone who said, "So why say it?" Has that expression been outlawed?
Some linguists object to it; but many don't. It remains a useful transitional phrase to introduce what follows, as useful as "It is needless to say." But use sparingly.

> **Note:** Some critics suggest, rather than "It goes without saying," *naturally* or *of course.* In a proper context those expressions are just fine, and they are economical besides. But the question is, Do they have as good a flavor in this particular spot?

good and

What do you think of the phrase *good and*?
Although not grammatically correct, as in "I am *good and tired,*" it is commonly used in spoken English to intensify the following point. A similar phrase is "nice and" ("It's *nice and warm* today"), except that *nice* here implies approval.

> **Note:** Grammarians condemn the phrase *good and,* as in "Randy is *good*

and drunk," because it implies two actions, whereas only one is being called for. But some arbiters of usage insist that *and* reinforces the idea, so that greater thoroughness or determination is thereby expressed (*"Try and* stop me").

good/well

1. We discussed the difference in usage between *good* and *well* at a social affair but reached no conclusions. Would you help us?
Good is an adjective ("to have a *good* meal," "to hear a *good* orchestra"). *Well* is both an adjective and an adverb. After the copulative verb *look,* both words serve as adjectives, although used differently. *Good* refers to quality or appearance; *well,* to a state of health. In "The tangerines look *good,*" *good* refers to their degree of quality. In "My brother looks *good,*" *good* means that I like his appearance. But in "My brother looks *well,*" the reference of *well* is to health, the sense being "My brother seems healthy." In "My brother works *well,*" *well,* an adverb modifying the active verb *work,* describes how he works.

> Note: Some authorities, but not all, insist that after the copulative verb *feel,* the predicate adjective *good* is required to signify good health or high spirits. Those authorities would accept "I *feel* well" as meaning only that a person's sense of touch is functioning satisfactorily.

2. Is one limited to "You look *well"* when referring to good health?
No, you may say, "You look *good,"* the opposite of "You look *bad,"* and be grammatically correct (both *good* and *well* are adjectives). But many writers and speakers prefer *well* to signify sound health as distinguished from *good* meaning attractive.

got to get

Is there any objection to *got to get,* as in "I have *got to get* a new job"?
The expression is colloquial. It is better, certainly in writing, to say, "I *have to get* a new job."

> Note: The sense of *have to get* is *need.* "I *need (to get)* a new job." The phrase *have got* is frequently heard but is inappropriate in edited writing, although some respected authors use it. Obviously, in "I have a new bicycle," *have* alone, which expresses the idea of mere possession, is all that is required.
>
> The idiomatic expression "I *have got* to go" is condemned by purists because it clearly involves a redundancy. Nevertheless, it is in common use even by some careful speakers.
>
> Both *got* and *gotten* are past participles of *get,* and both forms are used in the United States (England prefers *got*). The distinction in usage between these past participles is that *got* connotes possession ("I've *got* that girl's address"), with no indication of time, whereas *gotten* may point to a recent acquisition ("I've *gotten* my raise").

graduated

Would a college student say, "Salvatore graduated college today"?
In the best English one should say either *was graduated from* or just
graduated from. Using *graduated* by itself, as in the example, is unacceptable. To receive the approval of your English teacher, be sure to follow
graduated with *from*. If *college* is not mentioned, *graduated* needs no *from*
("He *graduated* in 1934").

> **Note:** The older form *graduated from* ("Paula *graduated from* Vassar yes-
> terday"), although still very much alive, is not so much in play as its
> passive cousin *was graduated from* ("Sydney *was graduated from* Yale last
> week"). It does not matter which of these combinations you choose—
> *graduated from* or *was graduated from*—so long as you don't forget *from*.

graffiti

**The headline said, "The graffiti reflects the illiteracy of its scrib-
blers." Would you comment on that sentence?**
Graffiti is the plural form of *graffito*. The sentence, especially on such
a literate matter, should be consistently singular or plural: the *graffiti
reflect* or the *graffito reflects*.

> **Note:** Be sure to spell *graffiti* correctly, with two *f*'s and one *t*. And be
> equally sure to treat *graffiti* as a plural noun meaning inscriptions on a
> wall or fence. The caveat in this connection is to make certain that the
> verb is plural. Those who use the term *graffitis*, pluralizing the plural,
> have acquired few followers among educated people and probably none
> among those of Italian descent.

grammatical error

**May one speak of good grammar or bad grammar, and is not the
phrase *grammatical error* contradictory?**
Yes to the first question because correctness is not implicit in the word
grammar. No to the second. A definition of *grammatical* is "that which
relates to grammar" and "the systematic description of the ways of
language." One may speak grammatically of grammatical errors.

> **Note:** Some critics deplore the expression *grammatical error* on the theory
> that an error in grammar cannot be grammatical; in fact it is ungram-
> matical. But other authorities laugh at that distinction, think it pedantic,
> and say that a grammatical error is no more wrong grammatically than
> a *musical error* or an *artistic error* or any other kind.
>
> *Grammar* is the science treating of the use and application of language
> rules or, to be more specific, the study of the forms and uses of words in
> sentences of a particular language. The following are probably the most
> common mistakes made in grammar: 1. faulty agreement, 2. wrong case
> of pronouns, 3. wrong tense, 4. using an adverb for an adjective, 5.
> wrong form of the verb.

great grandfather

How should the word *great* be treated when it modifies *grandfather*?
Depends on the meaning. A grandfather whose grandchild had a baby
is a *great-grandfather* (hyphenated). A grandfather adored by his grand-
children is, to them, a *great grandfather* (no hyphen).

> Note: *Great* is used, as in the foregoing, in the names of relationship of
> the generation before and after: a *great-grandfather*, a *great-grandson*.
> These names are hyphenated.

grisly/grizzly

1. Do we say the accident was a *grisly* or a *grizzly* sight?
The former. *Grisly* means horrifying or gruesome. *Grizzly* means gray
or flecked with gray, like a gray beard or a gray bear. "That murder
was one of the most *grisly* on record." "The *grizzly* bear actually has fur
that is brownish." The word *grizzly* comes from the French *gris*, "gray."

> Note: Both *grisly* and *grizzly* are pronounced alike (GRIHZ-lee), with a z
> sound.

**2. I know that what is grisly is gruesome and what is grizzly is hair
flecked with gray. But when I come to spell them, I am not sure which
is which. Can you help me?**
You might remember that the word gruesome is often followed by the
word *sight* and that both *sight* and *grisly* have an *s*. If a gruesome sight
is not involved, use *grizzly*.

guarantee/guaranty

Which spelling is preferred: *guarantee* or *guaranty*?
Guarantee is never wrong, whether used as noun or verb. But business
practice is to use *guaranty* when referring to "a contract of guaranty" —
that is, an agreed responsibility for performance or payment of a debt.
The verb form is always *guarantee*.

> Note: The person who offers security is a *guarantee* or *guarantor*. Either
> form may be used as the agent noun for the verb *guarantee* but *guarantor*
> is simpler and, to many people, more explicit, since the *-or* ending indi-
> cates a doer. *Guarantee*, in this sense, is a needless variant.

guess

Would you use the word *guess* in "I guess I'll go home now"?
Probably. *Guess* is a common colloquialism, an equivalent of "think,"
"suppose," or "believe." I guess that almost everyone uses it on occasion. In formal writing, however, *guess* would not be suitable unless
employed to mean conjecture, estimate, or surmise—a real guess ("I
guess there are five hundred jelly beans in the red jar in the store
window").

Note: Shakespeare in *Henry VI* used *guess* to mean suppose. A somewhat common use of *guess* is to mean expect, a usage that is not well received in literate discourse. "Do you plan to go?" "I *guess* so," preferably should be rendered "I *expect* to."

guests

1. Are those who rent rooms at a hotel correctly called *guests*?

Not technically. Customers, those who pay for accommodations, are euphemistically called *guests*. A true guest receives service or entertainment gratuitously. But the term *guest* for hotel and restaurant customers has long been established.

Note: Dictionaries apply the word *guest* to those who pay and to those who do not pay, which could be a source of ambiguity. If the term *paying guest* is used, it distinguishes that guest from those who do not have to pay for board and lodging.

The expression *guest speaker* is often a favorite term used by the chairman of the evening when introducing the speaker. The chairman could economize: "May I introduce our speaker (not our *guest speaker*) of the evening?"

2. Is it correct to speak of *invited guests*?

That expression is redundant, since *guests*, by definition, have been invited, expressly or impliedly. There could, of course, be paying guests. In that case the term *invited guests* may serve as a contrast.

H

h

What do you call the _h_ that is sounded in such words as _hair_, _hero_, and _house_?

It is called an aspirated _h_, in contrast to an _h_ that is silent, as in _heir_, _honor_, and _hour_.

> **Note:** To aspirate is to make a breathing sound. An aspirated _h_ is pronounced with an emission of breath, as are _p_, _t_, and _k_.
>
> In everyday usage a question that disturbs some people is whether such words as _historic_ and _historical_ (the _h_'s of which are aspirated) should be preceded by _a_ or _an_. The general preference is _a_ (_a historic_ occasion).

had better

Should one say, "We _better had_ go now" or "We _had better_ go now," or doesn't it make any difference?

The difference is whether or not you wish to speak proper English. If the answer is yes, choose "We _had better_ go now."

> **Note:** It is a colloquialism, and not a good one, to use the word _better_ unescorted by _had_. To ensure better writing, be sure to precede _better_ with _had_. If confused whether to say _better had_ or _had better_, choose from among _should, must,_ or _ought to_. Any of those words will serve as well, and probably better. All this brings up another matter concerning the use of _better_. If you ask a man who has recently come from a sick bed how he is feeling and he replies that he is _better_ now, does he mean that he has improved or that he is fully recovered? If completely recovered, he should say that he is _well_, but idiom permits the substitution of _better_ (although imprecise) for _well_ in this situation.

hadn't ought

My boss frequently says, "You hadn't ought to do it that way." What do you think about the way he speaks?

He may be instructing you well, but, unfortunately, not in the best English. The expression _hadn't ought_ is nonstandard and is best avoided for "You _ought not_ (or _should not_) do it that way."

hailed

Does a person _hale_ or _hail_ a taxicab?

The person hails a cab. To signal is to hail. _Hail_ also means to shout a greeting, to salute, to cheer ("_Hail_ to the Chief"). To be healthy, to be robust, is to be *hale* ("A man may be both a *hail-fellow-well-met*" and "*hale* and hearty"). *Hale* also means to haul or to cart away ("The sheriff will *hale* him into court").

half

1. What is the rule governing the number given to the word *half*?
Half is treated as singular or plural according to the number of the noun in the following *of* phrase. If the noun refers to one object — "*Half* of the grapefruit *has* been eaten" — *half* is singular. If the noun refers to more than one — "*Half* of the oranges *are* spoiled" — *half* is plural.

> Note: Where there is no expressed *of* phrase — "*Half* (of the book) *is* torn," "*Half* (of the members) *are* gone" — the number of the noun following *half* must be mentally supplied. Whether to say, "cut in *half*" or "cut in *halves*" is a matter of taste. The latter is the technically correct formula, but "cut in *half*" is the more natural expression and is generally preferred.

2. Is this wording correct: "Clyde was there for a half a day"?
Using *a* before *half a* is considered a redundancy. Therefore, do not say, "a half a day," "a half a cup," or "a half an hour." Say, "a half day," "a half cup," "a half hour." The caveat is not to surround *half* with two *a*'s or *a* and *an*.

> Note: In written usage, although both "a half day" and "half a day" are acceptable to many authorities, prefer the first form — "a half day."

hamlet

"We lived in a tiny hamlet for many years," he said. What do you think of that? Is there such a thing as a large hamlet?
There is not. The phrase *large hamlet* is a contradiction in terms, and the phrase *tiny hamlet* is a redundancy, since *-let* means small. A *hamlet* is a little ham. At one time a small collection of cottages was called a *ham*, from which evolved the word *hamlet* to mean a small village.

hamstringed

When the hamstring of an athlete has been cut, has the athlete been *hamstringed* or *hamstrung*?
Technically, *hamstringed*; in prevalent usage, *hamstrung*. Fowler points out that verb *string* is not involved in *hamstring*; therefore the past tense, correctly put, is not *hamstrung* but *hamstringed*, a notion with few followers.

> Note: Dictionaries prefer *hamstrung* as the form for both the past tense and the past participle. They further indicate that these forms are usually employed in figurative constructions ("Our recent plans were *hamstrung* by a supplier's bankruptcy").

hanged/hung

We see the verb *hung* used of anything suspended, from Christmas stockings to human beings. Does this verb now cover all situations?
Not in standard English. *Hanged* is the only permissible verb when death by hanging is meant. For all other uses of *hang*, its past tense is *hung* ("The pictures were *hung* carefully").

> Note: Speaking of the verb *hang* brings up a point in the spelling of two nouns, *hangar* and *hanger*. Aircrafts are housed in *hangars* (with an *ar*); clothing is supported by *hangers* (with an *er*). Do not confuse.

harass

How is the word *harass* pronounced?
It may be pronounced HAR-uhs or huh-RASS. The former is more prevalent. Do not let *harass*, with its one *r*, lead to a misspelling of *embarrass*, which has two.

hardly

What, if anything, is wrong with the sentence "The United States cannot hardly adopt such a stand"?
Hardly has negative quality and should therefore not be used with another negative (*cannot*). The example is made correct if *hardly* is omitted ("The United States cannot adopt such a stand") or if *cannot* is changed to *can* ("The United States *can hardly* adopt such a stand").

> Note: Idiomatically *hardly* is followed by *when*, not *than*. *Than* introduces comparatives, of which *hardly* is not one. It is therefore incorrect to say, "We hardly had arrived home *than* the telephone rang." That statement should be rendered "We hardly arrived home *when* the telephone rang." The argument that *no sooner* takes *than* ("We no sooner arrived home *than* the telephone rang") to justify the use of *than* with *hardly* is invalid. *Sooner* is a comparative. Be careful of the less obvious negatives, as in "Without hardly a murmur, he agreed." Correct by dropping *hardly* or by changing *without* to *with*. These rules apply as well to *barely* and *scarcely*.

hate

1. Is there a fault in "I hate spinach worse than cabbage"?
Yes, the word *worse*. Although something like "I hate this worse than that" is far from uncommon, the word that should be used, rather than *worse*, is *more* ("I hate spinach *more* than cabbage").

2. Is there anything wrong with the word *hate* in "I *hate* oysters"?
A better word is *dislike*, since it is best not to intensify your aversions unreasonably. Seldom is *hate* justified. You might hate war, but generally *dislike* is a more suitable term.

headquarters

Is it proper to say that the company is *headquartered* in Atlanta?
Informally, yes. But *headquarter* is not employed as a verb in well-edited writing, although some dictionaries list it as an intransitive verb, "to have or set up headquarters (in)."

> **Note:** Noun *headquarters* (a place) is regarded by most critics as a plural ("These *headquarters are* large"); other critics say that the choice is the writer's ("The headquarters of the company *is* in Chicago").

healthy/healthful

Our travel agent recommended a visit to Arizona "where the climate is healthy." May *healthy* be used this way?
It should not be. Strictly speaking, *healthy* means possessing health, and *healthful* means conducive to health, that which encourages or promotes health. Careful writers distinguish between these words, although many travel agents do not. A climate cannot be healthy. It may be healthful, but since *healthy* has a better ring (a healthier ring?), colloquially it is displacing *healthful*. Some dictionaries now regard the words as equivalents.

he (or she)

1. Should the move to replace *he* with *he or she* be supported?
It is a writer's choice. English has no arbiter to say what is right and what is wrong and to issue edicts when there is a choice. However, the masculine *he* has been well established through the centuries as being inclusive of both sexes and to designate a person whose sex is unknown or immaterial ("Find out who's on the phone and tell *him* to call back"). Of course dual pronouns should be used where they seem logical, although those occasions are rare. A good illustration is where the work force is composed of men and women equally: "Before the employees leave today, every person must sign *his* or *her* time card."

> **Note:** The word *man* is generic for human being and for mankind. It has no connotation of masculinity when used in those senses. Where words that refer to no sex can replace those that do, without causing awkwardness or blurring meaning, the move is recommended. A writer should avoid, if possible, offending the sensibilities of feminists or of anyone else. We must remember that using plural words in some instances is an easy way out. Instead of "A member can appeal to the committee if *he* has a grievance," say, "*Members* can appeal to the committee if *they* have grievances."

2. Is it correct to use *his or her* to distinguish between the sexes?
It is, but "Each person had to make up *his or her* mind" sounds clumsy. Traditionally *his* alone has said the same thing, *his* being considered

generic, comprehending both sexes. If *his* is objectionable, use a plural noun if possible.

> **Note:** The problem with *his or her* corresponds with the one involving *he or she.* As has been pointed out many times by authorities, the use of *he* (or *his*) does not denote predominance of the male sex. It is simply a convenient and conventional designation of both sexes. No one is downgraded because of the employment of *he* (*his*), and no one is elevated by it either.

help but

Is *help but*, as in "I couldn't help but overhear her," accepted phrasing?

Verb *help*, meaning prevent oneself, should not be followed by *but*. Although often heard in common speech, its sense being avoid or fail to, in formal language prefer "I could not help overhearing her," omitting *but*. Here a gerund (*overhearing*) replaces the infinitive (*overhear*).

> **Note:** A companion expression is "Don't spend more than you can help." The construction seems illogical, but many critics look behind it and regard it as idiomatic.

herb/herbaceous

How are the pronunciations of *herb* and *herbaceous* distinguished?
The word *herb* is pronounced by most people with a silent *h—uhrb*. *Herbaceous*, which means like an herb, always has its *h* sounded huhr-BAE-shuhs.

highly possible

1. Is there anything wrong with "It is highly possible that it will rain"?
Yes. *Possible* is an absolute term and may therefore not be qualified. Rain may be *highly probable* but not *highly possible*. The example is rescued if *highly* is omitted.

> **Note:** The frequent use of the phrase *highly possible* does not justify its wide acceptance. It runs counter to established usage and offers nothing except confusion. Good writers should not permit themselves to be stampeded into turning an absolute term into a nonabsolute.

2. What I often see is the expression *possibly may*. Would you use it in your writings?
No indeed. The combination *possibly may* is redundant, since both *possibly* and *may* imply a contingency. One or the other should be used: "It will *possibly* be done" or "It *may* be done."

historical present

I have read about the historical present. What is that?

Placing an incident in history, an episode, the contents of an essay, or the like, in the present tense, even though it concerns past action. "Thomas Jefferson *tells* us much about how life should be lived. He *admonishes* gently, seldom *scolds*, and always *offers* practical solutions to practical problems." The point behind this device is to impart vividness by making the contents seem current.

> **Note:** The *historical present* and the rule governing the expression of a *universal truth* are similar in one respect, in that the present tense, not the past, is used to convey the message. The usual sequence of tenses is to use a past tense form in the dependent clause to correspond with that in the main clause. A statement in the historical present is always written in an independent clause. With that construction there is no problem. But with a statement of universal truth, the tense employed in the dependent clause is the present, despite the use of a past tense form in the main clause. For example, "We *were* told that water *freezes* at thirty-two degrees Fahrenheit"; "Columbus *proved* that the world *is* round."

historic/historical

Do we say that the President's visit to this small town was a *historic* or a *historical* event?

The event was *historic*. Use *historic* (Greek *histor*, "learned man") when the thing referred to is important, memorable, or famous. True, it may figure in history and may, in fact, be historical. But *historical* is a broad term meaning concerned with or relating to history. In other words, *historical* has to do with history; *historic* usually pertains to the event or thing itself. Armstrong's walk on the moon was a historic event. It was history-making. The Alamo is a historic building; *Gone with the Wind* is a historical novel.

Use the article *a*, not *an*, before *historic*, *historical*, and *history*.

hoard/horde

Should the words *horde* and *hoard* be distinguished?

Of course. The words are unrelated. *Hoard* means accumulation, a secret store of something (the squirrel's *hoard* of nuts). *Horde* refers to a swarm or a multitude (a *horde* of locusts) or a threatening throng of people (a *horde* of rioters). Originally *horde* referred to nomadic tribes, like the *hordes* of Genghis Khan.

Hobson's choice

Is the phrase Hobson's choice still used and, if so, has its meaning remained the same?

Yes on both counts. A *Hobson's choice*, of course, is no choice at all. Being compelled to handle a matter one way—and one way only—is to be given a Hobson's choice, the choice given by the Cambridge liveryman to his customers who wanted to select a horse. "Take the one nearest the door," he would say, "or walk."

> Note: A person given a Hobson's choice is not in a dilemma, since there is something desirable or usable offered. True, the choice is between that which is offered or nothing. But a dilemma is a choice between two undesirable alternatives.

homicide

Is a homicide necessarily a criminal offense?
Technically, no. A *homicide* is simply a killing of one person by another. It does not imply criminality. As a specific legal term, *homicide* is the action of unlawfully killing another human being.

> Note: The term *homicide* comes from the Latin *homo*, "man," and *-cide* from *cidium*, "killer" and "killing." An accidental death from an automobile collision is a homicide. Those homicides that are unlawful are termed *manslaughter* or *murder*.

homosexual

Is the term *homosexual* applicable to males only?
It is not. The first element in that word, *homo-*, is Greek for "same," which indicates that *homosexual* designates sexual attraction between members of the *same* sex, whichever it may be.

> Note: The general misapprehension that the word *homosexual* applies to the male sex only probably comes from the belief that *homo-* means man. It does in Latin, but as previously pointed out, in Greek it means same. This latter *homo-* is the combining form used in *homonym*, *homogeneous*, and *homophone*; namely, the same kind, uniform. Those who believe that *homosexual* is a term applicable to males only are likely, when speaking of women sexually attracted to each other, to use the term *lesbian*.

hope

1. Is this sentence subject to grammatical criticism: "The steel workers are now undergoing what is hoped will be a temporary layoff"?
The problem that the example raises is whether the indefinite pronoun *it* may be omitted from the phrase *it is hoped*. The answer is that it may not be. Before a clause introduced by *what*, the entire phrase—*it is hoped*—is required.

**2. The President said, "I would hope that it never comes to pass."
Did he say it right?**

He did not. The word *hope* needs no crutch to lean on. The auxiliary *would* should be omitted. "I *hope* that (not *would hope that*). . . ."

hopefully

Is *hopefully* in "Hopefully, the train will arrive on schedule" used correctly?
It is not. What is being said is that the train will be arriving full of hope, and that's nonsense. *Hopefully* means in a hopeful way or manner, as in "The defendant looked *hopefully* at the judge." The example should be corrected to read: "We hope that the train will arrive on schedule" or "It is hoped that. . . . "
> Note: The misuse of *hopefully* generates emotional upsets among traditionalists, some of whom threaten dire consequences on those who abuse correct usage. That misusing *hopefully* is inexcusable, many will concede. But we must also recognize that, in popular speech, *hopefully* is being used by countless numbers of people as a sentence adverb on the analogy of such words as *arguably* and *regrettably*. Trying to correct the masses is probably a futile task. Which is no reason for an educated person to ignore correct usage.

horrible

"What a horrible performance." Do you object to the word *horrible*?
We know what *horrible* stands for in this sentence, but a precise descriptive would be better—*inadequate, awkward, incompetent*, and so forth.
> Note: Authorities point out that, in everyday, casual usage, a word with such strong emotional connotations as *horrible* is much too powerful. A more moderate, and precise, term should be selected.

hospitable

How should the word *hospitable* be pronounced?
Pronounce it HAHS-pih-ta-bl, stressing the first syllable. Think of *hospital*, which is also stressed on the first syllable.

host

Has the word *host*, when used as a verb ("Sam *hosted* five teachers"), been legitimatized?
Not by many discriminating speakers and writers. They would use *entertained* instead. But in general reporting, verb *host*, because it saves time and space without seeming offensive, has found a useful niche for itself ("Toledo may *host* a mayors' convention," rather than *play host to*).
> Note: Many nouns have become acceptable verbs (*diagnose* from *diagnosis*), and this process of conversion, or functional change, keeps the lan-

guage alive and progressive. The test, however, is whether the conversion is useful. Does it serve a need? Or is it merely a graceless shortcut to save a few words? Verb *host* is being employed more and more by respected writers, but it has not reached the point of complete literary acceptance. One may say that its credentials are being reviewed, that the committee is still pondering the matter.

hot cup

Does it matter, grammatically, whether you order a hot cup of coffee or a cup of hot coffee?
In today's usage the placement of the adjective is unimportant if the meaning is clear. Of course, technically, since it is the coffee that is hot, and not the cup, you should ask for "a cup of hot coffee." However, "a hot cup of coffee" borders on idiomatic usage, as does "a new pair" in "I bought a new pair of pants." The expression is widely used and is not confusing, even though the pants are new, not the *pair*.

house/home

1. Real estate agents advertise *homes* for sale. Are they misusing that word for *house*?
Unquestionably. A *house* is a dwelling, a structure in which people live. A *home* is the basis, the essence, of family life. It connotes warmth, love, security. A *house* is salable, not a *home*. Selling a home is like selling love. It can't be bought.

> **Note:** The foregoing bald statements do not necessarily reflect common usage of *house* and *home*, terms interchanged with no thought of distinctions. Real estate agents offer homes for sale because *home* is a warmer and more inviting word than *house*. Almost anyone would say, "I'm buying a *home* for my family" rather than a *house*; but most likely, when selling that same property, would say, "I'm putting my *house* up for sale." In some instances one or the other word seems to sound better. For example, a person buys a "house and lot," never "a home and lot." Firemen extinguish a fire in a *house*, not in a *home*. But when the structure needs a more inviting name, *home*, not *house*, is used: communal residences for older people are called *homes*, not *houses*.
>
> One more thing with reference to *home*. Authorities disagree on whether *at* must precede *home*, as in "I was (*at*) *home* last night." The argument advanced in behalf of *at* is that static verbs need it. Certainly in formal writing the advice has merit. In speech and in other writings, take your pick. But note further that "Mandy is coming *home*" is correctly stated. There *home* is an adverb. No preposition is necessary with the verbs *coming* and *going*—"Our son is *coming* (or *going*) home from his tour of duty."

2. Why is it correct to say, "I walked home," but not "I stayed home"?
In example one, *home*, serving as an adverb, needs no *at*. When *home*

follows a verb not implying motion—"I *was* (or *stayed*) at home," *at* is required.

> Note: When a position or location of rest is expressed, *at* should not be used. For example, "Where's the elevator *at*" needs *at* excised.

however/how ever

1. How do you know when to spell *however* as one word and *how ever* as two?
When the idea to be expressed is general, meaning in whatever manner ("*However* we decide, the plan is risky"), or the sense is nevertheless ("*However*, we must decide soon"), spell it as one word. If *ever* is used to emphasize ("*How ever* did you bake so large a cake?"), use two words.

2. May *however* begin a sentence?
It may. But bear in mind that the function of *however* is to indicate a contrast. When used within a sentence, *however* serves to stress the preceding word or words, contrasting them with something that follows. To carry this a step forward, *however* at the beginning of a sentence must logically stress the entire preceding sentence. If that form of emphasis makes no sense, *however* should not be used.

human/humane

1. Should I refer to a person as a *human* or a *human being*?
Although many good writers, as well as dictionaries, accept *human* as a noun synonymous with *person*, preferably in formal writing *human* should be restricted to its adjective sense, either pertaining to people or reflecting the nature and qualities characteristic of man. Certainly the term *human being* is more dignified.

> Note: Many authorities do not agree that the word *human* should be employed adjectivally only. Some say that *human*, as a noun, is acceptable on a formal level in the sense of human being. But, although *human* as a classifying noun is used of people collectively, when individuals are grouped with nonhumans, *people* is the word that normally serves, not *humans*. "There were five persons (or many people) and two dogs in the courtyard" (not "five *humans*" or "*many humans*").

2. The report said, "What a human thing to do—to treat a dog with such kindness." Is human the right word?
The word *humane* would be preferable, since *humane* denotes the qualities of kindness and compassion.

3. Is a humane person a humanitarian?
A *humane* person is not necessarily a *humanitarian*. A *humanitarian* is a benevolent, philanthropic person. He may be regarded as one who promotes the welfare of people.

hurricane/typhoon

How does a *hurricane* differ from a *typhoon*?
A *hurricane* arises east of the International Date Line and a *typhoon* west of the Date Line in the area of the Philippines, the China Sea, or India. They are atmospheric disturbances of about equal intensity. Their difference is only a matter of semantics.

hyphens

1. Which is preferable—"a ten minutes' run" or "a ten-minute run"?
I prefer the latter because it is more idiomatic. The number *ten*, with its plural sense, is connected by a hyphen to the word *minute*, a singular noun, here used adjectivally. But "a ten minutes' run," with the possessive plural *minutes'*, is acceptable. Use it if you prefer it.

2. I saw "The two week course begins on Monday." Was the sentence written correctly?
A compound adjective before a noun should be hyphenated. Correctly written: "The *two-week course* begins on Monday."

3. Should these words be spelled with or without a hyphen: *interscholastic, inter-collegiate*?
Except when the main part of a compound begins with a capital letter (*anti-American, pro-French*), spell the compound as one word (*interscholastic, intercollegiate*). Other examples are *reexamine, postdate, premarital*.

4. When *like* is added to a word, is it written with a hyphen?
The suffix *-like* is attached to the key word—*manlike, warlike, childlike*—unless it ends in a double *ll*—*mall-like, gull-like*.

5. What do you think of the hyphen in "Of all the plays we produced, those by Tennessee Williams were the longest-lived"?
It doesn't belong. Although *long-lived* takes a hyphen, the comparative and superlative forms (*longer lived* and *longest lived*) are not hyphenated.

6. Why do we write *man-child* instead of *manchild*?
A compound noun in which both nouns refer to a person or thing is hyphenated to give the words equal value. Hence *boy-king*; *city-state*; *man-child*. The following forms may indicate business or professional capacities: *secretary-treasurer*; *conductor-soloist*; *lawyer-banker*.

7. When is it correct to use hyphens with the word *much*?
Hyphenate in a compound modifier (*much*-loved teacher; *much*-maligned ambassador). But not when it itself is modified (a *very much* feared critic—no hyphen).

8. Is a fraction always hyphenated?
No, it is not. A hyphen is not used with a fraction that is not serving as

an adjective. "Today he paid *one half* of the tax," not *one-half*.

9. When do you hyphenate words ending in *-fold*, *-score*, and *-odd*?

Suffix *fold* is hyphenated when preceded by a numeral: *50-fold*; otherwise it is written solid: *threefold, fourfold*. *Score* used as an adjective is written solid—*fivescore* years, but "Of the men assembled, five *score* will speak" (*score*, a noun, is a single unhyphenated word). Hyphenate compounds of a number with *odd*: twenty-*odd*.

> **Note:** *Odd* should accompany only round numbers. Say, "There were thirty-*odd* books on the shelf." A specific number is inappropriate with *odd* (not "thirty-two-*odd* books") because *odd* represents an approximation. If there were thirty-two books, an exact number, *odd* should be omitted. Also hyphenate *odd* when part of a compound (*odd*-looking) to avoid ambiguity. Not "We have one hundred *odd* pages to read," but one hundred-*odd* pages to read."

I

-ic/-ical/-ics

1. Do we say *alphabetic* or *alphabetical?*

Take your pick, although *alphabetical* is commoner.

> **Note:** Generally adjectives ending in *-ic* are preferred to those ending in *-ical: energetic, dramatic,* rather than *energetical, dramatical.* But note such words as *grammatical* and *theoretical. Grammatic* and *theoretic,* both good adjectives, are rarely seen. On the other hand, consider *electric* and *electrical.* They are interchangeable ("It is an *electric* [or *electrical*] appliance"). Wherever there is no change in meaning, prefer the shorter form —*-ic* rather than *-ical (heroic* instead of *heroical, parenthetic* instead of *parenthetical).* Note that *economic* means having to do with economics (rarely thrifty) and that *economical* means thrifty, avoiding waste.

2. How do you determine whether a word such as *athletics* or *acoustics* should be considered a singular or a plural?

These words, plural in form, are, when referring to a branch of study or to activities, singular in meaning and they therefore take a singular verb: "*Athletics is* the most interesting form of exercise"; "*Acoustics is* becoming a more popular college course." But when these *-ics* words are used in a general sense, referring to practical activities or qualities, they are plural and require a plural verb: "The *athletics* at this school *are* varied"; "The *acoustics* in the auditorium and study hall *were* repaired."

> **Note:** When used in the plural to denote qualities, the *-ics* words are usually preceded by *the, such,* or *his (her):* "His politics *are,*" "Such politics *were.*"

3. If an adjective ends in *-ic,* how is its adverb counterpart formed?

In every case, except one, by adding *-ally (grammatic, grammatically; fantastic, fantastically).* The sole exception is *public, publicly.*

identical

Have you noticed that the word *identical* leads to verbiage?

Yes. Such phrases as the "identical same menu" contain an unnecessary word, presumably for emphasis. Since *identical* means the very same, all that is needed is "the *identical* menu."

> **Note:** Two things can be identical (two neckties), but two persons cannot be. When a preposition is needed with *identical,* it may be *with* or *to* (with gets the bigger play): "This watch is identical *with* (or *to*) my brother's". Caveat: Older grammars declare bluntly that only *with* may be used with *identical.* They say that a proposal may be similar *to* the one received

135

yesterday, but it cannot be identical *to*. If the proposals are alike, it must be expressed with *identical with*. The fiat, however, is losing much of its power. Most writers use *to* when so inclined.

idiom

What are idioms?

An idiom is an accepted expression having a meaning different from the literal. Consider the phrase "to catch a cold." It's idiomatic. Take *many a,* as in "Many a man has gone wrong." It makes no sense, since *many* is a plural form and *a*, a singular. And so with a *six-foot* man, who is six *feet* tall. But that is the illogicality of established idiom.

> Note: Phrases and expressions that defy grammatical rectitude can become the accepted form of conveying a meaning if many people use the phrase or expression long enough. The combination of words becomes peculiar to the language and its meaning becomes established. The name given this mixture in which the conjoined meanings of the elements make no sense is *idiom*.

i.e.

Is it proper to use *i.e.* in formal writing?

It is not. Since *i.e.,* which stands for Latin *id est,* means *that is* in English, use *that is*. You may use *i.e.* in notes and technical reports.

> Note: Some abbreviations may be used in the most formal prose. For example, *Mr., Mrs., Dr.,* and so forth, are established as standard. But others, such as *i.e.,* belong, primarily, in footnotes. And so does *e.g.,* an abbreviation for *exempli gratia,* meaning for example, and *viz,* an abbreviation for *videlicet,* which means namely. Always precede any of these Latin tags with a semicolon or a comma.

if

1. Are not all *if* clauses put in the subjunctive?

No, they are not. The indicative mood is used with *if* clauses to express a simple condition relating to the past ("If Paul *was* there, he was drunk"). The subjunctive mood expresses a wish or a contrary to fact ("I wish it *were* true"; "If I *were* a Hollywood star").

2. Which is preferable: "If you see Al, say hello for me" or "If you should see Al, say hello for me"?

The choice is yours to make, since both are grammatically correct. *If* with *should* suggests less probability, that it is less likely to happen, than *if* alone.

3. Are the words *if* and *whether* interchangeable?

Not in precise language. For example, it is inexact to say, "I do not know if I should go." *If* is used to introduce a condition *("If* we leave now, we'll be on time"); *whether,* to express alternatives ("I do not know *whether* or not to go"). The *or not* may be omitted if the sense of the sentence is unaffected. "I do not know *whether* to go" needs no *or not,* but "I will go *whether* it rains" makes no sense and requires *or not.*

> Note: *Whether* is a nounal conjunction that introduces clauses dependent on verbs like *ask, doubt, know, learn, see,* and *wonder* ("He will let us know *whether* we should go"). Some authorities see no objection to using *if* instead of *whether* in such cases. The recommendation here, as was pointed out, is to prefer *whether,* especially if alternatives are expressed ("We don't know *whether* we should drive or fly"). Everyone agrees that there is no choice when the clause begins a sentence; *whether* is then mandatory ("*Whether* he will run for office is uncertain"). It also is required when *or not* is included. It would be incorrect to use *if,* as in "I don't know *if* I can go *or not*" (*whether*).

4. What does this mean: "Let Gus know if Tom wants a loan"?
One can't be sure. If Gus is to be told *only* if Tom wants a loan, it is better to frame it that way, "Let Gus know *only* if Tom wants a loan," meaning that Gus is not to be informed if Tom does not want it. Using *whether* instead of *if* changes the intent. "Let Gus know *whether* Tom wants a loan" says that Gus is to be informed in any event; that is, one way or the other.

if and when

Do good writers use the cliché *if and when*?
Seldom, if at all, since employing both ideas is usually unnecessary. In "We will celebrate *if and when* we win," either *if* or *when* could serve. The context usually indicates which is preferable.

> Note: When consequence is to be expressed, use *if* alone: "*If* the trunk is not repaired, we won't be able to leave." If the consequence will be handled satisfactorily, use *when* alone: "*When* the trunk is repaired, we will be able to leave."
>
> A cliché similar to *if and when,* and subject to the same general criticism, is *unless and until.* Use one or the other idea, whichever seems more appropriate. This means that either *unless and* or *and until* should be dropped, a move that will make for a tighter and more economical statement.

illegible/unreadable

If you can't decipher someone's writing, is it *illegible* or *unreadable,* or both?
The preferred word is *illegible,* which means the quality of the writing is so poor that it can't be read. *Unreadable* also means that, but additionally it may mean that the material is boring (perhaps too technical) or offensive.

Note: A distinction in meaning between *illegible* and *unreadable* should be preserved to avoid confusion. *Illegible* should retain its one meaning, not clear enough to be read (bad handwriting), and *unreadable*, what is unfit or unworthy to be read (bad writing).

imagine/suppose

Are *imagine* and *suppose* interchangeable words?

Usually. But prefer *imagine* to indicate a mental image ("I *imagine* that Washington looked dignified") and *suppose* when the reference made is not concerned with its truth or falsity ("Let us *suppose* the earth is flat").

Note: The word *imagine* brings to mind *imaginary* and *imaginative*. The former refers to something conceived in the mind, in the imagination. It is unreal. The latter is used of persons who have the faculty of creating mental images in new combinations. The word *suppose* brings to mind *supposititious*, which means "based on conjecture, hypothetical," and *supposititious*, "put by fraud in the place of the genuine or original thing or person." Its synonym is spurious. Be careful when spelling this last — *supposititious* — to note the *titi* in the middle. Better yet, steer clear of this overblown word; use *spurious* or *fraudulent*.

I/me

1. Do educated people say, "It is *I*" or "It is *me*"?

In writing, they probably use the correct form, *I*. In speech, many use *me*, thinking *I* sounds stuffy.

Note: *I* is a personal pronoun. It is in the nominative case and is used as a subject of a sentence. *Me* is an objective-case form and is used as an object. This establishes the grammatical need for *I* in the example. Nevertheless, *me* is now conversationally standard.

2. This sounds odd: "It was I who said you were too fat." Is it correct?

The example is written in precise, grammatical English. But it does sound stilted. Recasting is a way out: "I said you were too fat" or "I was the one who said. . . ."

immature/premature

How do the words *immature* and *premature* differ in meaning?

Both words share the sense "not being ready," but the first means "not developed," "not full-grown" (a child is *immature)*; the second, "too soon," "not ready" (a *premature* report, a *premature* birth). *Immature* signifies that something is not completed; *premature* that something has occurred before the expected time.

immunity/impunity

Please distinguish between the words *immunity* and *impunity*.
Immunity means exemption (from a disease or from prosecution). *Impunity* also means exemption, but precisely, an exemption from punishment (Latin *impune*, "without punishment"). People who do as they please, knowing they'll suffer no unpleasant consequences, feel they may act with impunity (or safety).

impact/implement

Two serviceable nouns, *impact*, meaning to effect, and *implement*, meaning to carry out, are accepted as verbs by many dictionaries but not by many usage authorities. How should one handle these words?
It is better not to handle them at all, but to choose plainer words. In place of *impact* (a trendy word at best), use *effect* or *influence*. In place of *implement*, try *carry out, fulfill, execute, make,* and *accomplish*. Is there any doubt that these simpler words are clearer? Plain English is a goal worth striving for.

impatient

What prepositions does *impatient* take?
It takes *for, of, with,* or *at*. We are impatient *for* something we desire, impatient *of* preaching without practice, impatient *with* a person and *at* the person's actions.

impeached

Is it true that if Nixon had been impeached, he would have been ousted as President?
It is not. To *impeach* is not to remove, but to bring charges, to accuse a public official of wrong conduct during office. A person who has been impeached has to stand trial, which, of course, may result in removal from office.
> **Note:** President Andrew Johnson was impeached (impeachment is a function performed by the House of Representatives). He was subsequently tried before the Senate and acquitted by one vote.

important/importantly

Is it better to say *more importantly* than *more important*?
It is not. Prefer *more important*, with its elliptical sense of *what is more important*. "He won the race; *more important* (that is, what is more important), he broke a record." Here *important* is an adjective qualifying the understood pronoun *what*.

Note: Many writers prefer *importantly* to *important* in this kind of construction, contending it is idiomatic. If that is so, no one should argue about its ungrammatical structure because idiom may go its own way blithely ignoring the rules of grammar. But if it is not established idiom, whether it is grammatical then becomes a fair and appropriate question. From that standpoint, it may be observed that adverb *importantly* has no word to modify, whereas adjective *important*, as was pointed out, qualifies *what*. Futhermore, if it is agreed that the elliptical form stands for "what is more important," the proper word to use is *important*, an adjective, and not *importantly*, an adverb, because the word follows the linking verb *is*.

in advance of

What do you think of this sentence: "The oath was administered in advance of the dinner"?

The phrase *in advance of* is wordy for *before*. Since it is desirable to use as few words as possible, avoid *in advance of*. Use *before*.

Note: The phrase *prior to*, like *in advance of*, for the sake of economy is also best replaced by *before*. Writing that is neatly and effectively concise gains in force. Using several words where one will serve is soporific.

inclose/enclose

Are both forms, *inclose* and *enclose*, accepted spellings?

They are. These verbs, which mean to surround or to close in on all sides or to insert, are interchangeable. You may rightly say, "Please *enclose* (or *inclose*) a check with your order." But note that the preferred spelling is *enclose* and that *enclosure* predominates over *inclosure*.

Note: *Inclose* is preferable only as a legal term. In the expressions "enclosed herewith" and "enclosed herein," *herewith* and *herein* are superfluous. And "Enclosed herewith please find" is a throwback to yesteryear. Avoid it. Say simply, "I am *enclosing*. . . ."

in close proximity

Would anyone criticize the phrase *in close proximity*?

Precisians would. A barn *in close proximity* to a farmhouse is just as *close* to the farmhouse if the unnecessary *in* and *proximity* are omitted. *Proximity*, from Latin *proximus*, "near," means closeness.

included

Is it proper to write, "The faculty included Wallen, Ash, Miller, and others"?

It is not, because *include*, like *such as*, implies a sampling, an incomplete list, a part of the content. Therefore, "and others" should be deleted, with *and* inserted before "Miller" and a period after it.

> **Note:** Do not confuse *include* with such expressions as *comprise, consist of,* or *be composed of.* Those expressions refer to the whole; they are all-inclusive. *Include,* as pointed out, refers to a part, not all. It does not imply a totality, that all components have been enumerated.

in connection with

Is it preferable to use *in connection with* to *about*?
By no means. Do not use three words when a single preposition *(about, at, by, from,* or *of)* will do. Instead of "The mayor expressed approval *in connection with* the planning survey," make it "approval *of* the planning survey."

indict/indite

How do the words *indict* and *indite* differ in meaning?
To *indict* is to charge with an offense; to *indite,* to compose or put into writing. The first is a common word; the second, a bookish term, one that is best avoided.

> **Note:** The words *indict* and *indite* are pronounced alike—in-DITE.

individuals

My cousin complains that he dislikes the individuals he meets at his club these days. Would you have used the word *individuals*?
I would have used *people.* It is best to confine the use of *individuals* to persons singled out from a group; for example, individuals as compared with society, family, government, and so forth. "The individual has full protection under our laws" implicitly contrasts the individual with collective organizations, especially the government.

> **Note:** Just as the word *individual* is often used pompously for *person* ("He is a stingy *individual*"), so is *party* in the opinion of authorities. Except for the telephone jargon of operators ("Your *party* has been disconnected"), the proper use of the word *party* is of a person or organization that is either a litigant or a contractual member ("Tom is a *party* in a divorce suit"; "Gino is a *party* to a million dollar contract"). Speaking of a person as an individual or a party may be a way of making a pointed, contemptuous slight: "I want nothing to do with that *individual* (or *party*)."

infer/imply

Is *infer* used correctly in "Do you mean to infer I stole the money"?
It is not. The word called for is *imply.* To *imply* is to suggest, to express indirectly, to hint. To *infer* is to draw a conclusion—an inference—

from what someone has said or from circumstances. An implier is a pitcher; an inferrer, a catcher. A speaker implies; the audience infers. A person may imply that you're wrong. Or you may infer, by reasoning, that the person thinks you're wrong.

> Note: Be particularly careful of *infer*. It is often the culprit in an *infer/imply* choice-of-verb blunder, as in the posed question. Seldom does anyone misuse *imply* for *infer*.
>
> A word sometimes substituted for *imply* is *insinuate*, since both words mean to hint or to suggest. But the connotation of *insinuate* (Latin, *insinuo*, "sneak in") is bad; it suggests slyness and evil. This is not so with *imply*.

infinitives

1. Would you criticize this sentence: "We are to leave on Sunday, go to Mobile, and survey the site"?
All the infinitives should have been introduced by *to*. The rule is that the *to* of any of the infinitives in a series should not be omitted: "We are *to* leave on Sunday, *to* go to Mobile, and *to* survey the site."

2. Is the rule against splitting infinitives still in force?
Yes. The rule is, or the better practice is, do not split needlessly. But if an awkward construction is avoided by splitting, do not hesitate to split. A split infinitive allows an adverb to come between *to* and the main verb: to *speedily* run. This all boils down to a simple bit of advice: Let your ear be your guide. In "Howard tried to get the city to *at least* repair the streets," if *at least* is placed anywhere else in the sentence, it would affect the meaning.

3. This is a sentence about which our group has had some controversy: "The practice of proprietors to label their goods with differently colored labels can be confusing." What can you say about it?
The infinitive *to label* should be replaced with a gerund: "The practice *of labeling.* . . ." An infinitive is not to be used where a gerund clearly belongs.

in general/in particular

Is there any objection to the phrases *in general* and *in particular*?
There is none. The phrases are firmly established in standard English. Many authorities, however, prefer the single adverb equivalents, *generally* and *particularly,* to the preposition and adjective combinations.

> Note: The phrases have no advantage over the single words, which save a word but add as many characters as were conserved. Euphony and rhythm should govern, which means that your ear must become the guide.

ingenious/ingenuous

Is there a substantial difference between the words *ingenious* and *ingenuous*?

Decidedly. *Ingenious* means inventive, clever, original, resourceful. ("Len concocted an *ingenious* plan to save the shrubbery from the wintry blasts"). *Ingenuous* means artless, free from deceit, unsophisticated, innocent in a good sense ("Clyde has an open, *ingenuous* manner that attracts people to him").

> Note: A synonym for *ingenuous*, but one carrying a mild pejorative overtone, is naïve. It is preferably spelled with a dieresis over the *i*.
>
> Pronounce *ingenious* ihn-JEEN-yuhs and *ingenuous* ihn-JEHN-yoo-uhs. *Ingenuous* has an antonym—*disingenuous*, meaning crafty or devious.

in/into/in to

1. We often hear a sentence like: "Andy went in his house to get a glass of water." Is *in* used correctly?

Colloquially, yes; strictly speaking, no. Preposition *in* denotes position, usually a fixed position ("The butter is *in* the icebox"), or motion within an area ("The patient was allowed to walk *in* his room"). *Into* implies motion from one place to another, as in your example — "He went *into* his house to get a glass of water."

> Note: Certainly a person who jumps in a lake is not entering it. To jump in it, he must already be in it. But he may jump into the lake if that is the way he wants to enter it. A person who jumps into bed makes a leap. A person who jumps in bed is using it as a trampoline. Despite all that, in everyday accepted English, *in* is regularly used instead of *into* with verbs of motion. This equating *in* with *into* is supported by almost all dictionaries. Figuratively, *into* indicates a change of condition or form ("Don flew *into* a rage"; "The patient fell *into* a faint").
>
> When *in* and *to* are used separately, *in* is an adverb and *to* a preposition ("Adeline went *in to* see the boss"; "We sent the package *in to* them immediately").

2. My children say they're into computers, into rock music, into many things. Is *into* used correctly?

As so used, *into* is a fad word destined for a short life. Your children are interested in, devoted to, or are busy with. Tell them to pick appropriate phrasing and substitute it for *into*. They'll then get into better English.

in order that

What is the proper construction with *in order that*?

The phrase should be followed by *may* or *might* ("We will do our best *in order that* we *may* achieve our goal"; "She drove slowly *in order that* her cousin *might* follow easily"; "The committee will review the matter *in order that* it *may* see the difference"). But it is not followed by *can*.

> **Note:** *In order that* can usually be simplified to *that* or *so that*, replacements that make for a less pedantic, more natural sentence, and each justifying a different construction ("The committee will review the matter *so that* it *can* (or *may*) see the difference"; "She drove slowly *so that* her cousin *could* follow easily").

> *In order to* is often no more effective than its economical partner, the *to* infinitive. In many cases the first two words could be dropped with no loss in sense or emphasis. For example, in "He left early in order to wash his car," the words *in order* are unnecessary: "He left early *to* wash his car."

insure/ensure

Conceding that *insure* and *ensure* are synonymous, how would you distinguish their usage?
Ensure is used only when the notion is to make certain or to make safe. *Insure* is also widely used that way, but it is exclusive when the sense is to make financially secure, particularly that which involves insurance matters. "Using a seat belt will *insure* not being thrown against the windshield in case of an accident." But with equal correctness, you might say, "Wearing a seat belt will *ensure* your safety."

> **Note:** A close relative to *insure* and *ensure* is *assure*. The three words all mean to make sure or certain, but only *assure* means to make a person feel secure or confident. *Assure* takes an object. You do not assure that everything will be as planned. You must assure someone or some organization that everything will be as planned ("The principal *assured* the *parents* that no danger existed in the school building").

in the course of

What do you think of *in the course of*, as in "In the course of the discussion, we questioned. . . ."?
I think it is wordy for *during* ("*During* the discussion, we questioned . . ."). Verbiage should be avoided in anyone's writing.

inside of

1. My question is whether a good speaker would say, "This session will end inside of an hour"?
The phrase *inside of* is not a desirable expression with reference to time. A good speaker would say, "This session will end *within* an hour."

> **Note:** *Inside of*, meaning less than, has a wide colloquial following. It is used with reference to both time and distance (*inside of* an hour, *inside of* a mile).

2. "Inside of the room sat six persons." Is *inside of* the proper way of saying it?

No, because *of* is unnecessary, and dispensable words should be omitted. Say, *"Inside* (no *of)* the room sat six persons." This advice applies to *outside of* as well.

insignia

In "The insignia was removed," was *insignia* used properly?

Technically, no, since *insignia* is a Latin plural. Its singular form, *insigne,* however, is rarely seen. *Insignia* has become the accepted singular form and is regularly used with a singular verb. *Insignias* is the standard plural.

> Note: The U.S. Army recognizes *insignia* as a singular, using *insignias* as the plural form. Most dictionaries follow along.

insufficient

Is the wording correct in "The course was canceled because of insufficient registrants"?

No. *Insufficient* should qualify a quality, quantity, or amount (insufficient strength, insufficient heat). Restated: "The course was canceled because of *an insufficient number of* registrants."

> Note: Fowler admonishes writers to avoid using *insufficient* where *not enough* will do. This, of course, is in keeping with a basic rule for good writing: choose the plainer word where it will serve adequately.

intend/propose

Is it more forceful to use *intend* or *propose* in "I don't *intend* (or *propose*) to go through with this matter"?

It is not a question of forcefulness but of meaning. The primary senses of *propose* are suggest and nominate. If your meaning is to have in mind, you *intend,* not *propose.*

inversion

1. How can one, with certainty, use the correct verb form in an inverted sentence?

Simply be alert to the number of the delayed subject. Not "From these reports emerge one single idea" *("emerges one single idea").*

2. What might be said of this sentence: "Heading his collection of plaques is a Pulitzer Prize and two Emmy awards"?

A plural subject requires a plural verb, which is what the example needs *(are).* Inversion, a change in the natural order of words, can fool you if you are not careful.

Note: Inversions are contorted sentence structures and are therefore best avoided. The natural order of a sentence—subject, verb, object—reads more easily and is more quickly comprehended.

irregardless

What leads so many people to use *irregardless*?

Perhaps an association with *irregular, irresponsible,* or *irrespective. Regardless,* of course, is the word wanted. *Irregardless* is not a word in the English language.

> **Note:** Nonwords need not be analyzed or given undue time. But interestingly, if it is true that *irregardless,* as some word historians contend, is the offspring of *irrespective* and *regardless,* apparently the parents did not know that their child would be doubly negative. The prefix *ir-* means not and the suffix *-less* means without.

-ise/-ize

Why is it that I sometimes see some words written with *-ise* instead of *-ize*?

You have been reading British publications. Britishers use *ise (realise, criticise).* Americans use *ize (realize, criticize).* Of course, some American English words end in *ise,* too *(surprise, revise, compromise, televise,* and so on).

> **Note:** Be careful not to create useless words ending in *-ize.* It is easy to convert a noun into a verb by adding *-ize.* Don't do it. Not *documentize* (write down), not *prioritize* (put first), not *finalize* (finish). The *-ize* words that are part of our vocabulary have stood the test of time—*immunize, memorize, theorize,* and so forth.

-ish

Is it wrong to say, "She's fiftyish"?

Not wrong, since suffix *-ish* has wide acceptance in informal language. But it is undesirable in serious writing. When attached to colors *(reddish, greenish), -ish* is generally recognized as standard English.

is when/is where

Is it wrong to introduce a definition or an explanation with *is when* or *is where*?

It is because *when* pertains to time and *where* to place. Neither *is when* nor *is where* is a proper formula to define other terms. *When* or *where* should be replaced by a single noun. Not "A sentence *is when* you express a complete thought," but "A sentence is a complete thought." Not "Swimming *is where* you propel yourself in the water," but "Swim-

ming is a sport in which. . . ." To repeat: Don't forget the noun.
> **Note:** Equally undesirable is *where* used as in, "I see in the papers *where* a tornado set down in Kansas." Conjunction *that* should replace *where*. *Where*, in this usage, is considered an illiteracy.

it says

My college son often says, "It says in the paper," "It says in the book," "It says on my diploma." Should I dare correct him?
You're his parent. You may point out that the combination *it says* is undesirable. Have him say, "The paper says," "This book says," "The diploma says." He'll sound more like a college product.

its/it's

Why is it that *it's* is so often misused for *its*?
Perhaps some writers are deceived into thinking that the apostrophe makes *it's* a possessive form. It looks like one, but it is, of course, a contraction of *it is*. This statement needs its apostrophe deleted: "The cat was washing *it's* face."
> **Note:** None of the possessive pronouns take an apostrophe because their meaning is already possessive. You write, "The brown house is *theirs* (not *their's*)." "The ball is *yours* (not *your's*)." In "Although it's theirs now, its size would be better for us," we have both *it's* and *its*, the contraction for *it is* and the neuter pronoun *its*, the possessive form of *it*. Do not allow *it's*, with its apostrophe, to beguile you into using an unnecessary one with the possessive *its*. Another note. In formal writing prefer *it is* to *it's*.
>
> One thing further. Some indefinite pronouns take an apostrophe when forming the possessive case: *anybody's, another's, one's, somebody's,* and so on.

J

jargon

What is *jargon*?

The term *jargon* has two unrelated meanings, although each refers to a form of speech. Originally *jargon* was a mixture of several languages that employed almost no grammar or syntax. It was, to many people, unintelligible speech, gibberish. As widely used today, however, *jargon* is a special language peculiar to a group, the lingo of a trade or profession. To the members of the group, *jargon* is easily understood and is often verbal shorthand for lengthy terms or explanations. *Jargon* is especially useful to people in the scientific world.

jealous/envious

How can I tell whether I am *envious* or *jealous*?

It may be difficult, since the words *envy* and *jealousy* are so often interchanged. Yet the terms are not exact synonyms. An envious person is discontented because he does not have what someone else has—wealth, accomplishments, fame ("Anne is *envious* of her cousin's artistic ability"). *Jealousy* is a stronger word. Jealous people are unpleasantly suspicious or downright fearful, perhaps fearful that someone they love may love someone else or even that someone is encroaching on their possessions or reputation. But if envy, a somewhat mild desire toward another's possessions or position, deepens into an enveloping resentment, it may be said that *envy* has become *jealousy.*

> **Note:** Inherent in *envy* is covetousness. Inherent in *jealousy* is bitterness—bitterness toward a social or business rival, bitterness toward losing a loved one's affection to someone else.
>
> Both *envious* and *jealous* take preposition *of.*

jettison

What does the word *jettison* mean and where did it come from?

To *jettison* is to throw overboard. Its forebear was French *jeter,* "to throw." Observe that although its ancestor is spelled with one *t, jettison* has two.

> **Note:** A word derived from the same ancestor as *jettison* is *jetsam,* which refers to whatever was thrown overboard during an emergency to lighten a ship.

job/position

When my nephew became an account executive, did he get a *job* or a *position*?
Either word could be accurately applied. Usually a job, an activity performed regularly for pay, involves a menial or manual task. *Position* is considered a word of greater dignity. An account executive, I would say, holds a position. Certainly, the garbage collector would not be said to have a position. When employed, that person got a job, meaning a situation of employment. And yet there's nothing inherently deprecatory about the word *job*. One may add that if a person has a position, there's also a job to do.

join together

My minister sometimes says, "Let us all join together in singing." His idea is good, but how about his grammar?
The combination *join together* is almost always redundant, since *join* means "to unite" or "to connect." Either "Let's *join* in singing" or "Let's sing *together*" would say it precisely and more economically.

> **Note:** Some authorities maintain that *join together* is proper phrasing if emphasis is desired. Perhaps the thought is that *together* in "What God has joined together, let no man put asunder" is a stronger admonition than *join* alone. Or it may merely be a remnant of Elizabethan English. It is best, nevertheless, not to use those words in tandem. The phrase *link together* is subject to the same criticism; *together* doesn't belong. Avoid such combinations as *gather together, assemble together,* and *collaborate together.*

Jr./Sr.

Should I write "John Ester, Jr. is here" or "John Ester Jr. is here"?
If you know Ester's preference, the thing to do is to follow it. Otherwise, the choice is yours. There are no rights or wrongs. For many years a comma was preferred between the surname and *Jr.,* but a recent stylistic change is to drop the comma. Naturally you should treat *Sr.* the way you style *Jr.*

> **Note:** It has long been the general practice not to use a comma between a surname and the designation II, III, and so on ("He is Bradford Williamson II").

judge/jurist

1. Is a jurist a judge?
Not necessarily. A *jurist* is a person skilled in the law. A jurist may be a practicing lawyer, a law professor, or a judge. Which, of course,

means that all jurists are not judges and that all judges are not jurists, although all judges ought to be jurists.

> Note: Just as the terms *judge* and *jurist* should not be equated, so should *judge* and *justice* not be equated. A *justice* is a member of the U.S. Supreme Court and, as a general rule, a judge of the highest state appellate level. *Justice* may also denote the lowest-ranking judge: *justice of the peace.*

2. What is the full and correct title of the Chief Justice of the Supreme Court of the United States?

His title is *Chief Justice of the United States*, not *Chief Justice of the United States Supreme Court.*

> Note: The eight Associate Justices have a fuller title: *Associate Justice of the Supreme Court of the United States.*

judicial/judicious

Is it not true that *judicious* and *judicial* are synonyms?

They are not, even though both words stem from a Latin ancestor meaning "judgment." *Judicial* pertains to courts of law ("The *judicial* proceedings dragged on and on") and to judges ("He put on his *judicial* robe"). *Judicious* means using or showing sound judgment, that which is well calculated, wise, prudent.

> Note: Since in some contexts either *judicial* or *judicious* may serve appropriately, be careful that no confusion results. If the meaning is ambiguous, recast the sentence.

junction/juncture

Are the words *junction* and *juncture* interchangeable?

Although both words have the primary sense of "the act of joining or the state of being joined," each word enjoys a special use. *Junction* is widely employed to indicate a meeting or crossing of, say, wires, rivers, or railway lines. If you think of crossroads, you think of a junction. *Juncture* applies to a point of time or a critical moment ("At this *juncture* we must decide whether to buy or sell"; "We must consider at this *juncture* our military strategy because our position is critical").

> Note: It is usually a gaffe to begin a sentence with "At this *junction*, I would . . ." because probably what was meant was *juncture,* meaning a meeting or convergence of two happenings. And even *juncture,* though correct, is best replaced by "now" or "at this moment" (but not by "at this point in time").

junta

What is a *junta* and how is it pronounced?

A *junta* is either a group of military officers holding state power in a country after a *coup d'état* or a committee created to legislate. Pronounce it HUHN-tuh, although JUHN-tuh, its anglicized version, is acceptable.

jury

I have seen the word *jury* followed by *is* (the jury *is*) and by *are* (the jury *are*). Which is right?
Either may be. The word *jury* is a collective noun, a noun singular in form but plural in connotation, such as *class, committee, faculty, family, group,* or *team.* Collective nouns, generally, take singular verbs when the group is regarded as a whole, but plural verbs when its individual members are being considered. Hence *jury is* is right in "The jury *is* reaching a verdict" (the group is considered as an entity). And so is *jury are* in "The jury *are* disagreeing among themselves" (the individual jurors are disagreeing independently of one another).

> **Note:** If the combination *jury are* sounds awkward, amend the sentence to read "The *members* of the jury *are* disagreeing among themselves." This suggestion is applicable to other collective nouns. For example, rather than "The *committee are* now voting" (meaning the individual committeemen are voting), make it "The *members* of the committee *are* now voting."

just

1. Is the word *just* in "I'm just fine" used properly?
In strict formal prose, *just,* as so used, should be avoided. Except for that caution, the expression is an entrenched colloquialism, widely accepted by educated people.

> **Note:** Using *just* as an intensive in the sense of "very," "simply," or "quite" is regarded by many as idiomatic, but be careful. Saying "I'm *just* dying to tell her" is a colloquialism that should be kept on its proper level.

2. "Claude was honored just the same as his teammates were" is a sentence that disturbs me. Is it worded correctly?
No, a correction is needed. The phrase *just as* means "in the same way as," which makes "just the same as" a redundancy. The sentence should read: "Claude was honored *just as* . . ." or, if you wish, "was honored *precisely* (or *exactly*) as his teammates were."

3. The carpenter said, "It is just about what I expected." Should I hope his workmanship is better than his grammar?
You would be justified in hoping so. The combination *just about* is objectionable because it is self-contradictory. *Just* means "exactly" ("it is *just* right") and *about* means "approximately" ("I'll see you *about* two o'clock"). Regardless of what has just been said, the phrase, despite its illogicality, is respected idiom.

4. Is it justifiable to say, "He just recently arrived"?
Redundancies are never justifiable. One meaning of *just* is recently ("He *just* got here"); one meaning of *recently* is just ("He *recently* arrived"). Clearly the words do not belong in tandem. Use one or the other, *just* or *recently*.

5. Where in a sentence should the word *just* be placed?
Place it close to the word, phrase, or clause it modifies, and if possible immediately before it to prevent ambiguity. As *just* moves about, the sense of the sentence changes. "Today we *just* visited my aunt" (but did nothing for her). "Today we visited *just* my aunt" (and no one else).

6. My cousin said, "He'd just as soon play as study." Does he need more schooling?
It is good to know that *just as soon* is a colloquial expression meaning "rather." In more formal discourse, *rather . . . than* would be preferable. But all colloquialisms are not to be condemned, although some merit condemnation. The one you point out has been so frequently heard, and used by so many educated people, that we should not be critical of it. Let your cousin continue playing, but he shouldn't forget his studies.

just/justly

How are the words *just* and *justly* differentiated in their usage?
The adjective *just* and the adverb *justly* have the same basic meaning — that which is prompted by fairness, truth, and reason. We may say, "The mayor is a *just* man and his decency in office has been *justly* recognized." Note that the adverb *justly* precedes the verb.

just yet

My tennis partner uses the expression *just yet*, as in "I can't play just yet." Is this phraseology acceptable?
Colloquially, *just yet* is often used to mean "still" or "now," but either *still* or *now* would be a better choice when writing on a higher level. Select the word that would be most appropriate. For example, instead of saying, "The concrete is too wet to walk on *just yet*," say, "The concrete is *still* too wet to walk on."

juvenile

It seems to me that many people mispronounce *juvenile*. Am I right?
Some do stress the last syllable and rhyme it with *mile* or *smile*. The preferred pronunciation calls for a stress on the first syllable — JOO-vehn-ihl.

K

keel over

Is *keel over* slang for to cause to fall over suddenly or to faint?
It is not slang. Verb *keel*, usually with *over*, is now an accepted form, having been borrowed from its original sense in nautical language of overturn or capsize (a vessel).

key/quay

Is there a difference in pronunciation between *key* and *quay*, a wharf?
No. They both are pronounced KEE.

kibitzer

Whenever I butt in on my friends' conversation, they say, "Don't be a *kibitzer*." What's the precise meaning of that word?
The term *kibitzer* is a widely adopted Yiddishism for an onlooker at a card game who offers gratuitous advice. Such a person is, in short, a meddler. The meaning of *kibitzer* has been extended to include anyone who thrusts himself into another's conversation or presence without invitation. It need no longer apply to a talking nonplayer at a game of cards.

kilt/kin

1. My Canadian friend said, "A kin may wear my kilts today." He was speaking humorously, but was he also speaking correctly?
Not at all. The term *kin*, which refers to relatives collectively, is regarded as a plural. Since it does not represent a single person, the article *a* may not modify it. The one exception is the idiomatic expression "He is no *kin* to me," in which *kin* is employed as a singular. Whenever there is doubt about the number that *kin* takes, think of plural *relatives*, its equivalent.

Regarding the word *kilt* in the example, a Scot, or anyone else who fancies that article of clothing, wears *a* (or *the*) kilt, a singular term. A person wearing *kilts* would be wearing two garments. Some Americans have analogized *kilts* with *pants* or *trousers*, a single garment but a plural word ("His *pants* are too long"). They shouldn't. If you tell a man that you're laughing at his kilts, he may laugh back at your ignorance, for he is wearing *a kilt*.

Note: Be alert to the fact that some dictionaries regard *kin* as a singular.

153

However, the term is moribund and is heading for the mortuary of fallen words, where it will find its alliterative partner, *kith*, "friends and acquaintances."

2. Do the words *kinsman* and *relative* have the same meaning?
Not in all respects. A *kinsman* is a person related to another by blood ties (brother, cousin). And so may be a *relative*. But a relative may also be someone related by law (mother-in-law).

> Note: The word *kinsman* is heard less and less, perhaps because of the desire to avoid sexism. Instead of "She is my *kinsman*," a more likely phrasing would be "She is a relative of mine."

kind

"What kind of a date do you have?" my brother asked. How should I have answered?
Assuming that your question concerns your brother's grammar, you might have told him to omit *a* from his question — "What *kind of* date . . ."? The *a* is superfluous and makes the sentence sound dialectal. *Kind of* should never be followed immediately by either *a* or *an*.

> Note: Since *kind* indicates a class, it should be preceded by a singular demonstrative ("*This kind* of story intrigues me") not a plural ("*these kind* of stories"). A plural construction takes *kinds* ("*these kinds* of stories"). Shakespeare to the contrary notwithstanding (King Lear: "*These kind* of knaves I know"), be sure that *kind* and its referent agree in number. The plural lead word, *these* in this case, is a clue to what should follow. In the most formal English a preferred construction where a plural element is involved is to employ that element first; hence "Stories of this kind intrigue me."
>
> Although *kind of,* meaning rather or somewhat, is a favorite expression, even of many educated people, such usage is best avoided, since it gains nothing in precision and is less economical. It is as easy to say, "It is *rather* (or *somewhat*) warm today" as it is to say, "It is *kind of* warm today."
>
> One last thought. Using *kind* correctly as a singular noun is an aid to the correct use of other words indicating category, such as *brand, breed, class, quality, size, species, type,* and *variety.*

kindly

We frequently hear someone say, "Thank you kindly." Is that an approved expression?
Saying, "Thank you very much" is a better form. But "Thank you kindly" must be approved by many people, considering how often it is heard or read. The speech of people is what conditions usage. Yet because *kindly* means pleasantly or in a pleasant manner, the expression is illogical and should be avoided. Also, instead of "Will you kindly

send me a box of lined paper," one might say, with equal acceptability, "Will you be good enough to" or simply "Please send me."

> Note: All authorities do not disapprove of this usage of *kindly,* although many do. This would seem, therefore, to give a writer a choice. No matter. The best course to take is one that uses words according to their explicit meanings.

knot

Is it now acceptable to speak of a ship traveling at, say, ten knots per hour?

It is not. The expression "ten knots per hour" is incorrect and redundant, since a *knot* is one nautical mile per hour. One should say, "The ship was traveling at ten knots," with no "per hour" appended.

> Note: A knot is the equivalent of 1.15 land miles per hour. The term knot arose from the original seafaring practice of measuring speed. A line with equally spaced knots was reeled over the stern. The number of knots reeled into the water in one minute was then counted.

know/realize

Should one discriminate between the words *know* and *realize?*

There is a fine point of difference that demarcates the use of those words. Generally the words are regarded as synonyms, since their meanings overlap. To *know* is to be aware, to recognize, to understand. To *realize* also means to understand. The distinction between them lies in the degree of understanding. People know what they perceive or apprehend. If they apprehend so thoroughly as to grasp possible consequences, they are said to *realize.*

> Note: *Know* is widely used to mean "well informed," as in "Ralph is *in the know.*" Such usage is colloquial. The noun *know-how,* however, referring to technical knowledge with a knack, although viewed critically by some authorities, is nevertheless standard American English.

koala

Did my son say it right when he asked for a koala bear?

Not technically. A *koala* is not a bear but a marsupial that lives in trees in Australia and looks like a teddy bear. The animal should be called simply *koala,* with no *bear* appendage. But that might take the fun away from the kids.

kosher

How would you define the Yiddish term *kosher?*

Technically, the word applies to food conforming to dietary laws. It now refers, in general usage, to anything that is truthful or honest—aboveboard. If it is legitimate, if it is right, it's *kosher*.

kudos

The report said, "The Governor was entitled to all the kudos heaped upon him." Would you criticize that sentence?
Yes. The word *kudos,* a word best confined to crossword puzzles, means "praise, fame, or glory." It is a singular word and therefore may not be preceded by *all,* a word that indicates more than one. The word *all* should be deleted.

> **Note:** Many people, especially some newspaper reporters, regard *kudos* as a plural and give it a singular form—*kudo.* There is no such word as *kudo.* And there is no plural form for *kudos.* To repeat and exemplify, not "*Kudos* always *seem* to gravitate to Bob Ryan," but *seems.* And not "*Kudos* go to Steven," but *goes."*

L

lamentable

I have heard *lamentable* pronounced several ways. What is its correct pronunciation?
Dictionaries show a stress on either the first or the second syllable. Preferably stress the first, though it is easier to stress the second. Some words, however, must be stressed on the first. Consider HAHS-piht-abl; MIN-ee-uh-chuhr. And so LAM-ehn-tuh-bl.

last/latest

1. Should one say, "The *last* three days are important" or "The three *last* days . . ."?
The word *last* should come first ("The *last three* days"). There could scarcely be three last days. All this despite Coleridge's "The fifty or sixty last years of her life."

2. Are the words *last* and *latest* interchangeable?
Although both *last* and *latest* mean coming after all others, their applications differ. *Last*, meaning final, refers to position (the *last* row) or to time (the *last* show). *Latest* connotes not so much finality as the current or the most recent ("My sister's *latest* boyfriend will not be her *last*").
   Note: Despite what appears above, *last* and *latest* are interchangeable where there is no chance for ambiguity. We speak of an author's last or latest book. There *last* and *latest* serve equally well to mean the most recent. An unjustified fear is that if you ask an author for a copy of his last book, you are implying that he will never write another. With *latest*, of course, there would be no such notion. But that thinking is stretching a point a little too far.

lawyer/attorney

I hear a member of the bar called *lawyer* and sometimes *attorney*. Is there a difference?
Not in the legal profession. The words mean the same thing, even though the term *attorney* may sound more elegant. There is another aspect to this, however. Although a lawyer has been admitted to practice before the bar, this is not necessarily true of an attorney. An attorney is a person authorized to act for another. Such person need not be a lawyer, though often this is the case. The full expression for a nonlawyer attorney is *attorney in fact*.
   Note: When admitted to practice, a lawyer is designated "attorney and

counselor." In Great Britain, there is a distinction between an attorney and a counselor. An attorney is called a *solicitor,* and a counselor (there spelled *counsellor)* is called a *barrister.* A solicitor performs all kinds of legal work for clients but does not appear in court. The barrister, the counselor, is the trial lawyer.

lay/lie

1. Is it correct to say, "Stella laid down for a half hour"?

No. The past tense of *lie* is *lay,* not *laid. Laid* is the past tense of *lay* ("Stella *laid* the books down"), but "Stella *lay* down."

> Note: The problem with the word *lay* is that it serves two verbs in differ-
> ent capacities. It is the present tense of the transitive verb *lay* (meaning
> to put or place somewhere), which requires an object ("I lay the *newspa-*
> *per* on my Dad's desk every morning"). It is also the past tense of the
> intransitive verb *lie* (meaning to rest or to recline), which takes no object
> ("I *lay* down for a nap at four o'clock"). The parts of speech of *lay* are
> *lay, laid, laid;* of *lie,* they are *lie, lay, lain.*

2. My uncle said, "I had laid here on the hammock for an hour." Is that really what he did?

No. Your uncle had *lain* on the hammock. The past participle of *lie,* to be in a lying position, is *lain.*

3. If you lay a vase on the shelf, does it *lay* there or does it *lie* there? Confusing?

It is confusing, judged by the number of times we see *lay* misused for *lie.* Unfortunately, *lay* and *lie* have an identical form (*lay*), even though *lay* is a transitive verb (requires an object) and *lie* is an intransitive verb (does not take an object). Both the present tense of *lay* and the past tense of *lie* are *lay.* Therefore one rightly lays something down (an object), but if he lays himself down, he must say, to be correct, "I now *lie* down."

lead

Please explain and exemplify the past tense of *lead*.

The past tense of the verb *lead,* meaning to direct (not to be confused with the metal) is *led.* Therefore, "The guide *led* us today," not *"lead* us," and not "These events have *lead* us to our ruin," but "have *led* us."

> Note: What may be a cause of confusion is that the metal *lead* and past
> tense of *lead (led)* are pronounced alike. The principal parts of the verb
> are *lead, led, led.*

leave/let

1. Is there a distinction between *"Leave* him alone" and *"Let* him alone"?

There is no distinction between *leave alone* and *let alone* — both expressions mean to refrain from disturbing and are interchangeable when the key verb is followed by a noun or pronoun and the adverb *alone*. Without this adverb, the two verbs change their meanings: *leave* means to depart ("The train will *leave* soon") and *let* means to permit ("*Let* the child remain awhile").

> **Note:** Some writers feel that for the sake of clarity and style, *let alone* is preferable when the sense is to refrain from disturbing (and that is the formula they would employ in formal discourse) and *leave alone* when the sense is to depart and leave a person in solitude.

2. Should we say, "Leave it go" or "Let it go"?

"Let it go." Do not misuse *leave* for *let*. *Let* means to allow, to cause. The sense of the sentence is "allow it to go."

lend/loan

Which is preferred, "He *lent* (or *loaned)* me his book"?

The former *(lent)* is preferable. Verb *lend* (past tense *lent*) has long been established as the verb meaning to let another have or use for a time. But *loan,* originally a noun only, has, through its commercial indulgence, become established also as a verb. Dictionaries approve of this extension. We may now say, "I made a *loan* (noun) of five hundred dollars," and also "The bank *loaned* (verb) me five hundred dollars."

> **Note:** Although there seems to be no good reason why *loan* (past tense *loaned*) should not be interchanged with *lend,* especially with reference to money, many authorities object to any use of *loan* as a verb. It is a wise course to use *loan* as a verb only in connection with banking transactions and *lend* in all other cases.

lengthy/long

Is it true that the word *lengthy* has been made obsolete by the shorter word *long*?

Not at all. Although *long,* which has widespread application involving time, scope, or distance, can replace *lengthy* in every instance, idiomatically we say Alaska is such a *long* distance from New York that the air flight is *lengthy*. The sense of *lengthy* is overlong, tedious. A boring meeting always seems *lengthy*. A wordy memorandum is said to be *lengthy*.

> **Note:** Many authorities hold that *lengthy* should not be regarded as a variant of *long,* but should be used only to express tedium. Others point out that *lengthy* need not imply only tediousness but may refer to time ("We had a *lengthy* but interesting discussion").

let/let's

1. What kind of help does this sentence need: "Let you and I leave now"?

Grammatical surgery. *I* should be replaced by objective case *me*. To test which pronoun is required, mentally omit *you and*. The sentence would then read, *"Let me* leave now," which is clearly a correct wording. You wouldn't say, "Let *I* leave now." This maneuvering leads to the proper construction: "Let *you* and *me* leave now."

> Note: If *let's* had been used in the example instead of *let,* the answer would be the same. "Let's *you and me* (not *you and I*) . . ." would be the required formula. But the reasoning would be different. With *let's* the following pronouns *(you and me)* are in apposition with *us,* which spelled out is "Let us, *you* and *me,* leave now." "You and me" is called for because an appositive takes the same case as its antecedent, here *us,* an objective case.

2. Is it wrong to say, "Let's us all go now"?

Let's is a contraction of *let us. Let's* may therefore not be followed by *us.* If it is, the *us* is redundant.

like/as

1. Does this sentence need correcting: "Howard acts like Richard does?" If so, how is it done?

The sentence is grammatically improved if *does* is omitted or if *as* is substituted for *like. Like* is a preposition that compares nouns and pronouns (Howard acts *like* Richard). *As* is a conjunction that introduces clauses, which—and here is the telltale clue—contain a verb, as all clauses do (*as* Richard *does*). Remember that if "similar to" or "similarly to" can logically be substituted, the word required is *like.* Neither of those phrases makes sense in the example unless *does* is deleted, which means that *like* is inaccurate. *As* means in the way that: "Howard acts *as* (in the way that) Richard does."

> Note: A common error is using *like* to serve as a conjunction. As a general proposition, *like* is a preposition and therefore must be followed with a noun or pronoun as its object ("Kohn looks *like* that boy"). But idiomatic expressions in which *like* stands for *as if* abound in the English language: "Randy's car looks *like* new"; "The audience applauded *like* crazy." However, the cliché "Tell it *like* it is," although regarded as a low colloquialism, is bound to stay. It has a mystique of its own.

2. Is there a difference in sense between "Paul plays *like* a professional" and "Paul plays *as* a professional plays"?

Yes, the first is a simile, meaning that Paul's playing resembles that of a professional; the second, that Paul has the ability of a professional and actually plays as a professional does.

3. Which is correct—"He whistles *like* me" or "He whistles *as* I do"?

Both are correct. In the first, *like* means similarly to and takes an object (*me*). In the second, *as* introduces an adverbial clause, the sense being in the manner that I do. Note that *like* is a preposition and therefore should be followed by a noun or pronoun. *As*, a subordinate conjunction, is used when a verb follows.

4. "I would like for you to go with me" raises this question: Is *for* used correctly?
It is not. A *for* phrase may not be the object of a verb. Delete *for* ("I would *like you* to go with me").

5. Is it proper to say, "Rhythm like in punk rock is hard to follow"?
The expression *like in* is pure punk. *Like* should introduce a noun or pronoun, not a prepositional phrase. Say, "Rhythm like *that* in punk rock is hard to follow."

6. Are there too many words in "I don't eat certain vegetables, like for instance turnips"?
Yes, the preposition *like*. The combination of words — *like for instance* — is nonstandard. It sounds provincial.

7. How does this sentence rate: "We've never seen the likes of anything like the new museum"?
Poorly. *The likes of* in the sense "of a kind" is substandard. If omitted from the example, nothing would be lost except three useless words. Try it.

likely

May *likely* be used by itself when its sense is *probably*?
Adverb *likely* (meaning probably), as in "They *likely* will leave soon," should idiomatically be escorted by a modifier, such as *most, quite, rather,* or *very* ("They will *very likely* agree with our plan"; "*Most likely* Andrew will come early"). *Probably* or *in all likelihood* may serve instead of *likely*, in which case no qualifying word is required ("Probably they will leave soon"). In a sentence such as "It is *likely* to snow today," *likely* needs no qualifier because it is an adjective joined to the subject by a linking verb.

limited

Is it all right to say, "He had a limited acquaintance with his neighbor"?
The word *limited* is too general in that construction and is being extended beyond its normal province. Say a *slight* acquaintance. *Limited* should not displace such more precise terms as *few, small, scant,* or *meager.*
Note: In formal language *limited* is employed only in a literal or concrete

sense ("By rules of Council, we are *limited* to what we may spend on decorations"). Saying, "We can expect *limited* help from Council" is not standard English. Saying that a student has limited learning ability and that a person has limited means are euphemisms, idiomatically acceptable, but fuzzily informative.

linage/lineage

The words *linage* and *lineage* are confusing. Please clarify.
The similar spellings and pronunciations of these words account for the confusion. *Linage* is preferably used to mean the number of lines of written or printed matter and *lineage* to mean lineal descent from a common ancestor. But note that *lineage* is, according to the dictionaries, an accepted variant spelling of *linage*.

> **Note:** *Linage* has two syllables and *lineage* three. The recommendation is to use *linage* only with reference to the number of printed lines and to use *lineage* when the reference is to ancestry.

literally/figuratively

What caveat applies when using the word *literally*?
Do not use it to mean *figuratively*. *Literally* means actually; that is, true to the meaning of the exact words. Saying that a teacher was so upset that he literally tore his hair out is fine if the teacher thereby became bald. Otherwise, use *figuratively*, which means metaphorically; that is, not in the words' exact sense.

> **Note:** The desire of some people to make a point obvious, to make it emphatic, or even to make it shocking is what frequently leads to the misuse of *literally* as an intensifier. Instead of saying that something is figuratively so, the word *literally* is transposed to gain the desired effect: "He *literally* hit the ceiling"; "He *literally* exploded"; "She was *literally* bathed in tears." Of course none of those things are true. A corrective step is to omit *literally* or to adopt a more moderate phrasing to replace *literally*: "He *seemed to* hit the ceiling"; "He *all but* exploded."

live

What preposition follows the verb *live*?
Many prepositions may follow the verb *to live*; for example, *in, on, at,* and *by*: "I *live in* Pleasantville"; "I *live on* Pine Street"; "I *live at* 1322"; "I *live by* writing."

> **Note:** *Live* rhymes with *give*. Both *live* and *give* have a short *i*. If you live a long time, you are *long-lived*, (*lived* has a long *i*). A person whose life span was short was *short-lived* (but the *i* was long).

livid/lurid

I have heard *livid* and *lurid* used in so many ways that I now wonder what those words mean.

Livid means a bluish leaden color. But few people think it means anything but red, a bright red at that. When a person is enraged (*furious* is a popular meaning of *livid*) and his face becomes livid, it should be ashen. But instead it has become flushed, which means to become red suddenly. To satisfy both the populist and the etymologist, the only thing to do is to avoid the word *livid* entirely.

Originally *lurid* meant pale yellow, like a sallow, wan face with the hue of death. A lurid light is ghastly, as flames seen through smoke. But, figuratively, the word has come to imply sensationalism (*lurid* headlines) or weird lighting (*lurid* effects of a discotheque) or shocking (the *lurid* details of the murder).

loath/loathe

The spellings of sound-alikes *loath* and *loathe* are often confused. Is the problem solvable?

Yes. To *loathe* is to despise, to hate. When thinking of something abhorrent or of something you detest, let the final *e* of synonym *hate* and *despise* direct you to a final *e* in *loathe*. For the record, *loath* means reluctant, unwilling, or disinclined ("The teacher was *loath* to admit her mistakes").

Note: A variant spelling of *loath* is *loth*: "The boy was *loath* (or *loth*) to leave his puppy." Adjective *loathsome* (no internal *e*) means hateful, disgusting, or repulsive.

locate

What do you think of "We will *locate* in Omaha"?

In the sense of settle or become established, *locate* is colloquial. Preferred to *locate*, in particular speech or writing, would be *settle* or *live*. But "Our house is *located* in Omaha" is standard according to some usage panelists. Of course you might say, "Our house is *in* Omaha," and save a word.

Note: When the reference is to the place where a person will live (a residence or other living quarters), the preferred word is *settle*. *Locate* is also acceptable in this context but is less refined.

Locate also means to discover the place of. It is a distant, a very distant, synonym for *find*. We say, "Can you *locate* the place on the beach where you were sitting? If you can, we may *find* your eyeglasses there." To *find* is to come upon by chance or to recover something. One added thought. Avoid using *located*, meaning situated, after the verb *be*. Not "The school building is *located* near the police station," but "The school building *is* (not *located*) near the police station."

lot

Is *alot* in "Vernon bought alot of goods today" accepted spelling?
It is not. Although frequently seen, *a lot* should be rendered as two words: *a lot*. And observe that *a lot*, meaning much, a great deal, or a great many, although widely used informally and found in the works of some respected writers, is not an approved expression in edited writing. It has a tinge of colloquialism about it.

> **Note:** The phrase *a lot of* is common to suggest a quantity. What must be observed is that *lot*, as the grammatical subject, is followed by a singular verb if used by itself ("These days *a lot is* being imported from Japan"), but a plural verb if the noun in a following *of* phrase is plural ("*A lot* [or *Lots*] of *bananas are* now on sale"). If followed by a singular noun, the verb naturally is singular ("*A lot* [or *Lots*] of *food is* on the table").

loud/loudly

Should I say, "He sang *loud*" or "He sang *loudly*"?
Take your pick. After the verb *sing* (*laugh, say, shout,* and *talk*) the adverbs *loud* and *loudly* are interchangeable. Prefer *loudly* in formal usage, but be sure in any usage to use *loudly* after the verbs *boast, insist,* and *proclaim*.

> **Note:** One should say, "He sang *loud* and *strong*," not *loudly* and *strongly*. But observe that after some verbs, the adverbs *loud* and *loudly* are equally acceptable. We may say, "The lion roared *loudly* (or *loud*)"; "The frightened child screamed *loudly* (or *loud*)." Idiom, however, demands that we say, "He bragged *loudly* (not *loud*) about his accomplishments." Formalists employ adverb *loudly* more often than adverb *loud* because in general they prefer the adverbial form to the adjectival.

love/lovely

1. Some people say they love everything on the menu. Is the word *love* used properly?
It is being used loosely. A more precise word is *like*. If you *like* chopped herring, say it that way, not "I *love* chopped herring." Use *like* wherever it will do.

2. Everything good is *lovely* to some people. Is that word being used properly?
Lovely, called a feminine intensive, is a greatly abused word. If it does not refer to something worthy of winning affection, something delicately or exquisitely beautiful, the answer is no. Colloquially anything agreeable, pleasing, or delightful is said to be lovely—a lovely house, a lovely meal, a lovely handbag. Try to find a more suitable descriptive.

3. Is there anything wrong with saying, "We had a lovely time"?
The established colloquialism *a lovely time* is frequently used by edu-

cated people. But saying, "We had an *enjoyable* time" is more specific — and preferable.

loving/amorous

May the words *loving* and *amorous* be freely interchanged?
No indeed. Although each word may refer to lovers or to lovemaking, *amorous* has a more sexual connotation and therefore a narrower use.

luxurious/luxuriant

When should one use *luxurious* and when *luxuriant*? The words are confusing.
Use *luxurious* to mean characterized by luxury or sumptuousness. It also means costly. *Luxuriant* is equated with fruitful, teeming, and abundant. A profuse growth, whether in a garden or on top of the head, is luxuriant, not luxurious. Living in a chateau is luxurious, not luxuriant.

-ly adverbs

1. What care should one take regarding the placement of *-ly* adverbs?
The sound of a repetitive *-ly/-ly* has a disagreeable effect. Therefore, not "We are usually especially fond of turkey at Thanksgiving," but "We usually are specially fond. . . ." In a sentence in which one of the *-ly* words can be changed to one without an *-ly* ending, consider doing so.

2. What might you say about hyphens after adverbs ending in *-ly*?
Avoid them. A hyphen should not follow an *-ly* adverb because it serves no purpose. Not "He is an equally-good man," but "*an equally good man*" (no hyphen).

3. Isn't *-ly* a good sign to know that the word is an adverb?
It is a sign to heed because many adverbs end in *-ly*. But some do not; for example, *here, now, so*. And remember that some adjectives end in *-ly* (a *friendly* man, a *brotherly* act).

> **Note:** The adverbial form, the one with the *-ly* ending, is always grammatically acceptable. But in many cases idiom bypasses this form for the adjectival form of the adverb. Formalists prefer the *-ly* appendage, and the *-ly* form is the safer one to use when not sure whether the adjectival form is established idiom. However, no one will dispute that adverb *slow* is preferable on signs saying, "Go slow." And then there is *sell cheap* and *sweep clean; drink deep* and *ship direct; play fair* and *turn sharp*.

M

maître d'

Why does the term *maître d'* end in *d'*?
The term is an abbreviation of *maître d' hôtel,* which means master of the house. But in today's usage it applies to the headwaiter of a fancy restaurant.
Note: Pronounce this term MEH-truh doh-TEHL.

majority

Do we say, "The majority of union members *were* (or *was*) opposed"?
The answer is *were.* With the word *majority,* the thing to do is to decide whether the reference is to a totality, which takes a singular verb, or to separate items or individual persons, which take a plural verb. We say, "The *majority* of the union *is* composed of senior citizens," construing *majority* as an entity, but "The Western *majority were* unwilling to change their minds," meaning individually.
Note: *Majority* always takes a singular verb if it is followed by a specific number ("The majority *was* seventy-five"). It is rightly used to mean more than half, but in matters pertaining to elections, the term is best avoided in favor of *most* or *the greater part* unless an exact count has been made.

Although the expression *great majority,* meaning most or considerably more than half, is acceptable in any context, the expression *greater majority* may be used only where two precise numbers are being compared. And do not use the word *majority* where numbers are not involved. For example, rather than "The *majority* of the time she spends watching television," say *most* or *the greater part.* Rather than "The *majority* of his suits are blue," use *many* or *most.*

The overused combination *the vast majority of* is best put in storage. Besides, it uses three words where one may serve, either *most* or *many.*

majority/plurality

How does a *majority* differ from a *plurality*?
A *majority* of votes is more than one half the total cast. A *plurality* is the difference between the highest and the second highest vote-getter, there being at least three candidates. If Tom received sixty votes, Bill fifty, and Ralph twenty, Tom's plurality was ten.
Note: Two things to note about *plurality.* One, a *plurality* is less than half of the votes cast. Two, if a majority of the votes is required to be declared the winner, the candidate winning a plurality of the votes has not won.

make

Is there anything wrong in "Are you going to make lunch now?"
Although *make* is unambiguous, "Are you going to *prepare* lunch now?" would be more desirable. *Make* has many senses, but its usefulness should not be abused. And so rather than "Are you going to *make* a party?" prefer *have, plan,* or *arrange.* Reach for the appropriate verb.

malapropism

What is *malapropism*?
It is the use of a wrong word that sounds similar to the right one but has an entirely different meaning. ("I escaped by *alluding* him" instead of *"eluding* him").

> **Note:** Richard Sheridan, who in 1775 wrote *The Rivals,* coined the term *malapropism* from the French *mal à propos,* which means unsuitable or out of place. An endearing character in this play, Mrs. Malaprop, enjoyed impressing her friends with elegant words that, unfortunately for her, she was constantly misusing. She would warn, "Don't attempt to extirpate yourself from that matter. . . ." Or say, "I would by no means wish a daughter of mine to be a progeny of learning."

manner/manor born

1. Was Hamlet to the *manor born* or to the *manner born*?
When Hamlet said, "Though I am native here/And to the manner born," the word, as just indicated, was *manner,* meaning custom or habitual practice. True, Hamlet was born in a manor, but that was not what he was saying.

> **Note:** Hamlet was referring to his familiarity with the custom of celebrating each drink taken by Claudius, the King, by sounding trumpets, firing guns, and beating on drums. Hamlet disapproved of the custom, even though he was "to the manner born"; that is, grown up with this practice. Hamlet then concluded with another often-repeated quotation: ". . . it is a custom/More honored in the breach than the observance."

2. Doesn't "more honored in the breach than in the observance" mean that a custom is more often broken than observed?
That meaning is the one accepted by most people. But Shakespeare meant that it was best to break custom (stop drinking) than to observe it (and get drunk).

3. Which wording is correct: "Not by any manner *of* means" or "Not by any manner *or* means"?
The first one: "Not by any manner *of* means."

> **Note:** Be careful not to use the word *manner* unnecessarily. It may often be eliminated by converting an adjective into an adverb: in a haughty manner (*haughtily*), in a joking manner (*jokingly*).

many

1. What do you think of this contortion — *many another*?

The contortion is an accepted idiomatic expression. Idiom, of course, need not conform to the rules of grammar. *Many* has a plural sense and *another* a singular. We say, *"Many another* boy *is* deserving of a scholarship." Illogical, but we understand it.

> **Note:** Idiomatic *many a*, like idiomatic *many another*, takes a singular verb: *"Many a* man *seeks* a better position in this organization." But if the sentence is restructured without the *a*, a plural verb will be required, since *many* is a plural: *"Many seek"* or *"Many men seek."*

2. Can this sentence be improved: "A good many citizens failed to vote"?

Yes, if more precise detail is available; for example, "About 45 percent of the citizens failed to vote." Prefer concrete terms to those that are general and imprecise.

married

Is there any reason for persons who got married to be concerned with the grammar in this sentence?

Although it won't affect the marriage, *were married* is regarded as preferable wording to *got married* ("Rob and Jane *were married* yesterday").

> **Note:** Traditionally, a man married a woman and the woman was married *to* the man. Whatever the reason behind that phrasing might have been, it certainly no longer holds. Today a woman marries a man, just as a man marries a woman. But be careful not to say that last Sunday your neighbor married his wife. He didn't. He married a woman who thereby became his wife.

martinet

What is a *martinet*?

A martinet is a strict disciplinarian, a taskmaster. The word comes from Jean Martinet, an inspector general under Louis XIV. Martinet was a punctilious drillmaster who was thoroughly despised because of his uncompromising demands.

> **Note:** During the siege of Duisburg in 1672, Martinet was killed by a shot from his own artillery. Whether the shot was fired at him accidentally or intentionally has not been determined.

masterful/masterly

May I use the terms *masterful* and *masterly* to describe a great violinist?

Preferably not. *Masterful* means powerful, forceful, domineering, whereas *masterly* means possessing the skill of a master, highly proficient. It is more appropriate, and more precise, to say that a great violinist is *masterly* rather than *masterful*.

> **Note:** The adverb form of *masterful* is *masterfully*. *Masterly* has no adverbial form. To compensate for the lack of an adverb for *masterly*, some writers use *masterfully* as the adverb, a practice not recommended. Rather than saying, "He played the violin *masterfully*," avoid any possible criticism by recasting the sentence, even at the expense of a few more words.

may be/maybe

Is it correct to write, "*May be* he will come early today"?

May be is a two-word verb form and needs a subject—"*It may be* he will come early today." Its meaning corresponds with that of adverb *maybe;* that is, perhaps or possibly. The sentence, with no change in thought, might have read: "*Maybe* he will come early today."

may/might

1. Does it matter whether I say, "I *may* attend the seminar tonight" or "I *might* attend the seminar tonight"?

It matters to this extent. Although both words—*may* and *might*—connote possibility, the possibility inherent in *may* is greater than that in *might*. *May* indicates that thought has been given and that there is a likelihood that something will come about. *Might* suggests a remote possibility. It indicates an unsettled idea—you might, but then again you might not. A person told that his hat *may* be in the locker room has more reason to go and look than if told that it *might* be there.

> **Note:** *May* is an auxiliary verb in the present tense and *might* is its past tense. This distinction has no bearing when possibility is being considered. But in normal grammatical sequence, *might* is required when the sentence is framed in the past ("She *thinks* she *may* go," but "She *thought* she *might* go"). When a direct statement is changed to indirect discourse, *may* becomes *might*. "She says she *may* purchase a new car" becomes "She said she *might* purchase a new car."

2. Does this sentence seem right: "The mayor said that possibly the road may open next week"?

It does not. The sentence should be amended to avoid the redundancy *possibly . . . may*. The sense of *possible* is contained in *may*. Use either *possibly* or *may*, not both.

means

Should the word *means* be treated as a singular or a plural?

When *means* refers to resources (money or property), it is a plural noun

("His financial *means* seem unlimited"; "The *means* available *are* not enough to warrant such a trip"). When *means* refers to a way to an end, a way of achieving something, it may be regarded as a singular or a plural noun. What determines its number is the modifying word preceding *means*. A singular verb is required after *a means, one means,* and *every means* ("Every means is* to be taken"; "A good *means* to a movie career *is* modeling"). A plural verb is necessary after *all means, several means, other means,* and *such means* ("Such means *are* to be taken as will save our venture"; "There *are* other means to solve the problem").

meantime/meanwhile

Is there a preference between the words *meantime* and *meanwhile*?
Preferably use *meantime* as a noun to describe the interval between one event and another ("In the *meantime* I'll rest") and *meanwhile* as an adverb for intervening time ("My wife was late; *meanwhile* I prepared dinner").

> **Note:** Dictionaries list both *meantime* and *meanwhile* as nouns and adverbs. But as a practical matter, *meanwhile* is used only as an adverb and *meantime* as a noun, object of the preposition *in*. *In the meantime* is idiomatic; *in the meanwhile* is not.

media

I'm sure that this has often been discussed, but do we refer to television as the *medium* or the *media*?
Television, like the newspapers, is a form, or *medium,* of communication. Plural *media* is rightly used only when referring to many or all forms collectively. Reference to one calls for *medium,* which means that television is a communication medium.

> **Note:** Although standard English requires that *media* be followed by a plural verb, popular usage does not see it that way. *Media* is regarded as a singular noun which then, quite naturally, is followed by a singular verb ("The media *is* challenging the President again"). In edited writing *are* would be required. If *media* seems more like a singular noun than a plural, to be grammatically correct, simply drop the word and say, rather than "The news media *is* doing a fine job of uncovering corruption," that *the press is* or *the television coverage is* if only one medium is to be commended. If all the agencies that disseminate information deserve commendation, then refer to the *media (the media are)*. The standard plural forms of *medium* are *media* (not *medias*) and *mediums*. But the latter term is more applicable to spiritualists.

metonymy/synecdoche

Would you explain the meanings and use of *metonymy* and *synecdoche*?

In some cases it is difficult to distinguish these rhetorical figures of speech from each other. *Metonymy*—a part suggestive of the whole, such as "The White House" for the incumbent administration; "the Hill" for Congress; "Wall Street" for American financiers. *Synecdoche*— using a part to indicate the whole: "a sail" for a ship; "head" for cattle; "hands" for workmen. "Do you have wheels?" for an automobile; "Let's get our bread-and-butter" for go to lunch.

me too

Whenever my daughter asks for a cookie, my son always chimes in, "Me too." Should his English be corrected?
Although "I too" is grammatically correct (an ellipsis for "I too want a cookie"), idiom has entrenched *me too* so deeply that *I too* now sounds pompous. Let him continue his *me too's*.

mighty

I get sneers from my English-sensitive aunt when I say, "I am mighty pleased." Should I sneer back?
By no means. You are employing *mighty* to mean very or extremely, a justifiable replacement for either of those words in everyday speech. Most of us find *mighty* mighty useful. But bear in mind that your aunt's English may be more formally structured. In the sense discussed here, *mighty* is an informal expression. In formal discourse "I am very much pleased" would be a proper phrasing.

million

Should the word *million* be treated as a singular or a plural form?
It may be either; it depends on idiom. If a specific number or the word *several* is used before *million*, idiomatically the singular form is required ("Two *million* dollars was spent"; "Several *million* people marched"). If no number precedes *million* or the word *many* or *few* precedes it, the form *millions* is required ("There *were millions* of counterfeit dollars to burn"; "*Many millions* stood and watched"; "A *few millions* more or less won't matter").

> **Note:** Actually the plural form of *million* is either *million* or *millions*. A million is one thousand thousand. Two million *and a half* is preferred to two and a half million.

minus

"I'm home minus my money" is the way my husband expresses it after a session at the casino. Isn't he wrong?

I have no comment to make about his visits to the casino, but he's betting wrong on the English language. Using *minus* to mean without or having lost is colloquial, and on a low level at that. It would be better if he raised his sights.

> Note: *Minus* is a word belonging in mathematical and statistical contexts. When used otherwise, it is often a weak attempt at humor ("Jack had a hairy experience; he discovered he was *minus* his toupee and his wallet").
>
> A distant relative, *minuscule,* which refers to something small, has its own problems, some not so small. For one thing it is often misspelled *miniscule,* the *mini* representing something small like a *miniskirt.* But the word begins with *minus,* not *mini,* and therein lies a second problem. The word is preferably pronounced mih-NUS-skyool, although some dictionaries prefer MIHN-uh-skyool, stressing the first syllable.

mirabile dictu

What does *mirabile dictu* mean?
It literally means wonderful to relate, its sense being amazing as it may seem (*"Mirabile dictu,* the price is the same this year as it was last year"). But hearkening back to Ripley, it now means "Believe It or Not."

> Note: Pronounce it mihr-RAB-leh DIHK-too. This Latin phrase was used many times by Vergil in his epic poetry. A sister phrase is *mirabile visu,* "wonderful to behold."

mitigate/militate

Is *mitigated* used correctly in "The color of his skin mitigated unfairly against him"?
The word required is *militated,* which means to have an adverse effect or influence on ("His slovenly appearance *militated* against an advancement"). *Mitigate* means to moderate, to soften, to assuage, to lessen the severity of. A judge, responding to a tearful plea, might mitigate (reduce) the sentence ("The effects of the terrible deed were somewhat *mitigated* by the remorse shown by the criminal").

> Note: To *militate* is to operate *against* something. Rarely is it used to mean *for* something. *Militate* came from the same ancestor as *militant* and *military,* from Latin *miles,* "a soldier."

momentarily

What does "Anne will be there momentarily" mean?
It's hard to say. *Momentarily,* when used with the future tense, means either for a moment or in a moment. Hence the ambiguity: Anne may either be there very soon *or* remain for a short while.

> Note: Unless the context makes the meaning of *momentarily* clear, do not use it. When employed with the present or past tense, this adverb causes

no problems, for it then has the one sense of for a moment or for only a short while.

monopoly

What can be said of the phrase *complete monopoly*?
It contains an unnecessary appendage—*complete*. Drop it. A monopoly has exclusive control, which is entire, and that makes it complete. Incidentally, the phrase *entire monopoly* is just as redundant.

moot

I think the word *moot* **raises a moot point. Do you agree?**
Moot is a strange word. It means both arguable and nonarguable. Generally speaking, a *moot* point is one that is debatable. It concerns a point that is doubtful and therefore arguable. Yet in courts of law a point or case that is *moot* is no longer subject to argument; it lacks legal significance because previously decided or settled.

Note: Law school students try hypothetical cases before a "moot court," the case serving as an exercise in a training program.

morphine/hypnotism

Is it true that the words *morphine* **and** *hypnotism* **are related?**
They are by consanguinity. The word *morphine* was named after Morpheus, the god of dreams. His father Hypnos, the god of sleep; whence *hypnosis* and *hypnotism.*

Note: Do not confuse the terms *hypnotism* and *hypnosis.* Either term may be correctly used to name the art of mesmerism. But *hypnotism* refers only to the act or process of putting someone into a sleeplike state, whereas *hypnosis* refers either to the practice (the hypnotic trance) or the state of consciousness itself. Therefore, do not say, "He is under *hypnotism,*" but "He is under *hypnosis.*"

The cliché in "I'm so tired that I hope I fall into the arms of Morpheus right away," meaning to go to sleep, is inaccurately stated. Morpheus was not the god of sleep. His father, Hypnos, was. However, one who is dreaming may be said to be in "Morpheus' arms."

most

1. A remark often heard is "Most everyone knows my father in this town." How does that remark sit with you?
Not very well. *Most* in this usage is widely employed in colloquial speech, although, surprisingly, a few authorities do not disapprove of it. Undoubtedly, however, it is more precise, and grammatically acceptable, to say "almost" or "nearly."

Note: Most grammarians contend that *most,* meaning nearly, is not an acceptable replacement for *almost.* In fact they say that such usage is an example of slovenly speech. It is equally undesirable to say, "most always," "most any time," or "on most every occasion." The correct adverb, *almost,* is just as easy to use. Further, employing *most* as an intensive meaning *very,* at least in writing, is another questionable practice. Use sparingly, if at all. Overuse is a stylistic fault. Rather than "Spencer was a *most* interesting speaker," say, "a *very* interesting speaker" or, without the intensive, "an interesting speaker."

Confusing *most* with *mostly* should be carefully guarded against: "It was the overbuying that was *most* (not *mostly*) to blame for our financial problems." Restrict the use of *mostly* to mean in the main, the greatest part, or almost entirely, as in "After five days of constant work, the manuscript was *mostly* completed." Observe that *mostly all,* as in "It is *mostly all* gone," is a colloquial substitute for *almost all* or *nearly all,* either of which makes for better English.

2. What is the number of the verb that *most* takes?

Most takes a singular verb when it refers to quantity *("Most* of his hair *has* fallen out"; *"Most* of the food *has* been eaten") but a plural when it refers to individual persons or things *("Most* of the apples *were* saved"; *"Most* of the players *are* here").

much less

What do you think of this statement: "It's hard to listen to him, much less to agree with him"?

The sentence confuses *much less* with *much more* (". . . *much more* to agree with him"). Generally *much more* is used with positive statements ("We're surprised that such a rule was suggested, *much more* (surprised) that it was adopted"); *much less,* with negative ones ("Leona did not even examine the books, *much less* correct them").

much/very much

In "My son was very encouraged by his teacher," is *much* or *very much* required?

In general, *much* is used with participles (*much* admired, *much* disliked) and *very* with adjectives (*very* good, *very* pleasant). Some participles are now regarded as adjectives—that is, they have the force of an adjective. These participles may be modified by *very* alone: *very* pleased, *very* interested, *very* tired, *very* disappointed. Participles functioning as active verbs—that is, those used in the predicate with verbal force—continue to take *much* ("I was *much* encouraged by what I heard"; "Harold was *much* delighted by the award").

Note: The participles that are more verb than adjective and are modified by *much* may be more strongly emphasized by having *much* modified by *very*—"He was *very much disliked."* Or, rather than *much,* it could be *greatly, deeply,* or any other suitable adverb ("My mechanic was *greatly disturbed* by not being able to find the seat of the trouble").

The big question, the one that is not answered alike by all grammarians, is when does a participle become an adjective? Stated in another way, when may the questioned word be modified by *very* alone? The general answer is that if the word is commonly used as an adjective, then it has lost its verbal force and should be regarded as an adjective. But who determines that the word is in such common adjectival use as to justify a change in its status? A writer with a discerning ear.

mumps

Do we say, "Mumps *is* (or *are)* contagious"?

Mumps is contagious. Although *mumps* looks like a plural noun, it is singular. Hence *mumps is.* Be careful of other nouns that are plural in form but singular in meaning: *mathematics, measles, news.*

> **Note:** The word *measles* is treated the way *mumps* is, since it also is plural in form but singular in meaning (*"Measles is* a disease"). When referring to *measles* or *mumps* in formal language, if a pronoun is needed, it must be singular ("Measles. I had *it* [not *them*] when I was six years old"). The possibilities, however, are that in general conversation *mumps* and *measles* will be taken as a plural noun: "Did your son have the *mumps?"* "Yes, he's had *them."*

must

When something is important, my nephew says, "It's a must." Is it proper to use *must* that way?

The expression *must* is widely accepted in general English both as a noun meaning necessity (as in the example) and as an adjective meaning essential ("It is a *must* procedure"). Many authorities regard this use of *must* as standard English. Nevertheless, since *must* used this way has an informal ring, it is best avoided in formal writing.

N

named

In connection with the naming of a child, which is preferred —*named for* or *named after*?

The preference in the United States is the former: "Andrew was named *for* his maternal grandfather." In Great Britain *named after* is the idiomatic expression.

> **Note:** A person is honored by having a child named for him or her. In the United States, where Christianity is the predominant religion, the name bestowed on the child is commonly called a Christian name. But care must be exercised so as not to offend those of a different faith. For example, Jews, Buddhists, Mohammedans, and atheists have no Christian name. To be safe, therefore, it is advisable to ask for a person's first, or given, name.
>
> In other uses of *named*, do not follow it with *as*. Not "Samlin was *named as* the moderator for the evening," but "named moderator."

naught/nought

Should I use *naught* (or *nought*) to mean zero or nothing?

Depends. Use *nought* (the arithmetical symbol 0) for zero. ("*Nought* from four is four"). In other contexts use *naught* ("He cares *naught* for money or social life").

> **Note:** *Naught* is an archaic form of *nought*, best restricted to poetical contexts, but, although regarded as bookish, it is nevertheless available for duty wherever it may serve.
>
> A word that sounds similar to *naught* and *nought* and also means zero, not one, or nothing is *nary* ("We have *nary* a thing to say about it"). *Nary* has two strikes against it. It sounds provincial and, when used by educated people, sounds affected. Let's hope there is a strikeout. *Nary* is usually followed by *a* or *an*.

nauseous

Is it wrong to say "My uncle is nauseous"?

Depends on what you mean. He is nauseous if he makes other people sick. But if what is meant is that your uncle is ill, a more likely interpretation, then the required word is *nauseated*, not *nauseous*. A person who has a queasy stomach is nauseated. He is suffering from *nausea*, having become ill from something *nauseous*, gas fumes, for example. Just as a person is scandalized by something scandalous, so a person is nauseated by something nauseous.

Note: In a figurative sense, that which is *nauseous* is repulsive, disgusting: "That man eats like an animal. It is *nauseous*."

needs

Why is that we say, "Amos needs to rest longer," but "Amos need rest no longer"?

In the first example, the verb *needs* takes an infinitive in the accustomed way. In the second, *need* is an auxiliary like *must* and takes no *to*. The rule governing negative statements also applies to interrogatives: "Need Amos (no *to*) rest longer?" In these uses, as an auxiliary, the third person singular of *need* in the present tense is not inflected, not *needs*.

> **Note:** *Need(s)*, meaning of necessity, lends itself to some archaic constructions when accompanied by *must* (*needs must*, *must needs*): "Laura *needs must* find herself"; "We *must needs* inform him." Used this way, *needs* is an adverb, and its form is invariable.
>
> Although *need* and *necessity* are synonymous, idiomatically they take different constructions. *Need* takes an infinitive ("There's no *need to leave* so early"). *Necessity* never takes one. It is followed by *for* or *of* ("There's no *necessity for* leaving so early"; "We understand the *necessity of* eating nutritious food").

neglect/negligence

How are the words *negligence* and *neglect* differentiated?

Both *negligence* and *neglect* mean failure to attend to, to give too little care to. *Negligence* is repeated or habitual neglect ("The janitor's *negligence* is responsible for the sorry state of our elevators"). *Neglect* is most often used with reference to a particular instance. It is a specific failure or omission to act when required ("Wilder's failure to pay taxes when due can be attributed solely to *neglect*"). In some contexts *negligence* and *neglect* are equally acceptable terms. The stronger word, however, is *neglect*.

neither

May I trouble you to point out some of the pitfalls in the use of *neither*?

The commonest error is the use of a plural verb when *neither*, as a pronoun subject (which is always singular), is followed by an *of* phrase containing a plural noun or pronoun. Not "Neither of them *are* any good," but "Neither of them *is* any good." Second. If *neither* is an element in a correlative conjunction, the corresponding element must be *nor*, not *or*. Third. *Neither* is used with reference to two persons or things only. If there are more, use *none*. Fourth is the faulty adverbial use of *neither* when it creates a double negative, as in "Lou didn't and Jim didn't *neither*."

> **Note:** Some good writers use *neither* in relation to three or more persons or things. That practice is not a good one to adopt. But we must be aware that some authorities approve of it.

neither . . . nor

1. Why do we say, "Neither trains nor an airplane *travels* fast enough for me," but "Neither an airplane nor trains *travel* fast enough for me"?

The rule is that if two subjects differing in number are joined by *neither . . . nor*, the verb agrees with the nearer subject. Hence *airplane travels* and *trains travel*.

> **Note:** It is good style, when one subject is singular and the other plural, to place the plural in the second slot. "Neither Jane nor the boys *are* coming" is preferable to "Neither the boys nor Jane *is* coming." The former construction seems more natural and flows better.

2. Could this sentence be improved: "We neither saw Father nor Mother"?

Yes, because *neither . . . nor* conjunctions should be set out in grammatically parallel form. Make it: "We saw *neither* Father *nor* Mother." Balanced constructions improve readability, since they make sentences flow with no jolting interruptions.

> **Note:** The rule is that the grammatical weight given *neither* should also be given *nor*. This practice places the alternatives in structural balance. For example, "Sonia *neither* is pretty *nor* smart" needs recasting: "Sonia is *neither* pretty *nor* smart." Changing the position of the verb usually will solve the problem.

3. How does this sentence sound: "Neither Bolivia, Peru, nor Chile should be visited in the winter"?

The conjunction *neither . . . nor* should refer only to two alternatives, not to more. To be correct, make it "Bolivia, Peru, and Chile should not be visited in the winter," omitting *neither . . . nor* entirely.

4. May *neither* ever take *or*, and may *either* take *nor*?

The answer is no in each case. The correct combinations at all times are *neither . . . nor*; *either . . . or*.

nemesis

Is it permissible to call someone who always defeats you a *nemesis*?

Nemesis is frequently used in the sense reflected in the question, a traditional conqueror, and so it must be all right. Actually, Nemesis was the goddess of retributive justice who sought out wrongdoers and wreaked vengeance upon them. The word, strictly speaking, means an avenger, a person who punishes another for evil deeds.

> Note: In general usage *nemesis*, meaning an unbeatable rival, as in sports, is spelled with a lower case *n*. Of course if reference is made to the Greek goddess, a capital *N* is required.

never

"He never said yes when I asked him." Why should the use of *never* be criticized?

It should be because it does not belong. *Never* means not ever or on no occasion, and, although it is true that up to the moment he had not ever said yes, using *never* when a simple *not* is meant is uncalled for and regarded as colloquial. Recast: "He did *not* say yes when I asked him."

> Note: Bear in mind that *never* refers to a period of time, whereas *not* refers to one time. Hence the verb accompanying *never* should not be in the past tense as in "Grace *never saw* a dancing monkey before," but in the past perfect tense: "Grace *had never seen* a dancing monkey before." The desire to intensify *never* with *ever* ("They *never ever* went on vacations") should be restrained. Do not pair *never* with *ever*.

news

Do we say, "The news *is* (or *are*) bad"?

The word *news* is a singular noun and requires a singular verb. "The news *is* bad." Other singular nouns ending in *s* are *lens* and *summons*. "The *lens* is large." "The *summons* is for you."

> Note: The notion that the word *news* comes from the first letter of *north*, *east*, *west*, and *south* and means that the information was obtained from all directions has been discountenanced by word historians. They point out that the original spelling of *news* was *newes*.

nice

Why do many writers deplore the word *nice*?

Nice, except when it means precise or discriminatory (a *nice* distinction, a *nice* eye for color), is so vague as to convey little meaning. Prefer a more precise word. Not, for example, "We had a *nice* time" (enjoyable). Not "It is a *nice* day" (sunny). Not "He is a *nice* person" (pleasant).

> Note: Although all authorities do not agree, the consensus is that in the sense of agreeable, *nice* is regarded as standard (a *nice* afternoon, a *nice* teacher). Despite that unanimity of opinion, *nice* as a counterword of approval should be handled gingerly and then, in most cases, discarded for a more particular term. Think of *pleasing, good-tempered, delightful, kind, delicate, accurate, dainty, well-mannered, respectable*, and *refined*.
>
> Adverb *nicely*, in the sense of satisfactorily, has been elevated from a

colloquial status to the standard level of English in the eyes of some critics. But not all. Rather than "Our patient is getting along *nicely*," referring to improvement in health, prefer *satisfactorily* in precise English, and everyone will think you write nicely.

no business

Our coach once said, "Students not wearing sneakers have no business playing in the gym." Did he say it right?
Colloquially, yes. But properly he should have said, " . . . have *no right* to play in the gym."

> **Note:** The term *business* is a synonym for *commerce, industry, vocation, company,* and *employment,* among others. But it has become a blunderbuss word and used with many colloquial expressions: to get down to *business,* to mean *business,* to mind your own *business,* and, as in the question, to have no *business.*

noisome

Can you imagine a teacher at a discotheque saying, "What a noisome place"?
It depends on whether it was an olfactory or an aural reference. The comment was apt if the place was smelly. But if the teacher meant noisy, that's another matter. A noisome place is not noisy; it stinks. *Noisome* has a broader meaning: offensive, foul, harmful. ("The *noisome* weeds, that without profit suck/ The soil's fertility from the flowers" — Shakespeare, *Richard II*).

none

Why do we say, "Not one of our colleagues *was* sick" but "None of our colleagues *were* sick?
A verb must agree with its subject in number and person. In the first example the subject is *one*, a singular pronoun; hence *was*. In the second, *none* is being treated as a plural pronoun, which must take a plural verb, *were*.

> **Note:** Be not beguiled by the popular misconception that *none* should be treated only as the singular. *None* may be regarded as a singular or plural according to its reference. Some grammarians would have us believe that *none*, a contraction of "no one" or "not one," is always a singular, but that is not so. If the apparent intent of none is plural, it should be regarded as such ("*None* of the *boys have* arrived"), which means not any. When the reference is to a singular noun (meaning not one), *none* requires a singular verb ("*None* of the *food was* eaten"; "*None* of Danny's *work was* worth a farthing"). Most authorities today agree that *none* most commonly is a plural.

no one

Since *none*, a contraction of *no one*, may be a singular or a plural, does this flexible usage also apply to "no one"?
No one, as the subject of a sentence, is always singular and must take a singular verb and singular pronouns: *"No one* has control of *his* or *her* destiny," not "of *their* destiny." Be careful of the number given the pronouns.

Treat synonym *nobody* the same way. It is a correct replacement for *no one,* but *no one* is regarded as a more refined term.

noon/midnight

How are *noon* and *midnight* designated?
Noon is designated 12 *M.* The *M.* stands for Latin *meridies. Midnight* is designated 12 *P.M.* meaning *post meridiem* (past the noon hour).
> **Note:** Preferably designate exact noon or exact midnight by writing out the words. The words will eliminate confusion ("We will meet at 12 noon" or at "12 midnight"). Some people use the abbreviations *n* for noon and *m* for midnight. If *12 m* is used, the question in some minds would be whether the *m* stands for *noon* (*M.* for *meridies*) or *midnight,* an abbreviation of which is *m.* Some abbreviations are dangerous.

no place/nowhere

Is it preferable to say, "I could find it *no place* (or *nowhere*)"?
The phrase *no place* is often used informally for *nowhere.* In better English *place* should not replace *where* in such words as *anywhere, nowhere,* and *somewhere.* Say, "I could not find it *anywhere,*" not *any place.* "I saw it *nowhere,*" not *no place.* "His house is *somewhere* close at hand," not *some place.*
> **Note:** The term *nowheres* ("I couldn't find it *nowheres*") is dialectal. Do not attach an *s* to *nowhere,* or to *everywhere,* or to *somewhere.*
>
> Many careful users of the language do not substitute "place" for "where." Others discriminate between the use of those words as adverbs and nouns. They do not employ them adverbially but do not hesitate to use them as nouns.

no sooner

Is "No sooner had he recovered when he found a new job" written in good English?
To be so graded, *than* should replace *when.* "*No sooner* had he recovered *than* he found a new job." The established idiom is *no sooner . . . than.*
> **Note:** The idiomatic combination *no sooner than* is sometimes confused with that applied to *hardly, barely,* and *scarcely.* That threesome takes *when,* not *than* ("We had *hardly* entered the building *when* the fire alarm

went off"). The difference between them and *no sooner* is that *no sooner* is a comparative and comparatives take *than* ("He *no sooner* sped down the highway *than* the police stopped him").

nostrum/panacea

What is the difference between a *nostrum* and a *panacea*?
A *nostrum* (Latin, "ours") is a quack medicine known, according to its name, "to us only"–the quacks. A *panacea* (Greek, "universal remedy") is a cure-all, a remedy for all diseases, not merely a specific one, even though Grandma thought that chicken soup was a cure for all our aches and pains.

> **Note:** *Nostrum* (pronounced NAHS-truhm) is also used to mean a pet scheme for producing wonderful results. It may apply to economic or social matters; it need not be medicinal.

not

1. Would you write the following sentence this way: "He does *not* believe that there are *not sufficient reasons*"?
Although grammatically correct, the sentence would be clearer if *no* replaced the second *not:* "He does not believe that there are *no* sufficient reasons."

2. Why is it that *not* may not be used with *but*?
The sense of *but* in a *not . . . but* construction, when followed by a number, is "only," which has a negative connotation. In "Brian has *not* had *but* one vacation in two years," since there *but* means *"only,"* not should be excised to avoid a double negative: "Brian has had *but (only)* one vacation in two years."

> **Note:** Careful users of the language place *not* immediately before the word or phrase to be qualified. There is a big difference between *"Not* every driver will be given an eye examination this year" and "Every driver will *not* be given an eye examination this year."

nothing else but

"Nothing else but a touchdown will do the trick," said our coach. Did he say it right?
He could have improved the sentence by replacing *but* with *than,* "Nothing else *than* a touchdown. . . ." And while on the subject, note that *else* is superfluous in "No one *else* but Jim." Say, "No one *but* Jim."

not only . . . but also

Must *not only* always be followed by *but* or *but also*?
Normally, yes. But some writers occasionally substitute a semicolon for

but also to promote emphasis: "Not only must we write; it is important that we sell what we write." If this device is used at all, it should be used sparingly.

> **Note:** As with all correlative conjunctions, the portions of the sentence that *not only* and *but also* introduce should be in structural balance. This rule is known as parallelism. Not "She *not only* is rich *but also* talented," but "She is *not only* rich *but also* talented." You may use a noun, verb, adjective, or conjunction after *not only* provided you use the same part of speech, respectively, after *but also.*

not so/not that

1. May one say, properly, "It's not so cold in Wyoming this month"?
The use of *so* is undesirable as an intensive meaning very. Either use *very* or complete the thought. For example, "It's *not so* cold in Wyoming *as to* make one want to go South."

2. Is there anything wrong with the often heard remark "It's *not that* warm today"?
The statement is put correctly if *that* is changed to *very.*

> **Note:** Like its cousin *so*, *that* has grammatical sanction if the sentence is spelled out: "It is *not that* warm today as to make us feel uncomfortable."

not too

Is this sentence clear: "The director was not too pleased with my acting"?
Some usage experts would say yes, since *not too* clearly means not at all, not very, or not much. Others would have you say *not at all* rather than *not too.* But all would agree that "Ralph is not *very* likely to come today" is better than "Ralph is not *too* likely . . . ."

> **Note:** The expression *not too* is sometimes used as a negative statement to connote an affirmative ("Babe Ruth was *not too* bad a home run hitter"). This rhetorical device is called *litotes,* pronounced LIE-toh-tees.

no unmistakable

Was the teacher trying to speak emphatically when he said, "I'll explain it in *no unmistakable* terms"?
He was speaking erroneously. *Unmistakable* means clear. *No unmistakable* means muddied. The teacher was actually, although unwittingly, saying that his explanation is mistakable or ambiguous. The double negative suggests an affirmative assertion. He should have said, "I'll explain it in *no mistakable* terms."

nouns as verbs

May nouns serve as verbs?
In some cases yes. "We applied *pressure* (noun) on the boss." "We *pressured* (verb) the boss." Acceptable is "We *contacted* him," but most authorities object to "He *authored* a book and *hosted* a party." Before converting a noun into a verb, ask yourself whether good writers should do so in this particular instance. Be sure, in any event, that your conversion is not so unusual that it might shock your readers.

no use

How is the expression *no use* used correctly?
Correct formulas, in literary prose, are *no use in* and *of no use to*. "There's *no use in* objecting," rather than "There's *no use* objecting." However, *no use* is now an idiomatically established phrase without the preposition *in* or *of*.

> **Note:** One may say, "It is of no use to build a house in a desert," and be formally correct, or "It is no use (no *of*) to build a house in a desert," and be idiomatically correct.

nowhere near

1. My boss said, "It is nowhere near quitting time." I was tempted to correct him, but then I remembered that some usage authorities consider *nowhere near* standard English for "not nearly." Have you joined the ranks of those critics?
I have not. Although some wordsmiths may approve of that assembly of words, I cannot agree with them. The best that I can say for *nowhere near* is that it is informal. Prefer, however, on any level of speech or writing "not nearly," "not by a great deal," "far from," or "by no means." Pick the one most suitable, and avoid *nowhere near*.

> **Note:** Substituting *nothing like* for *nowhere near* is no improvement. Both those phrases are on the same level of unacceptability. Not "Simon is *nothing like* (or *nowhere near*) so athletic as he used to be," but *"not nearly."* And converting *nowhere* into a plural, so that the phrase reads *nowheres near*, is patently substandard.
>
> When used in a comparison in formal English, the combination *not nearly so* should be employed rather than the colloquial *nowhere near as:* "Practicing the violin is *not nearly so* (not *nowhere near as*) enjoyable as playing bridge."

2. I have been taught that using the word *nowheres* is wrong. However, our neighbor said, "We looked and looked but could find our dog nowheres." Since they looked in many places, were they not justified in using the plural form *nowheres*?
Nowhere has no plural form. *Nowheres* is not a word in the English

language. You were taught well. An *s* should not be appended to *no-where* no matter how many places are involved.

now pending

I read that a certain bill is now pending in the legislature. Would you comment on the phrase *now pending*?

Yes. Since *pending* means continuing, it is unnecessary to precede it with *now*. Omit *now*—save a word, avoid a redundancy, and improve your writing.

number

Is there a simple guideline to tell us when to regard the word *number* as singular and when as plural?

Yes. Treat the combination *the number* as singular (*"The number* of flowers in bloom this year *is* small") and *a number* as plural (*"A number* of guests *were* waiting for the governor's arrival").

> **Note:** The articles *a* and *the* govern the number of the verb in other instances. For example, *"A variety* of flowers *are* on display" but *"The variety* of flowers being shown today *is* small."

numbers, written

What is the general rule governing the use of written numbers?

Express them in words unless particularly long (*"We saw fifty men"*; *"It was 21,439 feet away"*). Never begin a sentence with a figure. Spell it out. Time may be expressed in words or figures.

O

objet d'art

I've seen magazines advertising *object d'art, object d'arts,* and *object darts.* Which phrase is correct?
None of them. The French phrase, now anglicized, meaning an object valued for its artistry, is *objet d'art,* literally object of art. Note *objet,* not *object.* Its plural form is *objets d'art.*

oblivious

My husband insists that *oblivious* has only one meaning: forgetful. Is he right?
Forgetful was its original meaning. Today, however, *oblivious* is taken more often to mean unaware or unconscious of ("He was so absorbed in his studies that he was *oblivious* to the noise around him"). It is safer, because of these disparate meanings, to prefer more precise terms. Use *forgetful* when that is what is meant and *unaware* or *heedless* or another appropriate term for its broader, popular sense.
   Note: *Oblivious* takes *of* when the meaning is forgetful. Otherwise, *of* or *to.*

obscure/abstruse

Do *obscure* and *abstruse* have the same meanings?
They do, in that each implies that something is hard to understand. *Obscure* means vague, like a document that needs explaining because it is not expressed clearly. *Abstruse* is applied to a statement, a document, or a study too complicated for a layman to comprehend ("A person lacking a good grasp of arithmetic will find algebra complicated and *abstruse*").

observance/observation

What is the distinction between the words *observance* and *observation*?
Observance is the act of complying with a rule, custom, command, or ceremony ("In *observance* of Memorial Day, the veterans will march"). *Observation* is paying attention or noticing. "From our *observations* we concluded that Monday nights are the least crowded."

off of

1. Doesn't *of* in *off of* make the following sentence more forceful: "Tod was seen jumping off of the roof"?

Decidedly not. The *of* is superfluous and should be omitted. Two prepositions next to each other *(off of)* seldom make for good English.

2. What do you think of this sentence: "We'll buy tomatoes off of the huckster today"?
Not much. The sentence is ungrammatical. A proper phrasing would be "We'll buy tomatoes *from* the huckster today."

> **Note:** The preposition indicating a source is *from*, not *off of*. Hence you get a loan *from* your brother, not *off of* your brother. The combination *off of* is usually redundant.
>
> Avoid the phrasing *off from*. It is as unnecessary as *off of*. Say, "My gardener got the cat *from* the roof" and "The old man stepped *from* the curb," not *off from*.

often accustomed

Is the phraseology in "The department head is often accustomed to getting her own way" acceptable?
It is not. Inherent in the word *accustom* is habitual practice, which makes the word *often* unnecessary. *Often* is also unnecessary in "Connie was *often* in the *habit* of visiting . . ." since *habit* denotes the doing of a thing over and over again, or quite often.

O.K.

If *O.K.* is to be used twice, what is its plural form?
The plural form is denoted by an apostrophe and *s: O.K.'s*. And so with *M.C.'s, F.O.B.'s,* and *V.I.P.'s*.

> **Note:** How to form the plural of letters and numbers is a stylistic decision. There are no rights and wrongs, merely eye appeal. Some writers would write the plural of O.K. with no apostrophe, and follow suit with the plural of letters (the three Rs) and numbers (the 1930s). Others think that the apostrophe makes for clarity (the three R's, the 1930's). Consider "Hooray for the YMCAs." Take your pick.

old adage

Is it wrong to speak of an *old adage*?
Certainly it is not desirable. Since an *adage* is an old saying or proverb, the sense of old is already built in. Drop *old*.

> **Note:** The expression *old adage* is a redundancy, a phrase that contains words unnecessary to the meaning. It is, in other words, a superfluous repetition. *Old cliché* is another. A cliché couldn't have gotten to be one if it weren't old.
>
> **Addendum:** Some critics say that *old adage* and *old cliché* are expressions so welded together that they are used even by educated people and English authorities.

one

1. Following the impersonal pronoun *one* with another *one* — the so-called *one-one* construction — sounds so awkward that I wonder whether it is best avoided.

Not at all. You may say, and correctly so, "One should follow *one's* own dictates." This construction is particularly desirable when *one* introduces a parallel clause: "If *one* is sick, *one* ought to see a doctor." Many writers shift to *his* — "One should follow his own dictates," or use *he* when it seems preferable. Which means that it must be a writer's decision.

> Note: *One . . . one* is technically correct and has been standard in literary prose for generations. But times have changed. The feeling among some current writers is that using *one* as the referent for *one* is, as was pointed out, somewhat awkward. And if repeated often enough, somewhat boring. Some writers evade the problem by using *you . . . you.* Bear in mind that in a proper case, *she* could be the corresponding pronoun: *"One who knows a bargain when *she* sees one is my next door neighbor."*
>
> The possessive case of *one* is *one's*. It is written with an apostrophe. *One* is a singular pronoun. Therefore, not *"One in every fifty people in the world are bound to have back problems,"* but *"One in every fifty people in the world is . . . ."*

2. Are the words *one* and *you* interchangeable, as in "One should" or "You should"?

You is used only when addressing a specific person; otherwise, *one*, meaning everyone. Not "The law says you should fasten your seat belt," but "The law says *one should* . . . ," since the law applies to every passenger.

one half

What tells you whether to say *one half is* or *are*?

One half by itself always takes a singular verb (*"One half is* all we want"). But if *one half* is followed by an *of* phrase, the number of the verb agrees with the noun in the phrase — *"One half* of the *barrel was* painted"; *"One half* of the *oranges were* shipped to Ohio."

> Note: Other combinations in English follow the same convention. For example, "A *lot* of gas *is* escaping," but "A *lot* of boxes *are* on the platform."

one of those

1. Should we say, "My dancing instructor was one of those teachers who *was* (or *were*) selected as best of the year"?

Despite the attraction of the singular *one*, the phrase *one of those who* does not take a singular verb. On the contrary, it always takes a plural noun and a plural verb. If the sentence is inverted, the need for a plural becomes clear—"Of those teachers who *were* selected as best of the year, my dancing instructor was one." The key word here is not *one* but *(those)* teachers and the verb must agree with it in number. Be alert to the fact, however, that although grammarians agree that the relative pronoun *who* is construed as plural and that its antecedent *(teachers)* and its corresponding pronoun should be plural, some authorities opt for the singular because of its widespread usage.

> Note: If the phrase *the only* precedes *one*, then a singular verb is required ("My dancing instructor was *the only one* of those teachers who *was* selected as best of the year").

2. My associate likes the phrase *one of those*. What do you think of it?
Usually it is superfluous. *"One of those* notions he has is to diversify the business" can be reduced to *"One notion* he has . . ." or even *"His notion* is to. . . ."* Verbiage lessens the effectiveness of an expressed thought.

one time

The brochures said, "He was a one time winner in the chess tournament." What does that sentence mean?
It means he was a victor only once. If what was meant was a former winner, the adjective that says that is *one-time* or *onetime*, not two-word *one time*.

only

1. How does the placement of *only* affect the sense of a sentence, and where should it be placed?
Only should be placed as close as possible to the word or phrase modified, preferably just before it. The placement of *only* may affect the meaning intended, for as *only* moves about, so the sense being conveyed changes. Consider the following: *"Only* Maxwell saw the accident," which means that no one else saw it. "Maxwell *only* saw the accident" means that he was not otherwise involved. "Maxwell saw *only* the accident" means he saw nothing else. In general speech, *only* is frequently placed before the verb, as in "I *only* heard about his bankruptcy an hour ago." No one is misled by that misplacement, but in writing, where opportunity exists to review, *only* should be more carefully placed ("I heard about his bankruptcy *only* an hour ago").

> Note: When used as a conjunction, *only* may mean *but* ("I would have gone sooner, *only* my car couldn't start"), but it should not be used as a preposition replacing *but* or *except* where it clearly may not serve. Change "No one could play it *only* John" to "*but* John" or "*except* John." And note that since *only* has a negative quality, it should not be combined with another negative. In "The gardeners will not work only after they're paid," *not* should be omitted.

2. Must *only* always precede the word or phrase it modifies, or may it sometimes rightly precede the verb?

Idiomatically *only* is placed before the verb in some usages and this practice has become legitimated. In those cases *only* sounds more natural in that position than it would in any other. For example, "We can *only* say, 'Don't do it'," not "We can say *only*, 'Don't do it'."

on the other hand

May one correctly say *on the other hand* if *on the one hand* had not been said?

Yes. *On the other hand* need not be preceded by *on the one hand*. But if you do say *on the one hand,* you are then obligated to follow with *on the other hand.*

> Note: Some authorities say that *on the other hand* reconciles the coming thought with the previous one or a fact to be established: "It is not raining now; on the other hand, rain is predicted for this afternoon." *On the contrary* emphasizes the differences between what is and what is not: "It is not raining now; on the contrary, it is quite sunny."

onto/on to

Please explain the difference in usage between *onto* and *on to*.

An employee walks *onto* an elevator, goes to the executive floor and then marches *on to* the boss's office. *Onto,* a preposition, implies change of position, a movement toward. It is written as one word. *On to* consists of an adverb and a preposition, in which the adverb becomes a part of a phrasal verb, not a part of a prepositional phrase. The words are written separately. *On,* in this case, means *onward* or *along.*

> Note: Since both *on to* and *onto* imply motion to a position or against an object, they are frequently interchangeable. But *onto* more clearly expresses movement toward something. "The crew jumped *onto* the upper deck." "Andy stumbled *onto* a solution." "The band marched *onto* the field." "Atlas sent the radios *on to* their southern depot." "Let's hold *on to* whatever seems best." "Greg went *on to* see his cousin."

on/upon

Which should it be : "I don't know *on* (or *upon*) what percent to base his commission"?

It may be either. It is simply a matter of preference. However, the preposition *on* is favored except where the meaning is upward motion (jumped *upon* a trampoline) or on top of (placed one *upon* another.)

> Note: Idiom makes some distinctions in the usage of *on* and *upon* ("We will *on* no account deal with him"), but *upon my honor* and *upon my word.* We say that a person was *put upon* but *imposed on.*

ophthalmologist

What difference is there between an *ophthalmologist*, an *optometrist*, and an *optician*?
An *ophthalmologist* is a physician who specializes in treating eye defects and diseases. An *optometrist* is a doctor who measures the range of vision and prescribes glasses. An *optician* makes lenses and sells eyeglasses.

> Note: *Ophthalmologist* is not an easy word to spell. Note the *hth*. At one time a doctor who treated diseases of the eye was called an *oculist*. This is no longer so, although the terms *oculist* and *ophthalmologist* remain synonymous. The profession prefers and uses the latter term. Pronounce *ophthalmologist* with the first syllable sounding like off, not op.

opposite

1. Are the phrases *opposite of* and *opposite to* distinguishable?
Very much so. Used as a noun, *opposite* takes *of* ("The *opposite of* tall is short"). Adjective *opposite* takes either *to* or *from* ("He took an *opposite* stand *to* [or *from*] mine").

> Note: Do not confuse the words *opposite* and *converse*. *Opposite* applies to things so far apart in position, nature, meaning, or other characteristics that they can never be made to agree. *Converse* means reversed in order, turned about. In "George loves Susan," the opposite is "George hates Susan." The converse is "Susan loves George."

2. Do any English words have two opposite meanings?
Yes. *Cleave* for one. It means to sever or split and, quite oppositely, to adhere firmly. *Ravel* is another. It means to become entangled and also to be disentangled. *Sanction,* if granted by an authority, is permission to perform an act. But not if a sanction is imposed on the activity in question.

oral/verbal

Recently I have been told that the words *oral* and *verbal* have the same meaning and may be interchanged. This confuses me. Would you please clear up this matter?
The lexical meaning of *oral* is "spoken," something said by way of mouth. The lexical meaning of *verbal* is "in words." This means that an oral agreement is also a verbal agreement, as is a written agreement. This overlapping in meaning could be a rich source of confusion. To be precise, therefore, and to avoid any chance of ambiguity, one should speak of an oral agreement (if spoken) and a written agreement (if in writing). Which means that *verbal,* properly should be contrasted with forms of communication that do not involve spoken or written words — smoke signals, semaphores, and so on. In general conversation, never-

theless, *verbal* is equated with *oral*. And almost everyone would assume that a verbal agreement was an oral agreement, something unwritten.

ordinance/ordnance

Do the words *ordinance* and *ordnance* have a related meaning?
None whatsoever. An *ordinance* is a regulation set by some authority, usually a city. *Ordnance* is military equipment—artillery, guns, cannons, and so forth.

Note: Be careful of this pair. They are surprisingly often confused.

orient/orientate

We talked about *orient* and *orientate*. Is one form preferred to the other?
Although both verbs mean to place or locate so as to face the East or, figuratively, to adjust to new conditions or surroundings, *orient* is the preferred form because it has the advantage of economy. Furthermore, *orientate* sounds pompous.

Note: The simpler form of spelling, where there is a choice, is usually preferable (*orient* rather than *orientate, preventive* rather than *preventative*). But this is not so with the shorter *interpretive;* the longer *interpretative* is more prevalent.

An *orientation* program may *orient* or *orientate* the participants.

origin of English

Where did the English language come from?
English is a conglomeration of many languages, having borrowed words from many sources. Philologists, however, say that half of English is Teutonic; the other half, roughly, is Romance (Spanish, Italian, primarily French, and much Latin).

Note: The three main historical periods are called Old English (Anglo-Saxon), from 800 to 1100; Middle English, from 1100 to 1500 (French was the official language in England for several hundred years after the Battle of Hastings in 1066); Modern English, from 1500 to the present.

or/nor

Which is preferable: "He noticed that not a secretary *or* (or *nor*) a clerk was absent"?
Use *or*. Since the negative *not* applies equally to *secretary* and to *clerk, or* should connect them. If the sentence structure changes, use *nor* ("He noticed that not a secretary was absent, *nor* did he notice a missing clerk").

Note: Some authorities approve of *nor* as well as *or* after a *not* negative where there is no structural change in the sentence, as in the example. But preferably use *or*.

Afterthought. The number of the verb following *or* is governed by the same convention as that governing *either . . . or* or *neither . . . nor;* that is, if both preceding elements are singular or plural, the verb is singular or plural, respectively. If the elements are different in number, the verb agrees with the nearer element: "An apple or grapes *were* all I wanted"; "Grapes or an apple *was* all I wanted." Unlike the correlative conjunctions, an *or* construction is not limited to two ("I'll take this *or* that *or* those over there").

or other

Is *or other* objectionable in "Somehow or other we will get the job done"?
It is not. The construction is idiomatic and is used by many good writers. The *or other* is unnecessary, but it is designed to, and does, emphasize *somehow*.

orphan

Someone said that Tom is an orphan because his mother died, even though his father is still alive. True?
Some dictionaries say an orphan is a child whose parents are dead *or* a child whose father or mother is dead. Others do not add that latter distinction. Be careful.
> **Note:** Most people would take it that an orphan has no living parents. Dictionaries aside, therefore, be sure your audience or readers understand what you mean when referring to an orphan. Webster came out with a compromise thought to indicate one living parent: *half-orphan*.

other

1. May we say, properly, "There is no other captain for our team except Tom"?
Not properly. *Other* takes *than*, not *except* ("There is no other captain for our team *than* Tom").
> **Note:** The phrase *other than* is used to express difference. It may be used adjectivally ("doctors *other than* pediatricians) or adverbially ("behaved *other than* properly"). But it is not an acceptable replacement for *apart from* or *aside from*. Rather than "He spoke little *other than* to suggest an early adjournment," make it *"apart from* suggesting."

2. The sentence read: "Of the eleven judges voting, three voted for Miss Illinois but the *other* eight voted for Miss Idaho." Is the mathematics right?
It is not. By using the word *other* the thought implied is that there was

a previous eight. Correct by rewording: ". . . but the eight *others* voted for Miss Idaho."

other/otherwise

I am confused about the use of *other* and *otherwise*. Please explain.
Treat *other* as an adjective meaning "different" ("The facts were *other* than we knew") and *otherwise* as an adverb meaning "in a different manner" ("The coach could not view it *otherwise than* a debacle" — not *other than*).

> Note: The continued usage of *otherwise* adjectivally is eroding its function as an adverb. Traditionally we said, for example, "My father's income, earned or *other,* was enough to see him through." But with the support of some dictionaries, many authorities would now replace *other* with *otherwise.* They contend that *otherwise* as an adjective has acquired idiomatic status.

ought

My neighbor said, "We ought cut down those branches." Please comment.
The expression *ought cut down* is dialectal. The auxiliary that should have been used is *should,* not *ought:* "We *should* cut down" or, as reworded, using an infinitive, "We *ought to* cut down."

> Note: The combination *had ought* and *hadn't ought* are unacceptable expressions. "It *had ought* to have been finished by now" is a typical example in which *had* should be excised: "It *ought* (no *had*) to have been finished." The caution is never to precede *ought* with "had" or "hadn't."
> Be sure to use *to* after *ought* ("We *ought to* do that") unless supplied through another verb form. However, in a negative statement *to* is permissible but preferably omitted: "We *ought not* (not *to*) do that."
> Addendum: The correct formula is *can and ought,* not *ought and can.*

ounce/viz

Why is it that *ounce,* which has no *z* in it, is abbreviated *oz.*?
The origin of the symbol *oz.* is unknown. Perhaps it is an abbreviation of *ouza,* Italian for *ounce,* or simply a printer's terminal mark. Another such instance is *viz,* an abbreviation of Latin *videlicet,* "it is permitted to see" or "namely."

out loud/aloud

Is it true that *out loud* in "We read it out loud so all could hear" is not the proper way to say it?
Out loud, a common colloquial expression meaning loud enough to be

heard, is best confined to everyday speech. In formal discourse use *aloud* or *loudly*, whichever would be appropriate to the context.

outside of

Should this sentence be criticized: "Outside of the six boys on our street, no one from our neighborhood went to college"?
Outside of, meaning with the exception of, is informal. Preferably say, "*Except for* the six boys on our street, no one went to college." In other uses, remember that the expression *outside of* is redundant. For example, "We live five miles *outside* Hicksville" is the way to say it, not "outside of Hicksville."

> Note: A slang use of *outside of* is to mean besides, as in *"Outside of the Browne twins, we have three good tennis players."* That sentence should read: *"Besides the Browne twins . . . ."* *Outside* is a preposition, which makes the additional preposition *of* superfluous to indicate physical limits or scope. The common remark, *"Outside of that,* I'll . . ." should be avoided in favor of *besides that* or *other than that.*
>
> Seldom is the placement of two prepositions next to each other justified. But note that *outside* is used as four parts of speech — adjective, adverb, noun, and preposition. When functioning as a noun, *outside of* is a proper combination: "He painted the *outside of* the shed." ·
>
> The same guidelines apply to *inside of*.

over

1. Would you object to *over* in this sentence: "Over half the men here don't play golf"?
I would not. *More than,* in the sense of collective quantity, is technically preferable, and pedants would insist on it, but *over,* meaning more than, is the popular term and has wide authoritative approval ("It costs *over* ten dollars"; "My father is *over* sixty years of age").

> Note: Be careful not to construe *over* as meaning *under.* This sounds like obvious advice, yet the frequent interchange of the meaning of *over* for *under* by advertisers has given credibility to that switch and, supposedly, understanding to the hearers and readers. The common advertising pitch is that this XYZ product is a better deal by hundreds of dollars *over* the nearest competitor. Using *over* when the sense is a decrease is out of place. And if an advertisement offers a 10 percent reduction on all merchandise, it should not conclude by saying that the customer will be saving 10 percent *over* the regular price.

2. Is the expression *over with* accepted in better English?
It is not. In the sense of completed, it sounds of slang. Prefer "Let's finish the job today" rather than "Let's get the job *over with.*"

overflown

The sentence read: "The Mississippi has overflown its banks again."
Is the word *overflown* being misused?
Yes. The participle of *overflow* is *overflowed:* "The Mississippi *overflowed* its banks again." *Overflown* is said of an airplane that failed to make the runway.

overly long

Is the sentence "His speech was overly long" too long?
It would be shorter and neater if it read "was *overlong*." It is best not to use *overly* when *over* will do, which is nearly all the time. *Overly* means to an excessive degree, a sense shared by *over*.

> **Note:** Grammatically there is no objection to *overly;* the objection is stylistic. However, adjectives and adverbs formed with *over-* are just as forceful as those combinations using *overly*—and more economical besides. Consider *overattentive* and *overly attentive; overcareful* and *overly careful*. But there are times when your ear must govern. It might sound more natural, and be easier to say, "She seemed *overly* excited" rather than *overexcited*. Or, "Joe was *overly* friendly today" rather than *overfriendly*.
>
> *Overly* is a separate word. It should not be hyphenated. Compounds with *over-* are spelled as one word: *overabundant, overconfident, overrated*.

owing to

Is the expression *owing to the fact that* objectionable?
Yes, because it is wordy for *because* or *since*. In "*Owing to the fact that* it's raining, we'll stay home," either of the suggested subordinate conjunctions is preferable.

> **Note:** *Owing to the fact that* can be given short shrift because it is obviously redundant for *because* or *since*. But *owing to* is another matter. Meaning because of or attributable to, *owing to* is an accepted prepositional phrase. It is often compared with *due to* which, in the opinion of some authorities, has not attained prepositional status. We may therefore say, "*Owing to* the weather, the game was postponed." But we may not say, unless we wish to be controversial, "*Due to* the weather, the game was postponed."

own

Does the pronoun *own* govern a singular or a plural verb?
It may govern either a singular ("We know that each *has his own* computer") or a plural ("We distributed the magazines so that all would *have their own*").

oxymoron

What is an oxymoron?

It is not a stupid ox. It is a rhetorical term, the name for two apparently contradictory elements in a single structure (a *sophomore,* "a wise fool"). The word comes from Greek *oxys,* "sharp," and *moros,* "foolish." Examples of oxymorons are a cheerful pessimist, an honorable thief, harmonious discord, make haste slowly, and cruel kindness.

P

pair

My aunt often says something like this: "I saw a pair of red-haired twins today." May the duplication of her words be excused as a colloquialism?

Excuse as you wish. But redundancies make no sense. All that she need do is drop *a pair of*: "I saw red-haired twins today."

> **Note:** Like the word *couple*, when *pair* refers to people, it takes a plural verb ("The *pair* of hoodlums we saw yesterday *were* arrested today"). A question sometimes asked is whether to speak of four *pairs* of gloves or four *pair* of gloves. The plural form is required in formal language, but informally either *pair* or *pairs* may be used after a numeral. With *few*, *several*, and *many*, plural forms are always required: *few* pairs, *several* pairs, *many* pairs.

panache

Although I don't recall ever using the word *panache*, I see it in print once in a while. How is it pronounced?

Panache, literally "a bunch of feathers," but used to mean verve or dash, is pronounced pah-NAHSH.

> **Note:** A panache originally was an ornamental plume, especially one worn on a helmet. Cyrano de Bergerac, in Edmond Rostand's play said—as he lay dying—that the only thing he could call his own—"*Et c'est . . . mon panache*" ("And that is . . . my panache")—a white plume, his symbol of uncompromising integrity and incorruptible honor.

parentheses

1. What kind of material is usually set out in parentheses?

Incidental or explanatory material to be segregated from the main sentence. Parentheses should be used sparingly—for they tend to distract the reader—and not used at all where commas can serve as well. Be sure to remember that parentheses come in pairs; do not forget the closing one.

2. Does a period belong within or outside a closing parenthesis?

Depends. A period goes inside the closing parenthesis when the parenthetical statement stands independently. Note that the statement begins with a capital letter. "I will go." (He did not say when.) If the parenthetical statement is within a sentence, it takes neither a final period nor an initial capital. "I will go" (a remark he often uttered).

3. What style do you recommend when writing both an amount written in words and a figure in parentheses?
Either "Four thousand three hundred dollars ($4,300)" or "Four thousand three hundred (4,300) dollars." A figure before the word *dollars* takes no dollar sign.

4. Is the parenthetical insertion acceptable: "Adam told Scott that he (Adam) would be happy if elected"?
Pronoun explanations set in parentheses are poor style. Restructure: "I would be happy if elected," Adam told Scott.

parenthetical phrases

1. What causes one to write a sentence such as "In 1840 Kennedy said the American people were mostly rural"?
A failure to recognize a parenthetical phrase. In 1840 Kennedy wasn't talking. Correct: "In 1840," Kennedy said, "the American people . . ." or "Kennedy said that in 1840 the American people. . . ."

2. My politician opined, "Sydney is the man whom I think should be elected." What do you think of my politician?
He may know his politics, but his grammar could stand a little beefing up. He should have said, "Sydney is the man *who* I think should be elected." The error he made was a failure to realize that *I think* is a parenthetical phrase and that the relative pronoun should have been *who*, not *whom*. *Who* is the subject of the following clause — *who should be elected*.

part

Why do we say, "A part of the crate *was* damaged," but "A part of the crates *were* damaged"?
The rule is that the verb following the word *part*, the simple subject, is singular or plural depending on the number of the noun in the *of* phrase that modifies it. Hence *crate was, crates were*.

> Note: Many similar constructions exist in English; that is, the grammatical subject does not govern the number of the verb, which instead is governed by the following noun in the *of* phrase. For example, "A *lot* of oranges *are* on the platform," and "A *lot* of food *is* on the table." "One quarter of the month *has* passed," and "One quarter of the members *were* absent." "Half of the book *is* soiled," and "Half of the pages *are* torn."

partake

My uncle always invites us "to *partake* of a meal." Is there anything wrong with that phraseology?

Not grammatically. Meaning to have a share in, *partake* is a rather formal word. It sounds stuffy in "We will *partake of* dinner shortly." The natural way of saying it is "We will *eat* (or *have*) dinner shortly." In other contexts more suitable words than *partake* are available. For example, in "In the light of government grants, many students will be enabled to *partake* in advanced studies," either *participate* or *take part* would do. Always prefer the simpler word.

Note: Authorities, disapproving of the use of *partake*, criticize it as stilted.

partial

What does this sentence mean: "It was a partial report"? We're all stumped.

Out of context, it is not possible to say. The two meanings of *partial* — consisting of part only and biased in favor of one side — are applicable to your sentence. Clearly, the meanings are unrelated and distinctive. The question to be resolved is whether the report was simply a part of a larger one yet to be written or one showing favoritism. If the sentence had read "It was an *incomplete* report" or "It was *partly* done," there would be no ambiguity. And, of course, if the sentence had read, "It was a biased report," it too would be unambiguous.

Note: Idiom in some cases determines whether to use *partial* or *partly*. For example, we say, "He was *partially* blind," but "She was *partly* to blame." *Partly* is in wider use, even though it may be interchanged with *partially* in many locutions ("The painter was only *partly* (or *partially*) finished"; "We noticed that the sorting of the cards was *partly* (or *partially*) completed").

A noun form of *partial* is *partiality*, an unambiguous word to express prejudice and a good replacement for adjective *partial*. The adverb form of *partial* is *partially*, which means to a degree or not completely. Its opposite number is *fully* — "The dancer was *partially* (not *fully*) clothed."

particularly/especially

Are the words *particularly* and *especially* always preceded by a comma?

When used internally to introduce parenthetic information, yes. "He likes seafood, *particularly* (or *especially*) lobsters." Treat *despite, perhaps, preferably, probably,* and *regardless of* in the same way.

party

Are the words *party* and *person* synonymous?

The words are loosely equated in general conversation, but this usage is inappropriate and not recommended. Of course, *party* is accepted legal terminology for *person* and is also a synonymous term within the domain of telephone operators. Otherwise, *party* should not replace *person*.

passed/past

1. Is there a simple rule that will stop me from misusing *passed* for *past*?
This is not a formula, but try using *passed* as a verb only, the past tense and past participle of the verb *pass* ("Lane *passed* his driver's test with flying colors") and *past* in all other nonverbal functions: "I knew him in the *past*" (noun); "That Porsche drove *past* me" (preposition); "In *past* years things were done differently" (adjective); "The boys ran *past*" (adverb).

> **Note:** Observe the difference between "With all his examinations *passed*, Walter left for home" and "With all his examinations *past*, Walter left for home." The latter sentence does not say whether Walter made passing grades, merely that all the examinations had been taken. You may say, "The time to submit the papers was *past*" or "The time to submit the papers had *passed*." Same idea, different parts of speech.

2. Is the sentence "Dennison has been a senator for the past twelve years" written well?
It could be improved by omitting "the past" ("Dennison has been a senator for twelve years"), since those words add nothing to the sense.

3. Is it correct to speak of a person's *past experiences*?
The combination *past experiences* is as redundant as *present incumbent*, *past records*, or *future plans*. Drop *past*.

> **Note:** Be careful before appending the adjective *past* to a noun to be sure that the sense of *past* is not inherent in it. For example, in "We will review the *past history* of this organization," *past* creates a redundancy. And since one's accomplishments were completed in the past, do not speak of *past accomplishments*.

peeve

Is the word *peeve* in good literary usage?
Peeve, now widely accepted, is a back formation from *peevish*. On that questionable ground, it is objected to by purists. Reputable speakers and writers do not hesitate to use *peeve* in informal discourse, but its use in formal writing is not recommended.

people/persons

Would you please differentiate the use of *people* from *persons*?
People are a group of persons—that is, many persons collectively are called *people*, as "the American people" or "We the people." Small

numbers or an exact number of individuals are called persons, not people. For example, we say there were six persons in the room, not people. Persons become people if the group becomes large ("There were five hundred *people* in the rotunda") or if the number is undetermined ("Crowds of *people* were pushing and shoving"), but people becomes persons if the number, other than a round figure of one hundred or more, is precise ("There were 206 persons in the garden").

Note: It has been said that persons, not people, must be used of small numbers or the result might be ludicrous. For example, if you were to say that four people were in the room and three people left, how many people would still be in the room? One people? But if of four persons three left, clearly one person would still be there.

per

1. The Latin word *per* has been criticized as commercialese, with the recommendation that it not be used. Do you agree?
I have no objection to using *per* when it is part of a Latin phrase, as *per diem* or *percent*. What I find objectionable is using *per* in ordinary writing where *a* or *an* would do. For example, *per hour* and *per year* are preferably written *an hour* and *a year* or *yearly* because in those latter phrases *per* sounds excessively technical.

Note: In widely established commercial discourse, *per*, meaning *by the* (*per* yard, *per* barrel), serves a useful purpose. What sounds bureaucratic in any use is the expression *as per* ("*As per* your letter, we will . . ."). Preferably write, "*In accordance with* your letter. . . ." One more. Rather than say, "We will travel *per* Amtrak," say, "We will travel *by* Amtrak." Avoid using *per* to mean *by*.

Percent, an abbreviation of Latin *per centum*, means rate per hundred. Since the term is in universal use and has been anglicized, it takes no period.

2. The phrase *per se* is so often misused that a clear example of correct usage would be helpful.
Per se in Latin means "through itself." In English it means intrinsically, its sense being of or by itself. "My watch is worth little *per se*, but much to me, for it belonged to my father."

personal

1. Is there any advantage to adding the word *personal*, as in the expression "in my personal opinion"?
There is none. In fact, the addition of *personal* militates against common sense. A person's opinion must be, ipso facto, personal.

Note: Things that are personal are clearly so and therefore the word *personal* needs no qualifying escort. A woman's charm is part of her person. It should not be said to be her "personal charm." A woman who says she's going to do something or to go somewhere is guilty of verbosity if she adds *personal* or *personally* to her activity. The phrase *personal friend* may be excused if a contrast is being made with a *business friend*. But such occasions are rare.

Addendum: The word *personally* is excess baggage to a personal pronoun. Avoid it. Do not say, "I *personally* think."

2. "He handled it in an exceedingly personalized manner." Good or bad?
Preferably say, "His handling of it was exceedingly personal." *Personalized* is a pompous-sounding word that grates on some people's ears.

perspicacious/perspicuous

The words *perspicacious* and *perspicuous* are sometimes confused. Why?
Possibly because they look and sound so much alike. *Perspicacious* means having keen mental perception, shrewdness, insight ("It was *perspicacious* of him to buy when he did"). *Perspicuous* means clear to the understanding, lucid ("His speech was *perspicuous*"). Their noun forms are *perspicacity* and *perspicuity*.
    Note: These words, *perspicacious* and *perspicuous*, are not everyday words. Therefore, like dressing for Sunday, they should be reserved for special, appropriate occasions. They have been described as being among the language's most confusable twosomes.

peruse

Is *peruse* a good word to keep in one's everyday vocabulary?
It is a good word, but it should be used only when occasion demands— that is, when reading is done with critical care. It should not replace the ordinary word *read* when *read* is called for, which is most of the time.
    Note: A synonym is a word that means the same or nearly the same as another word. *Peruse* and *read* are synonyms according to that definition. Yet the words are seldom interchangeable in a real sense. A man studying his income tax return may be said to be reading or perusing it (but more precisely *perusing*); but if he is looking at the comics, he could not be said to be *perusing*. You read what you peruse, but not necessarily peruse what you read.

philippic

Has the term *philippic* carried over into today's world?
The term is still with us, although its synonym *tirade* is commoner. If you use it, be sure to note its spelling—*ili* in the middle, followed by two *p*'s.

Note: The great Greek orator Demosthenes made speeches denouncing King Philip of Macedon to arouse the Greeks to defend themselves against the impending invasion. These declamations were called *philippics*, after the Macedonian king.

place words

It seems that almost everyone I know uses *place* for *where* in such words as *anyplace* and *everyplace*. Are "place" words in this usage accepted by good writers?

Some reputable writers and some authorities accord *anyplace* and *everyplace* the same level of acceptance as *anywhere* and *everywhere*. But others regard *anyplace* and *everyplace*, in this sense, as colloquialisms and do not sanction their use, certainly not in formal writing. Still others label *anyplace* and *everyplace* dialectal. A careful writer would be wise to use *anywhere* and *everywhere* and thus avoid criticism from any source — everywhere.

Note: The recommendation is to use the word *place* as the subject or the object of a verb or preposition, as in "*Any place* in the center of town will be fine for the reception"; "We can't find *any place* to park"; "I will look *in* every place possible." *Noplace* and *someplace* fall into the same category of criticism. It is best to use *nowhere* and *somewhere*.

Be particularly careful not to pluralize these adverbs. There are no such words as *anywheres*, *somewheres*, and so on. Do not say, "We couldn't find it *anywheres*," but *anywhere*.

plans on

Was my aunt's statement a good one: "The entire family plans on going to the shore"?

The idea was good, but the grammar could be improved. The correct expression is *plan to go* (a verb plus an infinitive), not *plan on going* ("The entire family *plans to* . . ."). Likewise, "wait for," not "wait on." *On* often insinuates itself where it does not belong.

Note: One thought about the word *plans*. It points to the future. Therefore words indicating futurity should not accompany it. Not, for example, *future* plans or *advance* plans. And as for *plan ahead*, it is just as redundant as *past records*.

plead

1. What is the proper past-tense form of the word *plead*?

It is *pleaded*. Today *pled* is heard frequently, but authorities regard it as a colloquial expression. As the usage of *pled* becomes more widespread, it will probably be on its way to greater acceptance.

Note: The form *pled* is sometimes seen spelled *plead*, the same spelling as the present tense *plead*, which may be a source of confusion. Avoid it.

2. May a defendant in a criminal case *plead innocent?*
Although it is occasionally reported in newspapers that a defendant pleaded innocent to all charges, there is no such plea in criminal law as a plea of innocent.

plenty

1. Commonly we hear remarks like "He was plenty wrong," "It is plenty cold today," and "Mr. McGovern has plenty of money." From a usage standpoint, would you say those statements are expressed acceptably?
I would not. *Plenty* is properly a noun, not an adjective or adverb, as would appear in the examples. The sentences should be recast without *plenty*: "He was *entirely* wrong"; "Mr. McGovern is *very* (or *extremely*) rich." "It is *plenty* cold" borders on idiomatic acceptance simply because of its frequent use. However, it has not as yet weathered the storm. Generally *plenty of* is what makes for correct English: "We have *plenty of* snow today"; "Mr. McGovern has *plenty of* money." If you follow *plenty* with *of*, you will not go wrong.

> Note: Any noun in English may serve as an adjective. And so with *plenty*. The thing to bear in mind in this regard is that *plenty* may function adjectivally in the predicate but not attributively before a noun. For example, "She has *plenty* reasons not to go" needs amending: *plenty of reasons*. But you may say, "Six books will be *plenty*." *Plenty* used adverbially is deprecated by all authorities: *plenty tired, plenty large*.

2. Should one say, "Plenty of apples *is* (or *are*) on the shelf"?
Plural *are* is required, since the number of the verb should be the same as that of the noun in the *of* phrase, which modifies *plenty*. And so "Plenty of fresh *air is* coming our way." "Plenty of *apples are* on the shelf."

plus

Is it correct to say, "Armand plus his family are strutting down the driveway"?
Not in formal language. *Plus* is a preposition meaning with the addition of. Therefore the sentence should read, correctly, "Armand *plus* his family *is* strutting . . . ," not *are*.

> Note: *Plus* is often mistakenly treated as a conjunction, the equivalent of *and*. However, although "The boy *and* the girl *are* here" is correctly put, "The boy *plus* the girl *are* here" is not. And so we say, "Two plus two *is* four," treating two as a unit. The rule that most authorities support is that a word or a phrase introduced by *plus* does not affect the number of the verb. You may rightly say, "The Athletic Committee *plus* the coaches *is* heading toward the field" or use *and* instead of *plus*: "The Athletic Committee *and* the coaches *are* heading toward the field." But

not "The Athletic Committee *plus* the coaches *are* heading for the field."
Avoid such expressions as "plus the fact that." Use *besides* instead.

portend

What do you think of this statement made by an economist: "Leading indicators portend an upswing in our national economy"?

A better choice of words would be *predict* or *presage*. *Portend* connotes an unfavorable prognostication. An upswing in the economy is something that would make us all happy.

possessives

1. How do you explain the sentence: "Bob is a friend of my brother's"?

The double genitive (*of* and *'s*) signifies one of several like possessions. The elliptical phrasing stands for "Bob is one of my brother's friends." This means that among his friends, Bob is one.

2. Would you find fault with this remark: "The analysis was agreed upon between his and my chemist"?

Yes. Grammatically, plural *chemists* is called for because possessive forms join, not separate, the ideas expressed—"between his and my chemists." If you wish to avoid the awkward plural, say ". . . between his chemist and mine."

3. Is the sentence "These are available at your jeweler" grammatically correct?

A change is needed, *at your jeweler's*, since what was meant, of course, is "at your jeweler's shop."

Note: The British preference is *jeweller's*, with a double *l*.

4. How do you form a plural possessive?

Convert the noun into a plural and then simply add an apostrophe if the ending is *s*: *ladies', girls'*, but add *'s* to *children, men*, and so on, since these forms do not end in *s*: *children's, men's*. And so with *women's* clothes, not *womens'* clothes.

5. How does one form the possessive of words ending in *ss*?

Add an apostrophe alone: the witness' testimony, the princess' gown, Strauss' waltzes, the hostess' hairstyle. But note that the possessive case is formed when a word ends in a single *s* by adding an apostrophe and an *s*: *'s* (Charles's son).

6. Should "The Seamens and Merchants Bank" have apostrophes (Seamens'/Merchants')?

Words that have become an established part of the noun need no apostrophes. They are more descriptive than possessive (State Teachers College; United States laws; Ohio roads; American Bankers Association).

7. The report read: "We saw the Smith's in their new car." Was the report written correctly?
It was not. A proper noun is made plural by adding *s* or *es*, as the case may be: the *Smiths*; the *Greens*; the *Joneses*; the two *Germanies*. An apostrophe is used only when the name is being made possessive.

8. How does an *apostrophe* indicate multiple ownership?
If a sentence read, "Herbert, Robert, and Sammy's VCR is not working," the *apostrophe* and *s* on the final member would indicate joint ownership, that the VCR was the property of the three boys. If there were three VCRs, each individually owned, the sentence would read, "Herbert's, Robert's, and Sammy's VCRs are not working," each owner getting his own apostrophe.
> Note: An *apostrophe* is used primarily to indicate the possessive case of nouns (the *man*'s hat), letters (two *s*'s), figures (four *4*'s), and the omission of letters (*won't*, *didn't*). Do not use it with personal pronouns. Not "it is their's," but *theirs*.

9. Do you prefer the possessive case to an *of* phrase where inanimate objects are involved?
The general rule is not to attribute possession to an inanimate object. Certainly, where such attribution would cause awkwardness, it should be avoided. Prefer the "legs of the chair" rather than the chair's legs, "the roof of the house" rather than the house's roof. But today editors are more lenient toward bestowing upon inanimate things the attribute of possession. No longer is there objection to "the team's management." It need not be "the management of the team." In fact, the reference more likely would be "the team management." And that would set well with most people.

10. If the Burns family lives in a house, how should their name appear on an outdoor sign?
In plural form: "The Burnses live here." But note the possessive, as in "This is the Burnses' house." Here you first write the plural and then add an apostrophe.

post hoc, ergo propter hoc

Please explain the meaning of *post hoc, ergo propter hoc*.
Translated from the Latin, the phrase means "after this, therefore because of this." It is a concept that believes if there are two successive happenings, the second must have resulted from the first. Of course, the reasoning is fallacious.
> Note: Fowler gives as an example of this fallacy: "On Sunday we prayed for rain; on Monday it rained; therefore prayers caused the rain."

posthumous

How should the word *posthumous* be pronounced?
Pronounce it PAHS-choo-muhs, stressing the first syllable. Be sure it does not sound like *post* in "postnasal."

> **Note:** *Posthumous* means happening after death. Two Latin words gave birth to a misconception of the origin of this word — *post*, "after," and *humus*, "earth." Since most corpses are buried in the earth, there seemed to be some logic to that derivation. But the fact is that the Latin word originally was *postumus*, "last *born*." The "h" was inserted simply to make the second element conform with *humus*.
>
> A posthumous child is one born after the death of the father.

practical/practicable

To be quite honest, I don't know the difference between *practical* and *practicable*. How should these words be differentiated?
These are good words to take stock of because they are sometimes confused. *Practicable* means feasible, able to be done, capable of putting into practice. *Practical* means useful or sensible, as opposed to theoretical. That which is practical is suitable to prevailing circumstances, such as "a practical suggestion," one that considers existing conditions.

> **Note:** Remember that an idea can be both practical and practicable. On the other hand, an idea can be practicable and not practical — that is, it could be done but would be too costly or would take too long to complete or would not be useful. In other words, just because something can be built or done does not prove its desirability. Bear in mind also that *practicable* is used only of objects, plans, and so forth, never of persons; *practical* applies to things and to persons.
>
> The negative form of *practicable* is *impracticable*; of *practical*, *impractical*, although all authorities do not agree. Some say the proper form is *unpractical*. However, if an idea or plan cannot be carried out, it is *impracticable*, not *impractical*.

practically/virtually

Should the words *practically* and *virtually* be distinguished each from the other?
As a practical matter, the words are synonymous, even though technically there are distinguishable differences. *Practically* means in a practical manner but has come to mean as good as or almost. *Virtually* too means very nearly, as good as, or in effect. If you have practically no sugar left, you're as good as or nearly out of sugar — or virtually out of sugar. Whether to choose *practically* or *virtually* in this situation is practically splitting hairs because their meanings are virtually the same.

> **Note:** Some authorities disagree with those who equate *practically* and

virtually. The meaning of *virtually*, they contend, is in essence or in effect, not almost. A Vice President serving while the President is physically incompetent to function is virtually—in effect—the presiding officer. Some critics would use *practically* when it serves only as a contrast to *hypothetically*. A sensible objection to *practically* as a replacement for *virtually* is in a sentence such as "The matter has been *practically* completed," in which *practically* might be construed as meaning in a practical manner.

precipitous/precipitate

My friend regrets his precipitous move. Would you use *precipitous* that way?

My guess is no. The word *precipitous* means steep, perpendicular, sheer. It implies a sharp descent or fall. The word probably required in the example was *precipitate*, which means hasty, rash, impulsive. *Precipitate* and *precipitous* have disparate meanings and should be treated accordingly, even though some dictionaries regard *precipitous* as meaning rash or hasty, thus making it a synonym of *precipitate*. The one thing those words have in common is an ancestor, Latin *praeceps*, meaning headlong. Most likely your friend's move was made with little thought, hastily—unless he had jumped from a precipice, in which case his move was both precipitous and, you can be sure, precipitate.

prefer

1. Is this expressed correctly: "We *prefer* oranges *to* grapefruit" and "We like oranges so much that we *prefer* them *than* grapefruit"?

Prefer idiomatically takes preposition *to*. The first example (with *prefer* ... *to*) is expressed correctly. The second is not—*to* should have been used instead of *than*. Conjunction *than* is only acceptable in the phrase *more than*, an established idiom when an infinitive follows *prefer*.

Note: The exception to the mandate that *to* should follow *prefer* occurs when the preference is expressed between two infinitives. If we like both to dance and to sing, but like dancing more, we might say, "We *prefer* dancing *to* singing." But if we used *rather than*, technically we should say, "I *prefer* to dance rather than *to* to sing," which of course is not only an awkward but an impossible construction. In this case the *to* is eliminated so that the sentence would read sensibly: "We *prefer to* dance rather than (no *to*) to sing." Constructions involving *prefer* should be balanced: "I prefer *to* jog rather than *to* run" or "I prefer *jogging* to *running*." Not "I prefer *to jog* than *running*."

2. Is it not true that the preposition following *prefer* must always be *to*?

It is not. When the object of *prefer* is not an infinitive, preposition *over* may serve as well, in the opinion of many critics: "I prefer chocolate *to* (or *over*) vanilla." The caveat is not to say, "I prefer chocolate *than* vanilla."

prefixes

Prefixes are usually attached to the base word: *postscript, predawn,* *cooperate.* **What rule governs their separation?**
Separate if attachment might deceive the reader; for example, *re-cover* (to cover again), *re-form* (to form again), *re-count* (to count again). Further, hyphenate if the second element is capitalized: anti-American, pro-Israel.

> **Note:** It is customary to hyphenate the following prefixes in all instances: *all* (all-star); *ex-* (ex-husband); *self-* (self-evident); *vice-* (vice-president). Exception: the Vice President of the United States is written without a hyphen. Some unhyphenated words do not read well. In those cases, judgment should be the rule. For example, *non-native* is clearer than *nonnative, co-worker* than *coworker.*

prejudiced in favor

May a person be prejudiced in favor of something?
Yes. Although the expression *prejudiced in favor* is seldom heard, it is a permissible phrase, since one need not always be prejudiced against. Bias is a two-way street—in favor of or against. However, we are more likely to say, "We are in favor of it" rather than "prejudiced in favor of it." Since *prejudiced* has a pejorative overtone, if, for whatever reason, you wish to use the word *prejudiced* (which means that you have prejudged, made up your mind in advance), say *prejudiced in favor,* not *prejudiced toward.*

preposition at end of sentence

Is it proper to end a sentence with a preposition; for example, "Where is he at?"
Although it is best not to end a sentence with a weak word, and prepositions are weak, nonetheless a sentence may properly end with a preposition. In fact, some sentences sound stilted when the preposition is buried within them. This is particularly so when idiom is being violated. Many cases require that the sentence end with a preposition or else the sentence will lose its effectiveness. Consider "Where is this man from?" "Fred doesn't know what it's all about." "The little boy had no one to play with." "This is the world we live in."

> **Note:** The superstition against ending sentences with a preposition stemmed from classical students who, in the eighteenth century, decided to make English conform with Latin, a language that did not end a sentence with a preposition. They took the word *preposition* (from Latin *prae,* "before," plus *ponere,* "to place") quite literally and determined that prepositions in English must be placed before their object, which foreclosed the possible use of one at the end of the sentence. In any event, Winston Churchill put this matter to rest with a cogent remark

when he was chided for ending a sentence with a preposition: "This is the type of arrant pedantry up with which I shall not put." But be aware that a sentence should contain no unnecessary words, and that a superfluous preposition at the end, like all deadwood, should be cut down. Therefore, "Where is he at?" needs *at* excised, just as *to* does in "Where did he go to?"

prepositions

1. This kind of sentence often tricks me: "Stuart has respect and confidence in the new treasurer." Are others so bothered?
Yes. It is not unusual to see a necessary preposition omitted. In the example *for* is required—*respect for*: "Stuart has respect *for* and confidence *in* the new treasurer." If the sentence had been so phrased that the two words joined by *and* took the same preposition, only one preposition would be required, and that one after the second word: "Stuart has respect and admiration *for* the new treasurer."

> **Note:** A preposition that can serve a series of objects should not be repeated. For example, in "Allen was criticized *for* coming *late, for* dressing poorly, *for* wearing a hat indoors, and *for* bothering a neighbor," the *for*'s do not make the sentence ungrammatical but, except for the first one, are needless.

2. Is the travel brochure that says, "Go with us because we go different places," worded correctly?
It is not. A preposition (a word that connects a noun with some other word—*to*, in this instance) is missing. Correctly put is ". . . we go *to* different places."

> **Note:** It is a solecism to omit a necessary preposition, just as it is to add an unnecessary one.

3. Is there anything wrong with using the same prepositions next to each other?
Not grammatically. We may say, correctly, "My brother was operated *on on* May 3" or "The weight lifter gave *in in* four minutes." As a matter of style, a rewording or a repositioning would be an improvement ("On May 3 my brother was operated on"; "In four minutes the weight lifter quit").

preposterous

What do you think of the word *preposterous*?
It's a preposterous word. It combines *pre-*, "before," and *post*, "after," which, as the Germans say, "puts the horse behind the wagon." That is absurd, of course, but that is what *preposterous* means: "absurd."

prescribe/proscribe

How would you differentiate the look-alikes *prescribe* and *proscribe*?
Those terms have almost opposite meanings. To *prescribe* is to order, to set down a rule or guide. To *proscribe* is condemn, to prohibit, to outlaw. A cardiologist when prescribing medicine may proscribe lifting. Note that the effect of *prescribe* is positive (you must do what has been prescribed), whereas the effect of *proscribe* is negative (you must not do what has been proscribed).

> **Note:** Either word may be used to the same effect in a given structure. A doctor may prescribe rules of conduct for a patient—for example, avoid tobacco and alcohol, or he may proscribe the use of tobacco and alcohol.

> The corresponding nouns are *prescription* and *proscription*.

present incumbent

"Speaking of the mayor, our present incumbent is Tom Roberts." Is that a fair sentence?
It should be graded poor, which is less than fair. The expression *present incumbent* is a redundancy because an incumbent is the present officeholder.

> **Note:** Critics point out that a writer who refers to himself or herself as "the present author" is using the third person singular instead of the first person (*I*) to appear humble or unduly modest. This is not a matter of redundancy but of taste. It is a practice not to be condoned.

pro and con

Why is it that *pro and con* means for and against?
The confusion that this phrase creates is in *con*. Clearly, *pro* means for and usually *con* means with. But in this phrase *con* is an abbreviation of Latin *contra*, which means against.

proceed back

What should one think of this statement: "We will proceed back to the starting point"?
Not much. To *proceed*, from Latin *pro*, "forward," and *cedere*, "to move," means to go forward. Logically, therefore, one cannot *proceed back*. One must return or go back.

> **Note:** The opposite of *proceed* is *precede*, which means to come before in rank, place, or time. *Proceed* means to go on, to continue. Notice the difference in spelling. *Precede* ends in *ede*; *proceed*, in *eed*.

prohibit/forbid

Are there particular rules governing the use of *prohibit* and *forbid*? They seem to mean the same thing.

Yes. *Prohibit* is followed by a noun as its direct object ("They agree to prohibit *sales* to children") or by preposition *from* and a gerund ("The children were prohibited *from entering* the building"). It is never to be followed by an infinitive (not "They were prohibited *to enter* the building"). On the other hand, *forbid* is followed by an infinitive or a gerund, never by *from* ("We will forbid you *to leave*" or "We will forbid *your leaving*," but not "We will forbid you *from* leaving").

prone

Is it correct for me to say, "Tony was lying prone on his back"?

It is not, because *prone* means lying face downward. A position in which a person is lying face upward, as Tony was, is *supine*.

> **Note:** Some dictionaries are becoming very loose concerning the meanings of *prone* and *supine*. Each word has had a long history of its specific sense. Holding, as some do, that *prone* means lying flat no matter what the position simply fosters lack of clarity with no compensable gain.
>
> As with *prone*, the use of *prostrate* has been extended to mean lying down. It need not be face downward. Which would mean that religionists prostrate in prayer may be lying on their backs. Pshaw!

proportion

Is it acceptable to say, "A proportion of the students were ill"?

It is not, because *proportion* may not substitute for *a few* or *some*. The sentence is grammatically rescued if *proportion* is modified by *large* or *small*: "A *large* (*small*) *proportion* of the students were ill."

> **Note:** Whether the plural form *proportions* makes for good English is controversial. Most critics accept the extended use of *proportions* in the sense of dimension, size, or extent, as in "A windstorm of hurricane *proportions*." A few critics contend that *proportions* is not a word related to size but to a relationship. Those critics are overwhelmed by the number approving the extended use of *proportions*.

propose/purpose

Should I say, "What I propose to do is leave tomorrow" or "What I purpose to do . . ."?

At one time the word meaning intend was *purpose*; *propose* was considered a misusage. Nowadays one may use either word for that sense; in fact *propose* has come into wider usage. One may say, since both *propose* and *purpose* mean to intend or to plan, "I *purpose* to continue with his plan" or "I *propose* to continue with his plan."

Note: *Purpose* is sometimes used redundantly. In "He is working hard with the purpose of earning enough to buy a car," all that need be said is "He is working hard *to earn* enough. . . ."

propositioned

"He propositioned me." How does that sentence sound?
The proposal may be a good one, but not the choice of words. As a verb, *proposition* is informal, connoting something unseemly, perhaps illegal or immoral. It is best avoided. As a noun, *proposition* is used indifferently as a replacement for more suitable words, such as *job*, *project*, or *proposal*.

protean

Protean is a word I came across twice last week in a magazine. Since its usage is current, please tell us something about it.
The term derives from Proteus, the Greek sea-god who was exceedingly knowledgeable. But to learn something from him, one had to catch him. Nabbing him was difficult because he kept assuming different shapes. Hence today something variable, shifting its form, is said to be *protean*. The term may be used of a person with attitudes and politics that keep changing.

prototype

Is there such a thing as an original prototype?
A *prototype* is an original model. Copies are made or products patterned after it. Hence "original prototype" is redundant, as is "the first prototype." Omit *original* and *first*.

In general usage *prototype* has come to mean an exemplar, an ideal type. Some critics do not go along with the general usage.

proved/proven

Is it better to use proved or proven as the past tense and participle of prove?
Prefer *proved* as the form for the past tense and *proven* for the participle ("I have *proved* what had to be *proved*; it is now a *proven* fact").

Note: *Proven* is a Scotticism used in legal parlance. Although some conservative linguists have refused to admit the word into the English language, others have taken an opposite tack. However, there is disagreement even among the dissidents. Some, possibly most, of those who accept the form *proven*, approve of its use only as an attributive adjective before a noun—a *proven* theory. Some would not limit its use in any way and would say, "He has *proven* his point." Others are more concerned with sentence rhythm and would select the word that serves it best. You may, of course, choose what appeals to you: "It has *proven* (or *proved*) true that the moon is a solid mass." My liking is expressed in the very first sentence, *proved*.

provided

Is it better to say, "We'll go *if* (or *provided*) it stops raining"?
Prefer *if* to *provided* where *if* will serve. Use *provided* only when a condition is implied. Certainly *if* is preferable in the example. If a condition or stipulation is stated, of course *provided* is the word required. We would say, "You may enter the mosque *if* you wish, *provided* you remove your shoes."

> **Note:** Purists insist that *provided* and *that* belong in tandem (*provided that*), but many linguists do not agree. Another question sometimes raised is whether *providing* may serve as a subordinating conjunction as well as, and in the place of, *provided*. Opinion is divided among word-usage authorities. Some say yes. Some say no. The noes contend that only *provided* may introduce a definite stipulation and that *providing* may introduce only a supposition, in which role it is easily replaceable by *if*. Among those who sanction the use of *providing* where a condition or requirement is stated, some require a following *that* (*providing that*); others do not.

put/place

Does a person *put* or *place* a vase on the table?
The verbs *put* and *place* are synonyms, but *place* connotes carefulness and exactness. *Put* makes no such suggestion. You give a little thought to where you place something. When the basket you're carrying becomes too heavy, you simply put it down.

Q

quantity

1. What, if anything, is objectionable in such a sentence as "We have a large *quantity* of books on hand"?

Many authorities contend that the word *quantity* is not an adequate substitute for the word *number*, which is preferably used of objects, like books, that can be counted in individual units. But there are truths and half-truths in all that. It is agreed that *number* should be applied when designating separatable items. If bulk or mass is being measured, then *quantity* is the suitable term. But according to current dictionaries, *quantity* may denote either a specific or an undetermined *number* or *amount* or an exact *amount* or *number*. This means that one may correctly speak of a large quantity of books. Which is not to say that using *number* instead would not be desirable. It would be.

2. I have two questions. Why do we say, "Two miles *is* a long way off" and "Twenty dollars *is* too much to pay," but "He is a six-*foot* man" and "We have a two-*car* garage."

At first glance the constructions do seem contradictory: miles *is*, six-*foot*. The answer to your first set of questions is that a subject, even though plural in form, requires a singular verb if the subject describes a fixed quantity or number, since the subject is considered a unit. Therefore, "Two miles (or the unit) *is*." In your second set, convention has long decreed that some singular nouns denoting quantity or measurement retain their plural sense and serve as adjectives when they precede other nouns. And so we speak of "a six-*foot* man" (although we say, "a man of six *feet*"). Other common examples are "a *hundred* copies," "a ten-*yard* loss," "two-*dozen* pencils," and "a ten-*room* house."

quasi

When is *quasi* hyphenated?

Quasi, meaning as if, more or less, or almost or somewhat, is hyphenated when serving as the first element in a compound adjective (*quasi*-judicial, *quasi*-scientific, *quasi*-humorous) but not in a compound noun (a *quasi* patriot, a *quasi* argument, a *quasi* union).

question as to

"The question was as to who should begin the program." Are all those words necessary?

No. Following the word *question, as to* is superfluous. ("The question was who should begin the program").

> **Note:** The phrasing *question as to who* runs second in "the most frequent surplusage race" to "question as to whether." Here, too, *as to* does not belong. Omit it. Rather than "There's some *question as to whether* McGuire will run again," say, "There's some *question whether* McGuire will run again."

question mark

1. Should a question mark follow this sentence: "Will everyone please rise when the principal enters"?
There is divided opinion, but the tendency is to omit the question mark when the question is really a request, one that does not seek an answer.

2. Where is a quotation mark placed if the quotation is a question?
It is placed inside the closing quotation mark because the quotation is complete unto itself (He asked, "Will you come with me?"). If the sentence is interrogative, but the quotation is not a question, place the question mark outside the quote's end–quotation mark ("You know what I heard recently, 'Ars longa, vita brevis'?").

3. Should a question mark ever be followed with a comma?
Most stylists say no. Rather than " 'Will you dance with me?', he asked," preferably omit the comma.

4. May a question mark appear within a sentence?
Yes. For example, "Ask 'What can we do for our country?' and there will be ready answers." "Will they accept? and if so, when?"

quid pro quo

What does *quid pro quo* stand for?
Literally, the expression in Latin means "something for something," but its sense is one thing in return for another. Doing a favor for a person who has recently done one for you is a *quid pro quo*.

quintessence

***Quintessence* refers to the best. Had its origin anything to do with that?**
The Greeks originally thought that four elements constituted all existing matter — earth, air, fire, and water. Pythagoras taught that a higher essence permeated nature and the planets: *ether* — the fifth essence — the quintessence, from Latin *quinta essentia*.

> **Note:** Today *quintessence* refers to the highest form of something ("My wife's cooking is the *quintessence* of culinary delight"). It is an exemplar.

quite

1. Is it all right to say, "The job is quite complete"?

Quite means completely, entirely, wholly. Saying "quite complete" is therefore like saying "completely complete," and that's nonsense. *Quite* has wider colloquial acceptance, meaning somewhat or to a considerable degree ("I was *quite* pleased with the review"), but formalists object to that usage.

> Note: The informal use of *quite* is so predominant that it verges on the standard, if it has not already slipped by that puristically clean threshold. Such statements as "It is *quite* warm today" are common among all classes of people. Widespread and continual usage is what makes for idiomatic acceptance.

2. Is this said in good English: "He's *quite* a politician"?

Although *quite a*, as in *quite a few* and *quite a little*, is regarded as standard English, when *quite* suggests unusual ability, as in the example, it is graded informal.

quixotic

What does the word *quixotic* mean?

It means impractically chivalrous, extravagantly romantic. An idealistic but unrealistic person is said to be *quixotic*. The word comes from the title of the satire *Don Quixote* by Miguel de Cervantes.

> Note: Pronounce *quixotic* — kwix-OT-ihk, and *Quixote* — kee-HOH-tee.

quotation marks

Where are periods and commas placed in relation to quotation marks?

They are placed inside quotation marks. "He said no." "He will go," he said. British writers place periods and commas outside quotation marks — "He said no".

quote/quotation

Is it correct to say, "His quotes were appropriate"?

Not in formal language. The common noun form is *quotation*. *Quote*, except in informal contexts, is a verb ("The prosecutor *quoted* from earlier testimony").

> Note: In the publishing field, noun *quote* for noun *quotation* is customary. Most authorities deprecate such use, but some dictionaries recognize it as standard.

R

raised/reared

Should one say that children are raised or reared? Or does it make no difference?

Choose the word you prefer. In yesteryear children were said to be reared or brought up; animals, to be raised. This distinction is now obsolete. Today to *raise* is to bring up or to rear, and it matters not what you raise.

> **Note:** Some dictionaries regard *raise* as an informal term for *rear* in the sense of bring up. *Rear*, no doubt, is the formal term. *Bring up* may be employed on any level of usage.
>
> *Raise* in the sense of moving upward or to a higher position is a transitive verb and requires a direct object ("I raised the windowshade"). Its companion, *rise*, is an intransitive verb. It takes no direct object ("The students *rise* when the dean enters"). As a noun meaning an increase in pay, either word may serve. *Raise* is preferred in the United States; *rise* in Britain.

rarely ever

My uncle never seems to get his language straight. He said, "We rarely ever visit that city." Does he need help?

The combination *rarely ever* is ungrammatical. Probably what was meant, and should have been said, is "We *rarely if ever* visit that city." Better yet would be "We *seldom if ever*. . . ."

> **Note:** Some dictionaries hold that *rarely ever* is an informal term, which is a hefty cut above one that is ungrammatical. In any event, *ever* is redundant whether you say *rarely ever* or *seldom ever*. Omit *ever*, especially in writing.

ravenously

Is "I am ravenously hungry" expressed too emphatically?

The objection is not a matter of emphasis but of redundancy, since *ravenous* means very hungry, famished. "I am ravenous" is sufficient, even though Webster cites *ravenously hungry* as an example of current usage.

re

Is *re* an abbreviated Latin term?

No, and it therefore takes no period. It is, to be precise, the Latin ablative of *res*, which means thing or matter, but which in English means concerning or in regard to.

Note: The Latin *re* is inappropriate in ordinary contexts. Its use is best left to the legal profession. This advice likewise applies to *in re*, which stands for in the matter of or in reference to. The prefix *re-*, when written by itself, as here, is followed by a hyphen. But not when it is serving as a prefix *(reelect, reinstitute, replace)* unless the prefix solidified with the basic element would mislead—*re-count* (to count again), *recount* (to tell or to relate); *re-claim* (to claim again), *reclaim* in all other senses; *re-cover* (to cover again), *recover* (to secure by legal process).

reaction

Is it a mistake to ask a correspondent for a reaction to your letter?
Yes, because a reaction, a scientific term, is a display of energy in response to a stimulus and does not generally apply to people. Ask a person who has had time to reflect for an opinion (a reflective statement), an impression, a thought, or simply a *reply,* but not for a reaction. *Reaction* is a widespread, popular, informal term for any response ("What was your *reaction* to your son's promotion?"). Handle cautiously.

Note: *Reaction* connotes spontaneity. One might rightly ask, "What was the country's *reaction* when war was declared?" Avoid the expression *immediate reaction.* It is redundant.

real

1. I read that *real* is an adverb because someone three centuries ago wrote, "It's a real fine day." Please comment.
Just because *real* (or any other word) was misused centuries ago (even by a distinguished writer) is no reason to continue the misuse. Say, "It's a *really* fine day."

Note: *Real* is an adjective meaning true, actual, genuine, as in "a *real* native Zulu." *Really* is an adverb meaning actually, truly, in fact.

2. I know I shouldn't say, "I'm real glad to meet you," but how can I be sure of the correct greeting?
Test by substituting *certain* and *certainly* for *real,* and see which one makes sense. You wouldn't say, "I'm *certain* glad," but *"certainly glad";* therefore, "I'm *really* glad."

3. Was "We attended a real exciting affair" said in good English?
It was not, because *real* was used colloquially as an intensive. Further, adverbs, not adjectives, modify adjectives. *Real* is an adjective. The simple adverb *very* would have served properly. Or it could have been *really.*

real/regular

Would you discuss the colloquial use of *real* and *regular*?
The use of *real* to mean very—"She is real (better *very*) nice"—is objec-

tionable, as is the use of *regular* to mean real—"Lois is a *regular* (better *real*) pal."

Note: If there is an established periodic happening (a daily newspaper, a weekly review, a monthly meeting), it is redundant to add *regular* when mentioning it. Say, "We will attend our monthly seminar," not "our *regular* monthly seminar." And "We have our daily newspaper delivered to our house," not "our *regular* daily newspaper."

really

1. My daughter uses *really* to intensify almost everything she says: "This is really good"; "It was a really funny movie." When I suggested that she stop abusing that word, she asked when it may properly be used. I was stumped. What should I tell her?

Really means "in fact," and it should be used only when that is the thought being expressed: "I *really* (in fact) failed the examination." Your daughter should switch her *really*'s to *very*. *Very* is not a *very* good word in many instances, but it is a better word than *really* in the examples.

2. My friend's favorite expression is "You look great, really and truly." Is that last phrase a good one?

Not really. *Really and truly* is trite and wordy. Prefer "You look really great." Better yet is the simple "You look great."

reason

What do you think of this sentence: "The reason we didn't object was because his father was the commissioner"?

The construction *the reason . . . was* (or *is*) is redundant, since *because* means for the reason that. To correct the example, either omit *the reason was* ("We didn't object, *because* his father was the commissioner") or replace *because* with *that* ("The reason we didn't object was *that* his father was the commissioner"). Technically, the expression *the reason is because* is objectionable on two counts: faulty predication as well as redundancy. As a subordinate conjunction, *because* usually introduces an adverbial clause; but in *the reason is because,* a combination is functioning as a nounal clause in which the same thing is said twice. *The reason is because* in effect says *the reason is for the reason that.*

Note: Avoid using such constructions as *the reason is because of, the reason is due to,* or *the reason is on account of.* Not "The reason we're bankrupt is due to our inability to borrow." The reason for the bankruptcy is not due to an inability to borrow; the inability to borrow *is* the reason. Be careful also of such a sentence as "Because you were absent is no reason why you should be dismissed," in which three words imply a cause. Say, "The fact that you were absent is no reason for your dismissal" or "Your absence is no satisfactory reason for your dismissal."

An associated, but controversial, problem arises in the expression *reason why* ("The *reason why* we lost is clear") because the expression is deplored by some English authorities, is considered colloquial by others, and is approved as standard English by still others. With this lack of consensus, it is best when writing on a formal level to eschew the phrase entirely except in a negative statement where it works well: "We don't understand the *reason why* he left." Of course, the sentence would be terser if *the reason* were omitted: "We don't know why he left."

recipe

What does the prescription sign with a capital R and a slash through its toe stand for?
It stands for *recipe*, a Latin word meaning take.
   Note: The anglicized equivalent of *recipe* is *prescription* or *formula*, especially in cookery. Historically the word for medical ingredients was *receipt*. It was changed to *recipe*, and the *R* in prescriptions symbolized it, the slant through the toe of the *R* representing the Roman god Jupiter, the patron of medicine.

recollect/remember

Is there a difference in the mental process between *recollecting* and *remembering*?
Decidedly so. Recollecting and remembering do not enjoy the same power of calling to mind. To *recollect* is to make a continuing, sometimes frustrating effort to bring to consciousness what has been stored in memory. You may struggle to recollect a classmate's name, but remember effortlessly the year you and the classmate were graduated. To *remember* is to call back to mind with no conscious effort. It may be termed instant recall.

reconcile

What prepositions go with the verb *reconcile*?
Pertaining to a condition, *reconcile* takes *to* ("He became *reconciled to* his fate"); to a person, *with* ("They became *reconciled with* each other").

redundant

I often read and hear the word *redundant*. What does it mean?
Redundant, from Latin *redundare*, "to overflow," means needlessly repetitive, using more words than necessary to express an idea; for example, *two twins, final climax, free gift, hollow tube*. A synonym is *wordy*.
   Note: William Strunk, Jr., in *The Elements of Style*, offered the best advice concerning the avoidance of redundancy: "A sentence should contain no unnecessary words, a paragraph no unnecessary sentences, for the

same reason that a drawing should have no unnecessary lines and a machine no unnecessary parts."

refer back

My supervisor frequently says that he is referring a document back to the initiating department. Would you care to comment on the expression *refer back*?

Your question indicates the obvious answer. Since *refer* means to turn back, the combination *refer back* is redundant. *Back* should be omitted.

> Note: Some people need their sense of security bolstered by saying again what has already been said. Some merely add an extra word, a redundant word, but that too makes speakers or writers sure that they've made their point. It is not uncommon to hear such duos as *refer back, revert back, remand back,* or *return back,* in which *back* is a useless appendage. The sense of *back* is inherent in all those words. And we often hear of a *redoubling* of efforts when what was meant was *doubling.* Which means that particular caution should be exercised before using a *re*-word.
>
> Just as *back* is unnecessary with words that contain that sense, so *again* is equally surplusage with certain words. What is the advantage of using *again* with *regain,* as in "Anne will *again regain* her leadership," unless you mean to gain for the third time? And so with *repeat again.* Something can be repeated again if it had been previously repeated. To *reiterate* follows the same pattern, since *iterate* means to say again.

referring to

Is this sentence punctuated correctly: "Mr Roberts's memo, referring to his schedule, will be reviewed"?

It is not. Except when *referring to (concerning, pertaining to,* or *relating to)* meaning about begins a sentence, it is an essential phrase and is therefore not set off by commas.

refute/rebut

The newspaper report said that when Tim McClatchy was accused by the union of being a scab, he refuted the charge by stoutly denying it. Can anyone deny that *refute* was the proper word?

A linguist would deny it. Although both *deny* and *refute* denote a contradiction of a statement made, there is an important difference between them. To *deny* is to assert that that which has been said or claimed is not true. To *refute* is to disprove. A denial is not a refutation. Tim McClatchy denied or repudiated the charge; he did not offer evidence to refute it.

> Note: *Rebut* should not be equated with *deny, contradict,* or *dispute.* To *rebut* is to answer in contradiction, but it is not so convincing or effective as to disprove completely the wrong that had been asserted. *Refute* is a

stronger word, since to refute is to disprove a charge that something is wrong. A sister word, but a bookish term, is *confute*. It means to refute decisively.

regard/consider

1. Roger said that he regards Thomas as a competent accountant. Whereupon Allan said that he considers Thomas as competent, too. Did both Roger and Allan speak correctly?

Only Roger did. The verbs *regard* and *consider* take different idiomatic constructions—*regard* takes *as (regard as); consider* does not. Allan should have omitted *as* following *considers* ("... he *considers* Thomas competent, too").

> **Note:** Idiomatically *regard* is followed by *as* when the meaning is consider or think ("Seth *regards* his neighbors *as* nuisances"). Idiomatically *consider* is *not* followed by *as* when the meaning is to regard as, think, or believe, but by a direct object ("The people *considered* him a *hero*"), and not a clause as a direct object ("The adjutant considers *the report is in error*"). Correct the last by deleting *is*.
>
> However, the construction *consider . . . as* is properly used when the sense is to look upon, study, or examine ("The judge *considered* the defendant's plea *as* having some merit"; "The psychologist said that he will *consider* the patient first *as* a frustrated teacher and second *as* a hapless father").

2. Would you criticize this: "He regards her as being the smoothest talker in the class"?

Yes, omit *being*. "He *regards* her as. . . ." In informal language *regards* is often followed by *being* or another similar participle, but not so in standard English.

regretful/regrettable

"What a regretful situation." Is the situation regretful?

It is not. *Regrettable* denotes a happening or a condition that causes regret ("The collapse of the grandstand was *regrettable*"), as was the *situation* mentioned in the example. *Regretful,* which refers to feelings of regret or sorrow, is applied only to people. "He is *regretful* that the *regrettable* incident occurred" (but don't use a sentence like this!).

> **Note:** *Regretful* is spelled with one *t*, *regrettable* with two.

relatively

"Today is relatively warm." That sentence bothers me because I'm not sure what it means. Do you get my feeling?

Your feeling is quite clear. When the word *relatively* is used, a reader has the right to know what is relative to what, since *relatively* implies a comparison. If the comparison is neither expressed nor implied, the reader will be in a quandary. But the example does suggest a comparison, that the temperature of today is somewhat warmer than it has been, which makes *relatively* not specific but understandable.

> **Note:** If in doubt, replace *relatively* with a noncontroversial adverb. Relative to temperature, you might say, "Today is fairly (or somewhat) warm." And do not use *relatively* with *percentage* or *proportion*, since inherent in those words is the notion of a part relative to a whole. The idea of a whole must be clear to justify the use of *relatively* ("The ship had many staterooms but the number occupied was *relatively* small"). The adverb *comparatively* is similar in meaning to *relatively* and is therefore subject to the same caution.

remain

How is the verb *remain* used properly?
Remain, a linking verb (one that links the subject and its predicate modifier or noun) takes adjectives, not adverbs ("In the face of danger, we *remain calm,*" not *calmly*). Active verbs take adverbs ("In the face of danger, we *leave calmly*").

> **Note:** The usual test to determine whether a verb is a linking verb is to substitute for it a form of the verb *to be*. If it can be done sensibly, the word involved is a linking, or copulative, verb. The test works out satisfactorily with *remain:* "In the face of danger, we *remain (are)* calm." The test will fail with the next example—no "to be" substitution can replace *leave*.

repel/repulse

Is this sentence worded right: "The campers were repulsed by the prospect of cooking their own meals"?
It is not. The campers were *repelled,* not *repulsed.* Both *repel* and *repulse* mean to drive back an opposing force, but *repel* also connotes aversion or disgust. The frequent misuse of *repulse* for *repel* is probably due to the false association of *repulse* with *repulsive,* which means causing extreme distaste.

> **Note:** Some unabridged dictionaries give the terms *repel* and *repulse* as synonyms. It is best to distinguish the uses of those verbs. A woman is bound to repulse a man's advances if he repels her.

replica

Was it proper for an advertisement to offer replicas of a Rembrandt painting?
Not if exact wording is a criterion. What they should have offered were copies or reproductions. A *replica,* in the fine arts, is an exact copy of a work made by its original creator.

Note: In general usage *replica* has come to mean the equivalent of *copy* or *reproduction*. It is also used of a *miniature*, such as a model. Many critics recommend that *model* or *miniature* be used instead of *replica*, first, because it is more accurate phrasing, and second, because some people do not know what *replica* actually means, whereas others who do might assume its literal definition.

respectfully/respectively

How different in usage are the words *respectfully* and *respectively*?
Very much so. *Respectfully* means in a courteous manner. A person addresses a clergyman respectfully. *Respectively* means each in the order given. "My children ski and swim in Vermont and Florida, *respectively*."

> **Note:** A problem with *respectively* is that sometimes it is unnecessary and sometimes it is confusing. In each case *respectively* should be omitted. *Respectively* is superfluous in "The opening dates for the 1990 and 1991 baseball seasons have been set for April 17 and March 24, *respectively*." It is confusing in "Mac and Ned received a tennis racquet and a golf bag, *respectively*." A clearer wording is "Mac received a tennis racquet and Ned, a golf bag."

rest

Should the word *rest* take a singular or a plural verb?
It may take either depending on the number of the noun in the *of* phrase following it. "The rest of the cars *have* been sold"; "The rest of the showroom *is* closed."

> **Note:** Many words used as a subject of a sentence do not control the grammatical number, as is so with *rest*. Be careful, therefore, to determine whether the noun in the following *of* phrase sets the number for the verb ("A lot of oil *has* been spilled"; "A lot of crullers *have* been spilled.").

reticent/reluctant

Is this sentence worded correctly: "Tom was reticent to speak about the matter"?
If Tom was unwilling to speak about the matter, which the sentence indicates, the adjective that should have been used, rather than *reticent*, was *reluctant*. *Reluctant* means averse or unwilling. *Reticent* means disinclined to speak freely and is usually applied to someone who is habitually silent or quiet.

right/rightly

Both *right* and *rightly* are adverbs. How does one choose between them?

When the meaning is properly or correctly, use *rightly* before the verb ("He *rightly* understood it") and *right* after the verb ("He said it *right*"). However, there are no hard and fast rules, merely preferences. One may say, "He answered it *right* (or *rightly*) or "Spell it *right*" (or *rightly*).

> Note: *Right* may serve as many parts of speech—a noun (a civil *right*), a verb (*right* this matter), an adjective (her *right* foot), or an adverb (*right* after the game). But *rightly* is an adverb only.

right along

1. What do you say about this: "The gardener makes the same mistake right along"?
The phrase *right along* is a colloquialism that is rejected by some usage authorities. It stands for "repeatedly," which is the recommended word to use.

2. Is it wrong to say, "Andy is moving right along"?
The popular expression *right along* is acceptable in everyday speech but not in formal writing. Say, "Andy is progressing" or "making progress."

rigmarole

What is the proper pronunciation of *rigmarole*?
Rigmarole, meaning confused or meaningless talk or complex and ritualistic procedure, is pronounced RIG-mah-rolle, with three syllables, not rig-a-mah-rolle.

rob/steal

How are the words *rob* and *steal* differentiated?
Rob has as its object either a person ("That shabby-looking man *robbed* Mr. Jones right in front of his office") or a place ("The neighborhood punk *robbed* the liquor store last night"). *Steal* has as its object the thing taken ("He *stole* two cases of Scotch").

> Note: To rob is to take feloniously from someone by force or fear of force. To steal is to take feloniously or furtively ("He stole the man's wallet"; "She stole a kiss") or to proceed furtively ("Ken stole into the room"). The thing to remember is that a person or place is robbed. What was taken was stolen, not robbed. A thief does not rob money from a bank. He robs the bank of its money.

route/rout

Does my son have a newspaper *rout* or *route*?
A *route* (pronounced root) is a way or course. A *rout* is an overwhelming defeat. A delivery boy follows a route and therefore has a *route*. But in

general usage *route* is more often pronounced rout (rhymes with out).

> **Note:** Critics say that *route* is acceptably pronounced root or rout. Even though *rout* is the commoner pronunciation for *route,* the phrase *en route* does not follow along. It is pronounced ahn-root.

runs

Would you correct this sentence: "Johnson runs the printing shop"? If so, what changes are recommended?

In the sense used, *runs* is colloquial. Colloquial expressions are not to be criticized, since they are commonly used in conversation by people on all levels of education. But this does not mean that all are ipso facto acceptable. To the contrary, some are vehemently deprecated by many authorities. Bear in mind that these expressions do not belong in structured writing.

> **Note:** In formal discourse do not use the word *run* to mean manage, as in "to run a business." Prefer *operate.* Its noun form is a good word to designate a proprietor *(operator).* Another replacement is *manage,* but its noun form *(manager)* usually refers to an employee.

ruthless

Ruthless **is a common word meaning without compassion. Is compassion** *ruth?*

The answer is yes. *Ruth* means compassion or sympathy for another. The word is seldom seen and therefore looks odd. It may be labeled obsolescent.

> **Note:** Many well-known words, such as *ruthless,* have comparativly unknown antonyms. For example, *unkempt* is known to mean not combed, untidy. But its opposite number, *kempt,* which means neat, well groomed, is also a good English word but is practically unheard of and would, in all probability, be misunderstood. And so with *unruly* and *ruly, uncouth* and *couth,* and *inept* and *ept.* All those terms are respected English words.

S

Sahara desert

My friend said she'll be seeing the Sahara Desert. Is that the correct name for that desert?

It is not, since *Sahara* in Arabic means desert. The addition of *desert* is a technical redundancy. Properly, she is going to see the *Sahara*.

> **Note:** Another commonly heard redundant expression is *Sierra Nevada Mountains. Mountains* is duplicative. Sierra Nevada means snowy mountains. Call it *the Sierras.* And so with *Rio Grande River*. In Spanish, *rio* means river. But be tolerant of those who use the full description, the popular name. It is so often used that, at worst, it is only a peccadillo.

same

1. May the word *same* properly replace a personal pronoun?

Excepting legal and commercial lingo, *same*, meaning the aforesaid thing, should not serve as a pronoun. "After you've read the memo, I'll read *same*" sounds stilted. Say, "I'll read *it*." And not "It is required that the *same* be presented by Monday."

> **Note:** *Same* is unnecessary in "I will do it if they will do it *the same* as I do." Make it " . . . if they do it *as* I do." But be careful of short-circuiting: "They did their work *the same* as the others" should be recast; "They did their work *in the same manner* as the others."
>
> When *same* means identical, as in "Each heir will get the *same*," it serves as a legitimate pronoun. In this use, *same* is always preceded by *the*.

2. Is it proper to use the phrase "the same difference"?

The phrase should be avoided in literary prose, since it is an oxymoron; that is, conflicting terms. But despite its illogicality, the expression is widely used, easily understood, and accepted by most people.

sanatorium/sanitarium

Does it matter whether a person goes to a *sanatorium* or a *sanitarium*?

It might matter to the person involved. Strictly speaking, a *sanatorium* is a place where people go to restore their health, a place for healing. It is an institution designed to care for patients with chronic diseases and to supervise their recuperation. A *sanitarium* is a place where people go to preserve their health, a health resort.

satisfied

"The firemen were satisfied that no one survived the explosion." Would you use *satisfied* there?

229

The sense of *satisfied* in the example is convinced, but since *satisfied* also means contented, a better word than *satisfied* would be *believed*, *concluded*, or *were convinced*.

save

"My daughter reads all kinds of books save biographies and science fiction." Do you approve of the word *save*?
The use of *save* to mean except is archaic. It might still have a place in poetry, but it does not belong in present-day writing.

scan

When the boss says, "You scanned the report, " is he being complimentary or critical?
Out of context, one can't tell, for *scan* means either to examine closely or, quite oppositely, to look through hastily. A person late for work will have time only to scan the headlines (*hastily*). But a person will also scan his income tax return (*closely*).
> Note: Words that have two diametrically opposed meanings, such as *scan* and *cleave*, must be considered carefully to avoid a misunderstanding of the meaning intended.

scarcely

1. Which italicized word is preferred in this statement: "He had scarcely finished reading the paper *than/when* his children burst into the room"?
Idiom has decreed that *when* be used after *scarcely*, not *than*. *Than* is used when a comparison is being made ("Charlotte is barely taller *than* I"). But in the example no comparison is being made.
> Note: Prefer adverb *scarcely* to *hardly* when quantity is indicated but *hardly* to *scarcely* to suggest degree. "He will *hardly* finish his studies before the test is given." "It is *scarcely* five minutes since he left."

> Like *hardly* and *barely*, *scarcely* has a negative connotation, its sense being "not quite." It should therefore not be used with another negative, *not* being the most obvious: "It is *scarcely* (not "it isn't *scarcely*") a week since Agnes resigned." Watch out for the less obvious negatives. "Without *scarcely* a murmur, he agreed to play" needs amending: "With *scarcely* a murmur, he agreed to play." And in "My daughter found it unnecessary to say *scarcely* anything about her absence," *scarcely* should be omitted.

schism

How is the word *schism* pronounced?
Pronounce this word, meaning a division or split, with a silent *ch* — SIHZ'm, not shihsm.

scrutinize

The sentence "He found a flaw in the report because he scrutinized it carefully" bothers me. Does it bother you?
It does because *carefully* is redundant after the word *scrutinized*. To scrutinize is to examine closely, to inspect carefully. Do not precede noun *scrutiny* with adjective *close, careful,* or *intense.*
> **Note:** *Scrutinize* and *scan* are synonymous. They both suggest a thorough going-over.

second best

What do you think of this: "The Mets are the second best team in the league after the Dodgers"?
The sentence should be restated: "The Mets are the second best team in the league" or "The Mets are the best team after the Dodgers," not "the second best after."

secondhanded

Is it proper to call a pre-owned car a *secondhanded* car?
The word *secondhanded* does not exist in the English language. You may call a pre-owned car a *secondhand* car.

seeming paradox

Does the phrase *a seeming paradox* make sense?
It does not. The word *seeming* should be omitted. A *paradox* is a *seemingly* contradictory statement that may nonetheless be well founded. A dictionary definition of *paradox* is "a statement that may be true but seems to say two opposite things."

select/selected

What difference is there between a *select* and a *selected* course of study?
A *select course* of study consists of courses carefully chosen from a larger number or from a variety. A *selected course* is a program of higher grade or quality than the ordinary.

self-confessed

A news report I thought ludicrous was "McLain is a self-confessed kleptomaniac." Have you ever read anything more laughable?
The writer did make a poor choice in structuring *self-confessed* as a compound, since one person cannot confess for another. *Self-* should

have been omitted. McLain *confessed*. He didn't *self-confess*.

> **Note:** Whether to attach *self-* to a base word to form a compound can be determined by omitting *self-* to see whether that word would suffice without *self-*. If it does, omit *self-*, for it would be serving no purpose. This is so with *self-confessed*, as it is with *self-admitted* ("He is a *self-admitted* perjurer"), *self-deprecating*, *self-conceited*, and so forth.

-self words

1. The invitation read "My wife and myself would like to have you for dinner next Saturday." I think the invitation needs correcting. Am I right?

You are, indeed. A *-self* pronoun should not serve as the subject of a sentence. The simple pronoun *I* should have been used in the example: "My wife and *I* would like. . . ."

> **Note:** It is as much an error to use a *-self* pronoun in the objective case as it is in the nominative. For example, "Dolores invites you to spend the weekend at her summer home with Sarah, Jayne, and herself" needs *herself* changed to *her,* an objective-case form, since *her* is the object of preposition *with.*
>
> *-Self* pronouns should be employed only as intensives or as reflexives. "I *myself* did it" and "You ought to do it *yourself*" are examples of intensive pronouns. They emphasize the doer. "I cut *myself*" and "Do you shave *yourself*?" are examples of the reflexive use of these pronouns. They turn the action back on the doer.
>
> Observe that *ourselves,* not *ourself,* is a proper reflexive-pronoun form: "We saw ourselves (not *ourself*) as martyrs to the cause. " And avoid *themself, theirself,* and *theirselves.* Those forms do not exist.

2. Are *-self* words, for example *ourselves,* ever hyphenated?

When *-self* is appended to a personal pronoun, no hyphen is used (*himself, themselves*). When *self* is employed as a prefix, it takes a hyphen (*self-evident, self-employed*).

semicolon

When is a semicolon required?

The most frequent use for a semicolon is to replace a missing conjunction between two independent clauses (those that can stand alone and end in a period). "I will go; he will stay." But "I will join the club *and* he will, too" (no semicolon). The second most frequent use is between two independent clauses when the second clause is introduced by a conjunctive adverb ("We will not go today; *moreover,* we don't intend ever to go"). Note that a conjunctive adverb is followed by a comma unless a one-syllable adverb is used: *thus, hence.*

sensual/sensuous

Is there a sensible way to avoid confusing the words *sensuous* and *sensual*?
Yes. Bear in mind their meanings (*sensuous*, "pertaining to the senses"; *sensual*, "applying to physical senses, primarily sexual") and note that *sensual* like *sexual* ends in *ual*. *Sensuous*, it may be said, suggests the refined; *sensual*, the lascivious.

> **Note:** In a broad sense, the words are synonymous, describing what a person experiences through the senses, primarily gratification. *Sensual* describes base feelings; *sensuous*, more aesthetic interests. *Sensual* pertains to sexual desires. *Sensuous* is used when senses, other than sexual arousal, are responding. Milton coined the word *sensuous* to distinguish it from sexual sensations.

sentence structure

1. What verb does a compound subject take if it consists of both an affirmative and a negative expression?
The verb should agree with the affirmative subject, whether singular or plural: "The coach, not the players, *was* wrong." "The players, not the coach, *were* wrong."

2. Which sentence is preferred: "I *gave* the book to *him*" or "I gave *him* the *book*"?
Verb *give* is preferably followed by an indirect object *(him)* and not by a "to" construction. This preference applies also to verbs *pay, send,* and *write.*

3. Is this correct: "Closing the gate, she left"?
Everyone would know what was meant. But actually she closed the gate and then left. It would be clearer to say, "Having closed (or "After closing) the gate, she left."

4. Is the construction of this sentence to your liking: "We had hoped to have found a larger house"?
It is not. Preferably say, "We had hoped *to find* a larger house." Use the present infinitive after *hope, plan, expect,* and *intend* when action planned for the past has not yet been completed: "I intended *to write* you (not *to have written* you) about the job."

5. What guideline is there when placing modifiers in a series?
If possible, graduate them according to length, the shortest coming first. It will make for more euphonious writing. Not "He was bedraggled, unkempt, and dirty," but *"dirty, unkempt, and bedraggled."*

6. This sentence doesn't sound right: "The best part of the play was the dancers." Please help.
Grammatically the sentence is correct. The verb *was* should and does

agree with the singular subject *part,* not the nominative predicate, *the dancers.* You might recast to avoid awkwardness: "The *dancers were* the best part of the play."

7. Are sentence fragments used by good writers?
Occasionally. *Fragments* can emphasize. Especially in a suitable context. Try one. Like this one. But with restraint.

8. Should the important point in a sentence be placed at the beginning or at the end?
The beginning is the more natural order. Placed at the end, however, it tends to create suspense ("He walked; he jogged; he ran — and then he dropped dead"). Use this kind of sentence, called periodic, sparingly.

9. If this sentence is not written well, please improve it: "Write short stories, sell each one promptly, and seek reviews."
Where possible, maintain the same number of the nouns and pronouns throughout. An improvement would be "Write short stories, sell *them* promptly, and seek reviews."

10. "They're off. Alice and Bernie D are out in front running one length behind each other." Was that said in understandable English?
The sentence is illogical. Only one of those horses can be behind; the other is ahead. But undoubtedly the bettors were not confused.

11. May I have your opinion on this sentence: "Sam called the purpose the money had been set aside for to the members' attention."
The sentence follows an unnatural order and is therefore awkward. It should be restructured: "Sam called to the members' attention the purpose for which the money had been set aside."

12. What do you think of "He traveled widely, enjoyed speaking with friends and colleagues"?
The sentence has two parts, and they should be connected by *and:* "He traveled widely *and* enjoyed speaking with friends and colleagues."

13. Please comment on this sentence: "The tree is tall and its branches long."
The verb *is* in clause one cannot be applied to clause two because the subjects do not have the same number. Say, "The tree is tall and its branches *are* long."

14. If you had to state in a simple sentence the important guidelines to good writing, what would you say?
I would rely on tradition and say that one's writing should be governed by *unity, emphasis, clarity,* and *variety.*

15. The sentence read: "He doesn't realize the significance of the problem or its likely solution." Please criticize.
An addition is needed, the prepostion *of.* Correctly stated: "He doesn't

realize the significance of the problem or *of* its likely solution." Necessary prepositions should not be omitted.

16. How would you treat this sentence: "Roy had suffered a relapse for two weeks when he died"?
The important point in a sentence should be at the beginning or its end. Minor ideas, not the principal statement, should be put into a subordinate clause or phrase. Try "After suffering a relapse for two weeks, Roy died."

17. Which is correct: "The football coach discouraged my throwing horseshoes" or "The football coach discouraged me from throwing horseshoes"?
Nothing is wrong with either sentence. The first is a gerund with a possessive; the second, a prepositional phrase. The prepositional phrase is preferable in this particular example.

18. Should both verbs in this sentence be in the past tense: "Galileo *believed* that the world *is* round"?
The second verb is correctly put in the present tense *(is)* because a general truth — an existing fact — is expressed. The world *is* still round. When a statement is historically, permanently, or universally true, use the present tense in the subordinate clause. "We *learned* (past tense) that water *freezes* (present tense) at 32 degrees."

19. A redheaded man in our office, when he sees my redheaded secretary, says, "Us redheads must stick together." If I were to correct his grammar, how would it be best to steer him right?
Tell him to repeat the sentence without the appositive *redheads*. No one is likely to say, *"Us* must" instead of "We must." And if you think this has any merit, tell him that the subject of a sentence is always in the nominative case *(we)* and not in the objective case *(us)*.

20. Should this sentence be criticized: "My employer was in a receptive state of mind to my proposal"?
The sentence is wordy. Without *in a* and *state of mind*, the shortened sentence retains its sense and with greater force: "My employer was receptive to my proposal."

separate

How should the word *separate* be pronounced?
Depends. Verb *separate*, meaning to divide, takes three syllables — sep-a-rate. Adjective *separate* is usually given only two — sep-rit. And note the spelling. *Separate* has a *par* in it, not a *per*.

sequence of tenses

1. How does one refer to a preceding event when writing in the past tense?

By using the past perfect tense; for example, "He *spent* (past tense) the money he *had won* (past perfect tense) last month." "We *had left* (past perfect tense) the area two weeks before the storm *struck*" (past tense).

2. How do "Bob was a broker for six years" and "Bob has been a broker for six years" differ in meaning?

The first says Bob is no longer a broker; the second that he still is. *Was* indicates past time, *has been* (present perfect tense) refers to action continued into the present. This means that when referring to something still going on, either *has* or *have* is required to indicate the continuation.

3. Which is correct: "She said her name *was* Nancy" or "She said her name *is* Nancy"?

The former, "She said her name *was* Nancy." The tense of the verb in the subordinate clause follows the tense in the main clause.

> **Note:** There are three ways to report what someone has said. (1) Direct speech. "I am hungry," Andy said, "but I will not eat." (2) Parenthetical. In this construction *he said* does not govern. "Andy is hungry, he said, but he will not eat." (3) Indirect discourse. "Andy said he was hungry but he would not eat." or "Andy said *that* he was hungry but *that* he would not eat." Notice the change of the verb *is* to *was* and of the auxiliary from *will* to *would*.

serendipity

What is the origin of the word *serendipity*?

The word, meaning a discovery of something pleasant quite by chance, was coined by Horace Walpole after reading the fairy tale *The Three Princes of Serendip*. Walpole wanted an English word to describe this fortunate facility. *Serendip* is an ancient name for Sri Lanka (Ceylon).

sewage/sewerage

Do the words *sewage* and *sewerage* mean different things?

Yes, they do. *Sewage* is waste material, refuse matter, the contents of a sewer. *Sewerage* is the system of sewers through which sewage is removed.

> **Note:** More and more the word *sewerage* is falling into disuse, and *sewage* is becoming increasingly predominant as both noun and adjective. Although it is correct to say, "The *sewerage* was unable to handle that tremendous downpour," most likely it would be given "The *sewage system* was unable to handle. . . ."

shall/will

Is the distinction between *shall* and *will* still maintained?
In careful writing, yes. *Shall* expresses futurity in the first person ("*I* shall leave later") and *will* in the second and third person. Determination is expressed by reversing the order ("*I* will do it"). As a practical matter, in declarative sentences, *will* is used by most people in all instances. Which does not make it right, merely common.

> **Note:** Some critics say that General Douglas MacArthur destroyed whatever life the prevailing *shall/will* rule had when he said, regarding his intention to recapture the Philippines, "I *shall* return." But some people do not believe that MacArthur's statement was a death blow because, as they point out, MacArthur was a military genius, not an English academician.

should/would

Which is correct: "I *should* (or *would*) like to see you tomorrow"?
The auxiliary that precedes *like* in the first person is *should* (I *should*, we *should*), not *would*.

> **Note:** The conditional forms of *shall* and *will* are *should* and *would*. Only *should* expresses obligation or necessity. Of these two forms, *would* is much more commonly used where simple conditions are being expressed. In fact, *should*, as the conditional tense of *shall*, is practically extinct.

sibling

Is it better to refer to *brothers and sisters* or *siblings*?
Some usage experts decry the use of *sibling*, calling it pedantic. But its frequent use and its conciseness make the word welcome. Be aware that not everyone is familiar with the word *sibling*. It is a common word in some social disciplines, when "sibling rivalry" is considered as a cause of familial maladjustments.

sideswipe

What do word usage-authorities say about the word *sideswipe*?
Sideswipe, during these days of heavy traffic, has become a useful word to mean to strike the side while passing, but it has been objected to by those who dislike the sound or slang meaning of *swipe* (to *steal* or *pilfer*: "I *swiped* two apples from that pushcart"). However, *sideswipe* has come to be recognized as standard.

similar

Are two similar things the same things?
They are not. *Same* means precisely alike, like Washington's face on

every one-dollar bill. *Similar* refers to a likeness that nearly corresponds. It is, it might be said, a partial resemblance.

> **Note:** Things that are identical are the *same,* not *similar* to one another. Therefore, do not say, for example, "My aunt, who slipped on the ice, broke her hip, and her daughter met a *similar* fate a year later." Make it "the *same* fate." Not "Three patients were waiting for Dr. Stein and a *similar* number for Dr. Gross," but "the *same* number." Since *similar* is an adjective, it may modify the subject of a linking verb ("That typewriter seems *similar* to the one in our office"). But do not make it do the work of an adverb. Not "That typewriter works *similar* to the one in our office," but "works *similarly to.*"

simple/simplified/simplistic

Shall I tell my pharmacist that he simplified everything or that he made everything simplistic?

Choose *simplified* over *simplistic.* Although dictionaries give both adjectives the same definition, "made simpler or made less complicated," *simplistic* has become a faddish word meaning oversimplified. It carries a pejorative tone and may be thought uncomplimentary.

> **Note:** Avoid the phrase *simple reason.* It may mistakenly indicate that you think even a moron could understand it. And remember that "for the simple reason that" says no more than *because* or *since.*

since

1. Is the sentence "We lived here since 1950" grammatically acceptable?

No, it needs correcting. When *since,* expressing time, is preceded by a verb, the verb must be in a perfect tense, not in the past tense ("We *have lived* here since 1950"). Be alert to the *have.*

> **Note:** The reason behind the foregoing rule is that *since* means "from" (a specified time) and is still continuing. Hence a present-tense auxiliary (*has, have*) and a past participle must precede it.

2. Did Don express himself correctly when he said, "I'm leaving, since I don't like what is happening"? Or should he have said *because*?

Don expressed himself correctly. Both *since* and *because* are causal conjunctions, and either one may serve in the example. In the sense used, *since* means because or for.

3. The statement read: "Since the librarian died, the library has purchased no books." Would you have reworded it?

Yes. *Since* makes the sentence ambiguous, for it may mean either because of her death or from the time of her death. A sentence should be so structured as to state clearly the desired sense.

> **Note:** Be careful with *since* where it may logically be considered either a

temporal or a causal adverb. In such case it is a source of ambiguity and should be avoided.

sincerely

I was taught that a letter may close with "Sincerely yours." Why is "Sincerely" now written without the "yours"?
Traditionally, a complimentary closing required "yours," as in "Very truly yours." A trend evolved during modern times to eliminate "yours," and it is now customary to close by writing "Sincerely" alone.

   Note: *Sincerely* is now the most generally used closing. *Cordially,* also widely used, is not necessarily followed by "yours" either. It is regarded as a friendlier closing than *Sincerely.*

size

Which is correct: *a medium-size room* or *a medium-sized room*?
Both are correct, since either noun *size* or adjective *sized* may form a compound adjective. "It is a large-size hat" or "It is a large-sized hat."

   Note: Authorities take slightly different views about the adjectival use of *size.* Some would agree that *medium-size* and *medium-sized* are interchangeable. Others would say that *size* is a noun and must not be used to form adjectives (even though nouns are regularly used to form adjectives). They would accept only *medium-sized.* One thing more. Since *size* is a noun, it should be followed by *of* in such cases as "that *size of* paper." Do not say "that *size* paper," although in commercial practice *of* is usually omitted.

slow/slowly

Are *drive slow* and *drive slowly* equally correct?
Yes, since both *slow* and *slowly* are adverbs. *Slow,* commonly used in informal speech and writing, has established idiomatic uses: the clock runs *slow;* the train is running *slow;* he drove *slow.* But in general and formal usage, *slowly* predominates. For example, we say, "The hearse was driven away *slowly.*"

   Note: Prefer *slowly* to *slow* where the words are interchangeable. In commands and exhortations, *slow* serves better because it is a crisp, concise word ("Be careful on those icy roads. Drive *slow*").

so

May *so* be used to start a sentence: "So we thought we would go"?
It may, but many careful writers object to this practice when it displaces *therefore. And so* beginning a sentence is somewhat more formal than *so* alone and, although not warmly received, is considered more acceptable.

Note: In informal speech *so* is commonly used as a replacement for *very* ("I am *so* warm"). In better English, certainly in written English, such statements should conclude with a *that* explanation; for example, "I'm so warm *that* I would like to jump into the pool."

so-called

How should the expression *so-called* be treated?

Hyphenate it when it precedes a noun—a so-called broker—but not afterward, "He is a broker, so called." The noun following *so-called* should not be put in quotation marks, not a so-called "broker."

Note: The expression *so-called* may imply sarcasm or irony. The context should make clear whether this was the writer's intention ("He's a so-called champion tennis player"). *So-called* means called by this term or so designated.

so far as

The sentence read: "So far as weight loss, this diet is effective." I'm left up in the air. What do you think?

You feel that way because the sentence is incomplete. Missing are the words *is concerned*—"So far as weight loss *is concerned*, this diet is effective." Words necessary to the sense of the sentence must not be omitted.

Note: Expressions must be complete or else they may make no sense. The curtailed statement "He couldn't cope," often heard these days, is an example of an incomplete thought. It should be, say, "He couldn't cope with personnel problems."

So far as may be contrasted with *as far as*. The first suggests a limitation, which may be of one's knowledge ("*So far as* I know, Andrew was not a sculptor"). The second suggests distance ("We ran *as far as* we could").

solely

Should this sentence be corrected: "The mayor's action was solely beneficial to his family"?

Like adverbs *only* and *even*, *solely* should be placed immediately before the word or phrase to be modified. Make it "The mayor's action was beneficial *solely* to his family."

Note: The inexact placement of *solely* may cause only momentary confusion, but even that should be avoided where possible. Regardless of that concern, it is neater to place *solely* where it properly belongs.

solvable/soluble

Should I say, "My problem is not easily *soluble* (or *solvable*)"?

Either word, meaning capable of being resolved or explained, is acceptable and each has its supporters. But usually *solvable* is used in reference to problems and *soluble* to substances in solvents. "Salt is *soluble* in water."

some

1. Is it wrong to say, "Some 346 students were there"?
The word *some* does not belong, since *some* means approximately ("more or less"). It therefore is incongruous when placed next to an exact figure.

2. Is *some* in "He certainly has grown some" and in "The day warmed up some" used correctly?
This usage of *some* sounds dialectal. Prefer *somewhat,* which means some part, amount, degree, and so forth.

3. The newspaper report said, "Some man walked up to Paul Watson and asked for directions." Is *some* a proper descriptive there?
It is not. The report would have improved wording if "*A* man" had been used instead of "*Some* man." The word *some* might have been chosen to indicate that the man was unknown. But it was not a good choice.

somehow or other

What objection is there to saying, "Somehow or other we'll get the work done"?
In general speech and informal writing, there is none. The *or other* emphasizes *somehow,* and this usage is idiomatically accepted, as is *sometime or other.* In formal prose *or other* should be dropped.

sometime/some time

Which is correct: "I shall arrive *sometime* (or *some time*) after four o'clock"?
The word required in the example is *sometime,* an adverb that refers to an indefinite occasion or expresses an indefinite time. An example is "Why not visit us *sometime* soon?" Two-word *some time* consists of an adjective and a noun. This form indicates an indefinite period of time ("The accountant said he would require *some time* to handle so voluminous a job").

> Note: A test to determine whether to use the adverb or the combination is to omit it from the sentence. If the sentence makes sense without it, as it does in "Why not visit us soon?" *sometime* is called for, even though unnecessary. If without it the sentence sounds nonsensical, then *some time* is required. For example, in "The accountant said he would require

some time to handle the voluminous job," the sentence would not survive without that adjective and noun. Try it.

Sometimes means an undetermined number of times ("Diane *sometimes* comes on Mondays instead of Tuesdays"). A plural adverb is unusual.

sort of a

Please criticize my daughter's favorite remark: "He's the sort of a man I'd like to marry."

The expression *sort of a* is not desirable on any count. First, prefer *kind* to *sort* or reword entirely. Second, since *kind* (and *sort* in a way) indicates a class, *a* does not belong. Say *sort of,* if you must, not *sort of a.*

Note: Some authorities do approve of *sort of a* because the expression has been used by reputable writers. But the best advice is not to follow *sort* with *a* or *an.* We must remember that even reputable writers make mistakes once in a while. Let us not use their errors to justify ours.

so that

In the sentence "Martha cooked all day so that there would be food enough for a week," should a comma precede *so that*?

No. The subordinate clause introduced by *so that* is a clause of purpose and therefore takes no punctuation. A clause of purpose is one that is essential to the sense of the sentence and is not, therefore, to be separated from the main clause. A test is to see whether "in order that" can logically replace *so that.* If it can (and it can in the example), the clause is a clause of purpose. A clause of result takes a comma: "She had heard Clifford lecture before, *so that* she was familiar with his style of presentation (*in order that* cannot sensibly replace *so that*). When *consequently, with the result that,* or *therefore* can replace *so that,* the clause it introduces is one of result.

Note: When words intervene between *so* and *that,* even though introducing a clause of result, no comma is used because the clause is considered essential to the meaning of the sentence: "The project is *so* far advanced *that* there is no turning back."

specie/species

Is it incorrect to speak of a certain specie of antelope?

Yes, use *species,* which refers to a classification in biology. *Specie* is hard money, coins. Caveat: *Specie* has no plural. *Species* is both a singular and a plural form ("This *species is* rare; those *species are* rarer").

Note: The word *specious* is not related to either *specie* or *species.* It means seemingly desirable, reasonable, or probable, but not really so.

spelling

1. Is *acknowledgment* or *acknowledgement* the approved spelling?
Both spellings are seen, but the preference is, when adding -*ment* to the base word *acknowledge*, to drop the terminal *e*: *acknowledgment*. And so with *judgment* and *abridgment*. But note that the *e* is retained before suffix -*able*: *acknowledgeable*.

2. My chief spelling problem is remembering whether a word ends in -*ary* or -*ery*. Can you help me?
To lick your problem just remember that the important words ending in -*ery* are *cemetery, confectionery, distillery, millinery, monastery,* and *stationery* (writing material). All the others end in -*ary*.

3. The plural of *attorney* is *attorneys*. The plural of *pony* is *ponies*. Why this difference in spelling?
Nouns ending in *y* form their plural by adding *s* if the *y* is preceded by a vowel (*attorneys, monkeys*) but by dropping the *y* and adding *ies* if the *y* is preceded by a consonant (*ponies, supplies*).

4. Is the plural of *bus*, a vehicle for transporting people, spelled *buses* or *busses*?
The former. Do not double the *s: buses, bused, busing. Bussing*, which means kissing, uses two: *busses, bussed, bussing*. Remember that kissing always needs two.
   Note: Monosyllablic words ending in a consonant double the final consonant when -*ed* or -*ing* is affixed (*bat, batted, batting; bug, bugged, bugging*). This convention has been bypassed with *bus*, a vehicle, to avoid confusion with *buss*, a kiss. The word for *kiss* follows the conventional forms throughout. *Bus* is a clipped form of Latin *omnibus*, meaning "for all," a vehicle designed to accommodate everyone.

5. Which is the correct spelling: *commonsense* or *common sense*?
Either spelling is correct. The adjective is spelled as one word ("a *commonsense* plan"). Two words are required when used as an adjective and noun ("John is known for his *common sense*").

6. Which is preferred, for *conscience' sake* or for *conscience's sake*?
The former. Eliminating the *s* eliminates an additional syllable. The rule applies to other *for . . . sake* constructions where the word preceding *sake* ends in a sibilant: *for justice' sake, for goodness' sake, for righteousness' sake*. Some stylists drop the apostrophe as well. They would write *for conscience sake*, with no *s* and no apostrophe.

7. When an adjective ending in *e* is converted into an adverb, what happens to the *e*?
It depends on the word involved. In most cases the final *e* is retained: *rare, rarely; severe, severely; negative, negatively*. But in these words the *e* is dropped: *true, truly; horrible, horribly; possible, possibly; whole, wholly*.

8. Which word in the English language do you think is the most

embarrassing to misspell?
I elect embarrass. To spell it *embarass* is most *embarrassing*.

9. Should *fiancé* and *fiancée* be written with acute marks?
They need not be, but preferably they should be. Most writers use the marks because these accents indicate that there are three syllables and that the third one should be distinctly pronounced. The marks help those unfamiliar with French rules of pronunciation. And they do create a panache that would otherwise be missing. Dictionary entries retain the accents.

> **Note:** Some foreign words keep their diacritical marks for the sake of proper pronunciation. For example, *résumé* is clearly distinguished from *resume* (to continue) because of the acute accents, even though *résumé* (a summary) is now considered an anglicized word and therefore needs no accent marks. But preferably the accent marks should be retained. Note that *resume* has two syllables, whereas *résumé* has three.

10. Which spelling is correct—*filet* or *fillet*?
They're both correct. But except when meaning "lace" or "filet mignon," use the double *l—fillet* (a slice of boneless meat or fish).

11. What formula governs the pluralizing of foreign words?
None. You must consult a dictionary unless you already know what to do. Some foreign words retain the foreign plural (*alumnus, alumni; addendum, addenda; datum, data*); others offer a choice (*curriculum: curricula* or *curriculums; stratum: strata* or *stratums; memorandum: memoranda* or *memorandums*).

12. Should we write "There are three *four's* (or *fours*) in twelve"?
The latter, "three fours," because the word has a meaning in that sentence. But write "There are three *four's* in the title," since plural *four's* is referred to as a word, not for its meaning.

13. Is *fulfil* or *fulfill* the correct spelling of the verb?
These spellings are regarded as variants. However, the former spelling predominates: *fulfil*.

> **Note:** Avoid these spellings: *fullfill* and *fullfil*.

14. Do I add an *s* to *ful* when I replenish my spoon with ice cream?
Yes, you are taking two *spoonfuls*. The plural of nouns ending in *-ful* are formed by adding a final *s*. There's no such word as *spoonsful*. Two-word *spoons full* means several spoons filled once. *Spoonfuls* means one spoon refilled.

> **Note:** The words most commonly seen ending in *-ful*, in addition to *spoonfuls*, are *cupfuls, handfuls,* and *teaspoonfuls*.

15. Which two common words do you think are most often misspelled?
I nominate *gauge* (often written *guage*) and *siege* (very often written *seige*).

Note: *Gauge* is occasionally seen spelled *gage*, a spelling listed as a variant in some dictionaries. It is best to avoid that spelling. A clue to the proper spelling of *siege* is think of the siege of Singapore. Both *siege* and *Singapore* begin with an *si*. A word that is in a close race with *gauge* and *siege* is the title of an ancient Egyptian king. Some people struggle to find it in the dictionary because they are misspelling it. It is *pharaoh*, not *pharoah*.

16. Why are the words *genealogy* and *mineralogy* so frequently misspelled?
Probably because they are mispronounced *geneology* and *minerology*. Note that those words have an *a* in the center, not an *o*.

17. Which is the correct spelling: *inadvisable* or *unadvisable*?
The correct spelling is *inadvisable*. But note *undiscriminating*, not *indiscriminating*. Yet we say *indiscriminate*, which proves how careful we must be with the prefixes meaning "not," *in-* and *un-*.

18. The sentence read, "Incidently, it happened accidently." Why do these misspellings occur so frequently?
Whoever pronounces the words that way is likely to follow suit when writing them. Of course the correct forms, in either speech or writing, are *incidentally* and *accidentally*.

19. What is the plural of *idiosyncrasy*? I have seen it spelled several ways.
The plural of *idiosyncrasy*, "a personal peculiarity," is one of the most misspelled words in the English language. It is not spelled *idiosyncracies*, as is often seen, but *idiosyncrasies*. Its final syllable is *sies*, not *cies*.

20. My question is, What are the approved forms: *in so far as, insofar as; in as much as, inasmuch as; none the less, nonetheless*?
Most critics sanction *insofar as*, but a few prefer separate words. Others point out that *in* is superfluous and write *so far as* open ("*So far as* we have heard, the game has been canceled"; "*So far as* we know, it will not happen"). Almost all, if not all, write *inasmuch as* and *nonetheless* as just given—solid.

> **Note:** There is little consensus on the proper use of *insofar as* or its spelling. The guide to follow is the authority whose opinions you most respect. In British English four words are used, *in so far as*, and some American writers prefer that spelling, too. But *inasmuch as*, with only two words, is standard in both British and American English. *Nonetheless* appears as three words, (*none the less*) in older American writings. But those words have coalesced during the last sixty years and have become a solid word.

21. Why do some people call the preschool class *kindergarden*?
Probably because, in German, *Garten* means garden. The correct word, of course is *kindergarten*, "a garden for children."

22. Do we write, "I was *leary* (or *leery*) about his proposition"?

The correct spelling for the word to be suspicious, distrustful, or wary is spelled *leery*. Think of *leer*, a sly look, which was the forebear of *leery*. But note that *leery* is an informal term and should be avoided in higher level discourse.

23. Do you agree that nothing is more embarrassing than to "mispell" the word *misspell*?
Agreed. One must be careful to use a double *s* and a double *l*. But note *dispel*. It has only one *s* and one *l*.

24. I don't know how to form the plural of words ending in *o* (*volcano, studio*). Can you help me?
Add only *s* to words ending in *io* or *eo* (*cameos, radios*), to musical terms (*sopranos, banjos*), clipped words (*photos*), and new words (*commandos*). Otherwise, *es* (*potatoes, cargoes, heroes*). And then to be safe, check with a speller.

25. How can I keep the spellings of *palate* and *palette* straight?
Remember that what you ate has passed your *pal-ate*, a part of your mouth, which leaves *palette*, a paintboard, as the other spelling. Another but less common homophone is *pallet*, a small, poor bed with no springs. Note the double *l* in the word.

26. A sign said, "Take a *parttime* job as a *passtime*." Are those words spelled correctly?
The word *parttime*, yes, but it is preferably hyphenated: *part-time*. *Passtime*, no. Although the word is a combination of *pass* and *time*, it uses only one *s*, *pastime*, not *passtime*.

27. What is the plural of *phenomenon*: *phenomena*, *phenomenas*, or *phenomenons*?
The accepted plural, meaning remarkable occurrences, is *phenomena*.

28. I see the islands that Marcos left spelled *Philipine*, *Phillipine*, *Phillippine*, and *Philippine*. How can we sure to spell the name correctly?
Remember that the islands were named for King Philip II of Spain, whose name has one *l* and ends with one *p*. Hence *Philippine* Islands — *Philip-pine* Islands.

29. Why is the past tense of *picnic* spelled *picnicked*?
A *k* is inserted before the suffixes *-ed* and *-ing* to make for easier pronunciation. And so with *traffic* (*trafficked, trafficking*); *panic* (*panicked, panicking*); *frolic* (*frolicked, frolicking*); *politic* (*politicked, politicking*).

30. Is *prophesize* an accepted variant spelling of *prophesy*?
Not to my knowledge. And even if it were, it would still be preferable to spell the verb *prophesy*. Observe that its past tense is *prophesied*, not *prophesized*.

Note: Be careful of the spelling of the noun and the verb forms because, except for one letter, they are spelled alike. The word meaning a prediction is noun *prophecy*. It rhymes with *see*. The verb *prophesy*, "to predict," rhymes with *sigh*.

31. Is there a simple way of remembering how to spell the "seed" words—*succeed, intercede,* and so on?

The only way is to embed them deeply in your memory. But you may note that only one word ends in *sede: supersede;* three words end in *ceed: exceed, proceed, succeed;* all the others in *cede: accede, precede,* and so forth.

> **Note:** The parent of the *ceed* and *cede* words is Latin *cedere*, "to go." The last syllable of *supersede (sede)* is from Latin *sedere*, "to sit," which means that combined with *super*, "above," *supersede* literally means "to sit on top." It is used in English, however, to mean to displace, to supplant, or to take the place of. *Supersede* is the most often misspelled of the "seed" words. Observe that it does not end in *cede* but in *sede*.

32. Why do we brush our teeth with a *toothbrush* instead of a *teethbrush*?

The first unit of two nouns that have been compounded is never pluralized. Thus we say *toothbrush,* not *teethbrush; footstool,* not *feetstool; man-hater,* not *men-hater.*

33. Should the past tense of *travel* be spelled *traveled* or *travelled*?

It should be spelled with one *l: traveled.* Also *traveling,* not *travelling.* The double *l* is British style.

> **Note:** *Cancel* is another word that should not have its *l* doubled when adding *-ed* or *-ing (canceled, canceling)*. However, its noun form is spelled with a double *l: cancellation.* The American rule is that with two-syllable words, the final consonant is doubled when adding *-ed* or *-ing* provided the consonant is preceded by a single vowel and the second syllable is stressed. Hence *infer, inferred, inferring.* But with *travel* and *cancel* the stress is on the first syllable. A word often misspelled with a double *l* is *marshal.* Whether used as a noun ("He is the *marshal* of the parade") or a verb ("He *marshaled* all the resources"), it should not be spelled *marshall,* but *marshal.*

spirituous/spiritual

My friend often confuses the words *spirituous* and *spiritual*. How do you define them?

Spirituous means containing alcohol. *Spiritual* pertains to that which affects the spirit or soul. Perhaps your friend would be more spiritual by becoming less spirituous-minded.

spit/expectorate

Do *spit* and *expectorate* mean the same thing?

The words are synonyms, but not exactly so. To *spit* is to expel saliva;

to *expectorate* (Latin *ex*, "from"; *pectus*, "chest"), to cough up phlegm from the chest.

split infinitives

Has the fuss over split infinitives subsided?

The general rule remains. Infinitives should not be split needlessly. But a split infinitive is preferable to a clumsy or vague construction. Infinitives are sometimes purposely split to emphasize the adverb — "to *strongly* criticize," "to *thoroughly* disregard."

> Note: There is no logical or grammatical reason why an infinitive should not be split. The rule against splitting grew up a long time ago simply because splitting an infinitive was impossible in Latin grammar. A Latin infinitive is a solid word. Fowler in 1926 destroyed the grammatical fetish against splitting, and, although the general rule is still widely observed, a sensible latitude has evolved: Splitting is desirable if the sentence gains in emphasis, smoothness, or clarity. An example is "She called *to quickly assure* her father she was safe." Do not hesitate to split in such combinations as "to readily understand" or "to fully intend."

squinters

How do grammarians evaluate a sentence like "To come late to work often militates against advancement"?

The question the sentence raises is whether *often* modifies verb *come* or verb *militates* ("to *come* late *often*" or "*often militates*"). Modifiers so placed — that can modify either a preceding or a following verb — are called squinters. To clarify the meaning of such a sentence, either split the infinitive (*to often come late*, in the example) or recast entirely.

> Note: Squinting modifiers create a more serious hazard to clarity than does the split infinitive or the dangling participle. A writer must be particularly careful not to sandwich an adverb between two verbs, so that the reader cannot know which verb is being modified. It is difficult, if not impossible, to determine what is meant in "How my wife wrote a story *completely* baffles me." "Oscar ran home *happily* calling for his dog." "The physician told his patient *frequently* to walk."

stalagmites/stalactites

How can we tell by the spelling of the words which way *stalagmites* and *stalactites* form?

In *stalagmite* there is a *g*. *Stalagmites* rise from the "ground." In *stalactite* there is a *c*. *Stalactites* hang from the "ceiling."

state

Is the word *state* a good choice in "I heard our cousins state that we should leave now"?

I think not. The word *state* in ordinary discourse sounds pretentious. In the example it is being inappropriately used for simple *say*. Reserve *state* for formal declarations and state occasions.

stationary/stationery

The sound-alikes *stationary* and *stationery* are often confused. How can I keep them straight?

You may note that the vowels in the words *letter* and *envelope* are *e*'s. and that the final vowel of collective noun *stationery*, which consists of letters and envelopes, is also an *e*. The adjective meaning a fixed position is *stationary*. It has no *e*'s.

stay

In better English should we say, "We will *stay* home tonight" or "*stay at* home," or doesn't it matter?

In formal prose, verbs that do not imply motion, such as *stay* and *remain*, take the preposition *at* (stay *at* home, remain *at* work).

stimulus/stimulant

Are the words *stimulus* and *stimulant* interchangeable?

Stimulus, the more general word, refers to anything that urges or rouses a person to action. It might be an incentive such as an extra week's vacation. A *stimulant* is something that temporarily quickens bodily action or mental process. It may be coffee or a potent drug.

Note: A stimulant has a short life. A stimulus can continue indefinitely. The plural of *stimulant* is *stimulants.* The plural of *stimulus* is *stimuli.*

stop/stay

Is it better to say, "I'm *stopping* (or *staying*) in St. Louis"?

You may *stop* in St. Louis on your way to Denver, but if you remain for a time, then, properly, you are *staying* there. To *stop* is to cease moving; to *stay* is to remain for a time.

Note: Although informal writing prefers *stay* to *stop* where "continue in the place" is meant, many, if not most, people pay little attention to it. Frequently you will hear even educated people say that they are stopping at such and such hotel for the next few days. The justification might be that while there, the hotel is their *stopover* — and so they are stopping there.

straightjacket/straitjacket

Is the jacket that violent criminals are placed in called a *straightjacket* or a *straitjacket*?

The latter, since it is restraining or confining, which is a sense of *strait*. A *straightjacket* would be one with no curves or wrinkles.

> Note: The only thing that *strait* and *straight* have in common is pronunciation. *Strait*, in its comparison here with *straight*, means tight or narrow (*strait* is used figuratively to mean prudish, as is a *strait-laced* person). Dictionaries accept *straightjacket* as a variant of *straitjacket*. Careful writers reject that variant.

subjunctive

I know that an untrue assertion is placed in the subjunctive mood. But I sometimes see such an assertion placed in the indicative. How do you explain that oddity?

It is not an oddity. True it is that an untrue or hypothetical condition is framed in the subjunctive mood: "*If I were* the boss, I'd vacation every other week." But I'm not. That condition refers to present time: "If I were the boss" means now. But an untrue simple condition that refers to past time (with a singular verb) takes the indicative form *was:* "If I *was* absent from the meeting, I must have been out of town."

> Note: More often *if* is followed by *were* than *was*, just because usually an untrue statement is being made, or, as is said, a condition contrary to fact. As previously pointed out, however, *if* may introduce a simple statement that will take the indicative. To cite another example, "If the doctor was not in his office, he was at the hospital." According to that statement, we do not know whether the doctor was in his office. He may have been there, but then again, he may not have been there. The statement does not assert a condition contrary to fact, and therefore takes the indicative form *was*. The phrasing *if I were* is possibly the subjunctive's last stand. The mood is fast disappearing. As Fowler said: "Subjunctives are nearly dead. . . ."
>
> A caveat is not to permit *would have* in *if* clauses to oust *were*. Not "If I would have been you, I . . . ," but "If I were you, I . . ." or "If I had been you, I. . . ."
>
> The combinations *as if* and *as though* always imply a condition or a hypothesis and should therefore be couched in the subjunctive ("The hospital is being run *as though* it *were* a country club").

substitute

We were told that the designer planned to substitute blue jeans with a more conservative style of dress. My question is, Were we told right?

You were not told in the best English. Verb *substitute*, when a preposition is called for, must be *for*, and no other. To *substitute* means to put in the place of. For that purpose the only combination is *substitute for*.

> Note: A synonym of *substitute* is *replace*. It means to take the place of. Although *substitute* may take only *for*, idiom has given *replace* a choice of

prepositions—*by* and *with*. Usually *by* is more suitable and is therefore more commonly used: "The Webster dictionary will be *replaced by* an American Heritage dictionary." Some grammarians contend that *replace* is not an exact synonym for *substitute* and therefore may not replace it, no matter what preposition follows. Others maintain, and the weight of authority is on their side, that although *replace* does mean to put back in the same place, which has no synonymity with *substitute*, another meaning of *replace* is supersede and to find a substitute for. These latter meanings accord with the meaning of *substitute*.

success

1. May one say, correctly, "Armand is a success"?
It depends on the authority you consult. Some authorities say that the word *success* should not refer to the person or thing that is successful. According to them, you must, at least in formal English, say, "Armand has been a successful architect," or whatever. Other authorities, including dictionaries, take a more lenient attitude.

2. Our boss said, "The initial phase of the project was a successful achievement." Something sounds wrong to me.
What sounds wrong is the phrase "a successful achievement" because that combination is redundant. An *achievement* cannot be a failure. All achievements are successful. *Successful* should have been deleted.

3. The newspaper account said, "The Secretary succeeded to keep control of the department." What is your opinion of that statement?
The sentence is poorly constructed, since *succeed* may not be followed by an infinitive. It should have read, "The Secretary *succeeded* in *keeping* control of the department."

4. A major journal reported that the Japanese had successfully developed a chip that will be competitive worldwide. Was that sentence faulty?
It was because of the unneccessary inclusion of *successfully*. One cannot develop something unsuccessfully.

such

1. Is it proper to say, "We have never seen such wonderful sights"?
Such, primarily an adjective, is being used here as an adverb, and on that ground has been derided by many grammarians. But this use has taken hold and is now idiomatically acceptable, the way other adjective forms are used as intensives.
   Note: Traditionalists will not accept the adverbial use of *such*. They would recast: "We have never seen sights so wonderful."

2. What is to be thought of the word *such* in "Chemistry is *such* a fascinating subject"?

Such is not to be used as a mere intensive. Use *very* instead ("Chemistry is a *very* fascinating subject") or follow *such* with a *that* clause ("Chemistry is *such* a fascinating subject *that* everyone should study it").

> **Note:** The combination *such a* is acceptable when it modifies a noun that is followed by a *that* clause ("It was *such a* hot day *that* even the air-conditioner did no good"). If *that* is not used, drop *such a*. A negative statement takes no *a*: "There is *no such* person as Santa Claus," not *no such a*.

such as

1. What are the general rules for the proper use of *such as*?

Such as requires a noun for completion: "I like sports, *such as* baseball." It does not belong before a prepositional phrase. Not "*such as* for traveling" but "*as* for traveling." Not "*such as* in promotions" but "*as* in promotions."

2. Where should *such as* be placed in a sentence?

Immediately after the word it qualifies. Do not, for example, say, "Citrus fruits are hard to peel, such as grapefruit." A grapefruit is not a peel. Say, "Citrus fruits such as grapefruit are hard to peel."

3. The speaker said, "Athletes are such men who know the value of nutritious foods." Do you approve of this wording?

The combination *such . . . who* is objectionable, as is *such . . . where* and *such . . . which*. The correct formula is *such . . . as* ("Athletes are *such* men *as* know . . .").

4. If you say, "I know many 'beauties' like Elizabeth Taylor," would Ms. Taylor be included in that group?

She would not, since *like* means similarly or similar to. This means the "beauties" are similar to her, but she is not among them. To include Ms. Taylor, say, "I know many 'beauties' *such as* Elizabeth Taylor."

suffer

Does a person suffer *from* or *with* an illness?

A person suffers *from* an illness or disability, not *with* it, since the trouble itself does not suffer — "Tom suffers *from* (not *with*) arthritis."

suppose/expect

1. Is *suppose* the equivalent of *expect*?

It is best to reserve the use of *suppose* to its meaning of guess and of *expect* to its meaning of count upon or look forward to. If you expect to go to the ball game tonight, be precise and say, "I expect to go," not "I suppose I will go."

Note: In the sense of expect, *suppose,* although regarded as informal, has had a long history and a widespread usage. Moreover, some authorities even go so far as to label it standard. But most critics do not agree, contending that it has an air of informality that has not as yet been dissipated.

2. How often have I read, "We are suppose to leave early." Is this usage now established?

Not in the least. The word *suppose* there was simply a slurring of *supposed* ("We are *supposed* to leave early").

sure/surely

Would this sentence be accepted in literary prose: "We sure swam fast today"?

Colloquial usage does not belong in formal discourse. *Sure* is an adjective; *surely,* an adverb. Since the modifier of *swam,* an active verb, must be an adverb, *surely* is the word required.

Note: Undoubtedly many educated people use adjective *sure* where adverb *surely* belongs. We often hear statements like "We *sure* will call you soon"; "He *sure* is right"; and "I'm *sure* glad to see you." In all these cases, *surely* is the grammatically required word.

This same problem is prevalent with adjective *real,* frequently used instead of adverb *really.* We hear "Antoinette played the piano *real* well"; "It's *real* cloudy today"; "This pie is *real* good." The word called for in each example is *really* or *very.* Or perhaps *certainly.*

sustain

Is there an objection to the word *sustain* in "If he continues to play football, he's bound to sustain serious injury"?

Sustain in this sense is in such widespread usage that almost everyone must use it occasionally. However, the traditional definition of *sustain* is to bear or carry for a long time. Figuratively, therefore, to endure without breaking under the strain is to sustain unyieldingly ("The city could easily *sustain* a three-month drought"). This sense is inapplicable to one who has received severe injuries. That person is not sustaining; he or she is suffering.

Note: The synonyms *suffer, receive, get,* and *undergo* are everyday words and preferable to *sustain* where they will do. "My son's left shin was bruised" sounds less elegant but is simpler and more desirable than "My son *sustained* a bruise. . . ." And so with *got* rather than *sustained* in "The damages I *got* from that sideswipe. . . ." The advantage of using an everyday word is that it avoids possible criticism from those who refuse to equate *sustain* with *suffer* — and there are many.

swap

May the word *swap* be used on all levels of writing?
The word *swap* (variant spelling *swop*), originally a slang term, has not yet been admitted into standard English by most discerning writers. However, it has its place in everyday English. In formal discourse the word to use is *exchange*.

swum

I heard a commentator say, "She swum the English Channel." Is *swum* an English word?
It is a variant form of *swam,* the past tense of *swim,* but regarded by many critics and lexicologists as dialectal. The same form, however, is recognized as standard for the past participle of *swim* ("She *had swum* the Channel last year").

synonyms

To avoid monotony, is it better to use a synonym for a word rather than repeat the word?
Be the judge. Bear in mind that repetition of itself is not objectionable, and a synonym may mislead. Many synonyms do not have exact meanings; their similarity may be shades away. Fowler pointed out that conspicuous variation is more to be decried than repetition.

T

talisman

Is it true that the plural of *talisman* is not *talismen*?
Yes. The plural of *talisman*, an object thought to have magical powers, is *talismans*. It is one of the few compounds of "man" that is not converted to "men" in the plural.

temperature

Is it in good English to say, "I kept my boy home because he had a temperature"?
Precisely speaking, since everyone has a body temperature, one should say "because he had a fever." But since "has a temperature" is the way most of us say it, it would be expecting too much, except perhaps on the highest levels of prose, to say anything different.

terribly

Since "It is terribly hot" is a common expression, is *terribly* a terrible word?
This sense, meaning very bad, is regarded as a colloquialism. *Terribly* means in a manner that causes fear or alarm, which cannot be said of a hot day. In careful speech prefer "It's *very* (or *extremely*) hot" to "It's *terribly* hot." Do not use *terribly* to intensify a point.

than

What pitfalls should be guarded against when using the word *than*?
Avoid "It is *different than* the others"—*from*; "The athlete is much *superior than* all the rest"—*to*; "Red is *preferable than* maroon"—*to*; "He had *hardly* entered *than* the bell rang"—*when*.

> **Note:** A pitfall involving conjunction *than* that must be viewed carefully is the case after a comparative. The case following *than* should be the same as the antecedent. In "Tom likes Anne more *than* I," *I* is in the nominative case because, spelled out, the sentence would read "more than I like Anne." But if Tom had a preference for Anne over me, then objective case *me* would be required: "Tom likes Anne more than *me*," since the comparison would be between *Anne and me*. Be particularly careful when a noun follows *than*. "Tom likes me more than Anne" may mean that Tom is fonder of me than he is of Anne or that Tom likes me more than Anne likes me. It is best to recast this kind of sentence.

than whom

What justifies the combination *than whom*?

Idiom. Conjunction *than* normally takes the same case after it as before it. But *than whom* in "Ralph, *than whom* no one worked harder, died yesterday" is an idiomatic expression, which, of course, needs no logical reason to justify it.

> **Note:** Many grammarians believe that *whom*, the objective case of *who*, is on its way to oblivion. Almost everyone uses *who* where *whom* belongs without giving any thought to it: "Hubert is the athlete *who* I like best"; "*Who* do you wish to see?" rather than the correct forms "*whom* I like" and "*Whom* do you wish to see?" But two combinations will, in the opinion of all grammatical prophets, survive. One is *to whom* ("*To whom* it may concern"); the other is *for whom* ("*For whom* the bell tolls"). Still another, reverting to the initial example, is idiomatic *than whom*.

that

1. The sentence read: "Suppose they wonder where we went?" Shouldn't *that* follow *suppose*?

The use of *that* as a conjunction is unnecessary in informal speech and writing. In fact, sentences move more smoothly without it. The best advice is, except in strict formal writing, to omit *that* if its omission does not harm the sense of the sentence.

> **Note:** Let euphony be the guide when determining whether *that* should be used before a nounal clause. Its use is never wrong, but its presence is usually not needed except where necessary to indicate time or date in a sentence such as "Hammerman said when Roger slowed his pace, he began to lose the race." A *that* after *said* would indicate that Hammerman did not say it when Roger slowed but said it later: "Hammerman said *that* when Roger slowed his pace. . . . " The rule: *That* must precede an adverbial clause of time and follow *said* when the clause is part of what was said. Here is another example of a sentence that needs correcting: "The economist said last month conditions began improving." The economist's statement was not made last month. The economic conditions began improving last month. Correctly put is "The economist said *that* last month. . . . "

2. Is this sentence to be criticized: "Mr. Feduce said that when the dogs return that he will feed them promptly"?

The second *that* should be omitted. Since there is only one noun clause, there should be only one *that*.

3. How is the plural of *that* expressed? Do we say, "There were too many *thats*"?

Most stylists would add to *that* an apostrophe and *s*: *that's*. Some words have established meanings in the plural and take no apostrophe: *pros* and *cons*; *whys* and *wherefores*; *yeses* and *noes*.

that/which

Our English teacher is distraught when we use *that* for *which* or vice versa. To help our teacher keep her sanity and to help us pass the course, please explain the difference in usage between *that* and *which*.

Your question is well written and accurately put. The answer is to employ *that* to introduce a restrictive clause — a clause that defines the subject by providing necessary information to fully understand the sentence: "It is a book *that* everyone needs." There the *that* clause is essential to meaning, for without it, the sentence would make no sense. However, in "The brown book, *which* is the third one on the shelf, is useful to everyone," the nonrestrictive *which* clause could be removed without impairing the basic meaning of the sentence. Note that a *that* clause is not set off by commas, whereas a *which* clause is.

> **Note:** Writers agree that it is stylistically preferable to omit the conjunction *that* where its omission makes for a smoother sentence: "We all say (no *that*) we must write"; "Alfred knows (no *that*) he cannot succeed." The question now raised is whether this convention applies to relative pronoun *that* as well? The answer: *that* may be omitted, but under different circumstances — where it is the object in a restrictive clause: "The house (no *that*) Johnnie bought is a bungalow." And it does not belong in "The sooner *that* we start, the happier we will be" because it has no antecedent. Adverb *sooner* modifies the verb *start*.
>
> One more idea. In a restrictive clause in which *that* or *which* takes a preposition, the preposition must come at the end of the sentence if *that* is used, but it may be interred within the sentence if *which* is used. For example, "It was a bad situation *that* he found himself *in*" may be converted into "It was a bad situation *in which* he found himself." Although the latter phrasing seems more dignified, the former is smoother. And there is nothing wrong in ending a sentence with a preposition.
>
> Afterthought. When choosing between *who* and *that* when persons are designated, prefer *who* to signify the individual and *that* to signify the group or kind, which is an indefinite number of people, a generic reference. We speak of the man *who* is the owner of the shop, for he is an individual, but of the man *that* refuses to vote, a type or class of man.

the

I understand that one should use a plural verb if two persons hold different positions, as in "The vice-president and controller *are* both here," and yet I was criticized. Why?

You omitted an essential *the*. You should have said: "The vice-president and *the* controller *are* both here."

> **Note:** The article *the* must be repeated before each person or thing when two or more persons or things are referred to in a compound subject or object. If one thing or person is referred to ("Thompson is the secretary and treasurer"), *the* is used before the first only. When two adjectives

modify a plural noun ("The fourth and fifth *chapters* have been written"), only one *the* is required, but if *the* is repeated, the noun must be singular ("*The* fourth and *the* fifth *chapter* have been written").

The primary function of *the* is to specify a particular thing, whereas the articles *a* and *an* designate one of a class. Do not capitalize *the*, even though part of the title, when the syntax requires a *the*. Not "We all read *The New York Times*," but "We all read the *New York Times*."

theirs

"I recognize Elmys' house, but my friend does not know it's their's."
What might be said about all that?

The possessive pronoun *their* never takes an apostrophe. Make it *theirs*. Do not allow a previous apostrophized possessive — Elmys' — to mislead you.

> **Note:** There is no such form as *their's:* "This house is *theirs*"; "*Theirs* is the prettiest house on the street." The possessive forms for *ours, his, hers*, and *its* are all written as just given, with no apostrophe.

then

I read: "Hawkins, the then Senator." The word *then* sounds peculiar.
Is it being used correctly?

It is, since *then* is serving as an adjective before the noun *Senator*. But it does sound peculiar. Another wording would be preferable.

> **Note:** *Then* usually serves as an adverb meaning at that time ("Hawkins was *then* the Senator"). Be careful not to confuse *then* with *than*, a conjunction used to make comparisons. Do not say, for example, "Esther swam better today *then* she did last week," but "*than* she did last week."

there is/there are

Do good writers begin sentences with "*There is*" or "*There are?*"

Occasionally, I'm sure. But they avoid this construction, called an expletive, wherever possible. Expletive *there* delays the true subject — "*There are* many patients waiting" needs only "Many patients are waiting."

> **Note:** Expletives *there* (*there are*) and *it* (*it is*) are filler words used to introduce intransitive verbs: "*There* are more books here than we need"; "*It* is the hour for lunch." Whether expletive *there* should be followed by *is* or *are* (or *was* or *were*) depends on the number of the deferred subject; that is, the following noun or pronoun. Use *is* if it is singular. Use *are* if it is plural or if followed by two or more singular nouns or pronouns. "*There is* a tavern in the town." "*There are* four boxes on the shelf." It is a person's choice whether to use *is* or *are* in a series of nouns when the first one is singular. Although technically a plural is required (*are, were*), the attraction of the initial singular noun may justify a singular verb. "*There is* a book, a pen, two pencils, and a ruler on the desk."

thing

I hear the word *thing* replacing all sorts of nouns. What do you think of it?

I prefer a definite noun if one is available. Rather than "A Florida sunset is a beautiful *thing* to behold," say, ". . . a beautiful *sight* to behold." Rather than "The *thing* I like about him is his smile," say, "His smile is his distinctive feature" or simply "I like his smile." There is no end to the use of *thing* as an all-purpose word. Omit it if possible. Its inclusion does not make for an effective or graphic sentence.

think

A frequent remark is something like "I was thinking to myself that I should call Aunt Leona." What is your opinion of that?

The words "to myself" are unnecessary because that is the only way a person can think. You can't think "to someone else." Grammarians say that "think to myself" is tautological. Scrub "to myself."

Note: Do not follow *think* with *that*. Say, "I think he is competent," not "I think *that* he is competent." *Think* followed by an infinitive is an unacceptable colloquialism. Avoid such expressions as "Did you *think to close* the gate?" Whether *feel* may replace *think* is a matter of controversy. Many distinguished writers have equated *feel* with *think* and some authorities approve of this synonymity ("I *feel* we ought to visit Aunt Leona"). What advantage *feel*, a word that applies to emotions, has over *think*, which applies to cerebral activity, is hard to see. Certainly "I *think* we ought to visit Aunt Leona" is as easy to put together and is more precise. However, because of its widespread usage, one should not criticize those who prefer *feel* for *think*, although no one need follow their example.

those kind of

Ned said, "Those kind of apples are best for baking." Did Ned err?

Ned may know his apples better than his English. Since the word *kind* is singular, it should be modified by the singular adjective *this*: "*This kind* of apple." The plural form takes *these* or *those*: "*Those kinds* of apples."

Note: An error when using the form *kind* apparently is induced, for some unaccountable reason, by the demonstrative adjectives *these* and *those* (*these kind, those kind*). *Kind* must be the more natural word to use. A typical misusage is "*Those* are the *kind* of instruments we need" in which the plural form *kinds* is required.

though/although

My question concerns the use of *though* and *although*. Is one preferred to the other? Or are they interchangeable?

In some constructions one is preferred to the other; in others, they are interchangeable. As conjunctions of concession, in the sense "in spite of the fact that," they may be interchanged: "We like our neighbors, *though* (or *although*) we don't want them as close friends." *Although* is more emphatic, but *though*, except at the beginning of a sentence, is commoner. *Though* is the preference to link single words or phrases: *poorer though wiser*.

> Note: *Though*, but not *although*, may serve as an adverb at the end of a sentence or clause ("The weather was bad. We enjoyed the hotel accommodations, *though*"). Many writers in formal discourse would avoid adverbial *though* for *nevertheless* or *however*—"We were promised an increase in interest rates; it did not occur, however," (rather than *though*).
>
> Idiomatically, *though* may be preceded by *even* ("We will not go, *even though* we have much to gain") or *as* ("*As though* it were spring . . ."). We do not say *even although* or *as although*.

thousand

Why is it that we treat *thousand*, in a phrase such as *a thousand pounds*, as a singular?

True, the notion of *thousand* is plural, but the rule is to consider collective nouns implying a unit, as well as numbers indicating a fixed quantity, as singular. Hence, "*A thousand pounds is* all we can carry." And so, "The *army is* ready to move." "My *family is* prepared to welcome you." But observe that collectives are regarded as plurals where they convey a plural idea. "*A thousand birds were* seen flying north." "My *family have* different jobs to handle."

> Note: The guideline is that if *thousand* is preceded by a number ("four *thousand* dollars"), it is a singular form. If no number precedes *thousand*, the plural form is required ("*thousands* of men").

through/throughout

1. "When I am through with the meal, I'll go to the library" raises a question in my mind. Is *through* the proper word to use in that sentence?

Colloquially, yes; in formal writing, no. Although some authorities would extend the meaning of *through*, so that it would be applicable in the example, most of them would hold that on a formal level *finished* is preferable. Likewise, rather than "I'm *through* with my course in biology," one should say, in more refined English, "I have now *completed* my course." And preferably, "I've *given up* smoking" to "I am *through* with smoking."

> Note: When the meaning intended is in every part, from end to end, it would be better to use *throughout* than *through*. Thus: "His political slogans are heard *throughout* (rather than *through*) the country."

2. Was the sports announcer speaking properly when he said, "The coach paced back and forth throughout the whole game"?

He was not. *Throughout* means in or to every part of and therefore carries the sense of whole or entire. Adding either of those words makes for a redundancy. In the example, *whole* should have been omitted. Then the sentence would have read: "The coach paced back and forth *throughout* the game." Equally bad would be "The coach did not miss a practice session *throughout* the entire season." Scrub *entire*.

titled/entitled

Is the word *titled* or *entitled* preferred in "The book is *titled* (*entitled*) 'I Must Say' "?

Either word is acceptable. Which to use is a matter of personal preference. Some writers who opt for *titled* do so on the assumption that *entitled* refers only to a right: "Each child is *entitled* to an equal part"; "Having fulfilled all the requirements, Barry is *entitled* to the reward." But *entitle* also means to give a name or title to. Although *titled* and *entitled* in terms of naming are synonymous, distinguishing between these words is sometimes helpful. For example, in "The author's new book is titled 'Phoenix,' and he is entitled to twenty-five copies free of cost," *titled* . . . *entitled* are more euphonious than *entitled* . . . *entitled*.

> **Note:** No punctuation mark should follow the words *titled* or *entitled* when introducing the name of a book: "We read a book titled *East of Eden*."

to

1. I recently read "We didn't know where they went to" and "I wonder where they will go to." How would you attack those sentences?

From the rear. The *to*'s are unnecessary and should be omitted. It is poor style to use a preposition needlessly.

> **Note:** Inserting *to* after such words as *been* or *going* is a grammatical blunder. Say, "Where have they been," not "been to." Say, "Where is Ruth going," not "going to." Compounds with *to* are hyphenated: *set-to*, *lean-to*.

2. Is *to* required in "His house came to within five feet of mine" and "Ralph helped his uncle to do the daily chores"?

Preferably *to* should be omitted. Some prepositional phrases (first example) do not need the preposition and some infinitives (second example) are often written without *to*.

together

1. What do you think of the speaker who, while berating a crowd, shouted, "We should all assemble together because if we mingle to-

gether we are more likely to cooperate together"?

He should have gotten his wits together. The sense of *together*, "in a single group," is inherent in *assemble*, *mingle*, and *cooperate*. It is redundant to hitch *together* to any of those words. They need no yoke.

2. Please give some examples of correct and incorrect uses of *together*.

Omit *together* when its sense is embedded in another word, such as *merge*, *collect*, *cooperate*, or *consolidate*. Do not say, "*Connect* the two pipes *together*" or "Let's *cooperate together*." But you may say, "*Put* the two pipes *together*" or "*Connect* the two pipes." You may say, "Let's *cooperate*" or "Let's *work together*."

3. Did the clerk write this right: "Debbie together with Jean are to report at 10 a.m."?

He did not. A noun or phrase introduced by *together with* immediately following the subject is considered parenthetical. It therefore does not combine with the subject, nor does it influence the number of the verb. It does not, in other words, convert a singular subject into a plural. Hence the clerk should have written: "Debbie, together with Jean, *is* to report at 10 a.m."

> **Note:** The rule also applies to *as well as*, *in addition to*, *along with*, and *with*: "The building, *as well as* the adjoining ground, *is* to be sold at auction"; "The library *along with* all its books *was* destroyed"; "The silo, *in addition to* the barn, *was* burned"; "The writ *with* the records of testimony *is* to be delivered tomorrow." But note that although it is often better to set off these expressions with commas, they are not always necessary. Bear in mind that a plural subject obviates the problem of punctuation and agreement of subject and verb, for naturally a plural verb is required: "The writ *and* the records of testimony *are* to be delivered tomorrow"; "The building *and* the adjoining ground *are* to be sold at auction."

token, by the same

Do you object to the phrase *by the same token*?

Generally, yes, since it is a cliché and is usually replaceable by *likewise*, *similarly*, *besides*, *moreover*, or *furthermore*. But although any one of these adverbs is more economical than the key phrase, the phrase is preferable if it makes the transitional flavor more palatable.

too

I have read that beginning a sentence with the word *too* is considered poor style. Do you agree?

I do. A sentence should not begin with *too*. Such words as *also*, *furthermore*, or *moreover* may ably serve in that position.

> **Note:** The proper use of adverb *too* is controversial in some respects.

For example, traditionally *too* was set off by commas ("I, *too*, would like to go"), but modern writers avoid the commas wherever the omission does not interfere with clarity. Hence: "I *too* would like to go" (no commas). When *too* comes at the end of a sentence, it more often is preceded by a comma ("I would like to go, *too*").

Perhaps a more serious question is whether *too* may modify a past participle, as in "He was *too* admired not to feel egotistical." Bear in mind that *too* is an adverb that denotes degree and is therefore avoided as a direct modifier of a past participle, since the participle is a verb of action, not of quality. Hence it is incorrect to say that a person was *too* admired or *too* depressed. An adverb of quality must come between *too* and the participle: too *much* admired, too *greatly* shaken, too *highly* seasoned, too *well* done. If, however, the participle is now used as an adjective, then *too* may modify it directly: "He is *too* tired to continue"; "I am *too* pleased to say anymore." The problem is to decide whether a participle is now functioning as an adjective. That is not easy to do. A guideline, nebulous though it be, is to decide whether the participle denotes quality or condition. If so, it is being used as an adjective and may be modified directly by *too*.

Adverb *very* follows the same conventions.

torturous/tortuous

Are the connotations of both *torturous* and *tortuous* unpleasant?
Torturous certainly is, since it means causing torture, tormenting. A synonym is *excruciating*. *Tortuous*, meaning twisting, winding, or crooked, is usually applied to streams or roadways. But figuratively its sense of crooked may be applied to devious persons. In that use, *tortuous* means not straightforward, and thus deceitful or crooked. *Torturous* is the adjectival form of *torture*, and both those words, unlike *tortuous*, have two *r*'s. Perhaps that will help distinguish the words.

Note: A word that sounds confusingly similar to *torturous* and *tortuous* is *tortious*. It refers to a civil wrong, in law called a *tort*.

total

How can I be sure to use the correct form of the verb following the word *total*?
Look at the article preceding it. The expression *a total* takes a plural verb; *the total*, a singular. "*A total* of six months *were* needed to complete the job." "*The total* of nineteen *was* unexpected."

Note: The number attributed to many words is determined by the article that precedes the word, just as *a* modifying *total* sets a plural stage, whereas *the* mandates a singular verb. Consider the word *number* ("A number of rabbits *were* there," but "*The* number of rabbits *was* under twenty") and *variety* ("*A* variety of flowers *are* on display," but "*The* variety of flowers today *is* meager.").

In current, popular usage, *total* has become a verb ("His car was *totaled*"), the sense being demolished. If the standard verbs *demolished* or *destroyed* are used, do not modify either one with *totally*.

toward/afterward

Which of these forms are the correct ones: *toward, towards*; *afterward, afterwards*?
They are all correct. Choose from them as you please, although the use of the words without the *s* is more prevalent. The same discretion applies to *upward* and *upwards* and *downward* and *downwards*. The presence of the *s* does not alter the meaning.

Note: The suffix *-ward* means leaning to or in the direction of. We say, "We are heading *eastward* (or *eastwards*)." And then there are the adverbs *backward* and *backwards*, meaning in reverse order or direction. Here euphony determines which form to use. But adjective *backward*, meaning poorly developed or bashful, has only this one form. Likewise with *forward*. Either *forward* or *forwards* may serve as adverbs — "He lurched *forward*" (or *forwards*) — but one form, *forward*, adjectivally: "a *forward* movement"; "a *forward* pass."

track/tack

Which is correct: *on the wrong track* or *on the wrong tack*?
The common expression is *on the wrong track*, a corruption of the seafarer's *on the wrong tack*, a phrase older than any railroad track. But you'll not be criticized for using either expression.

Note: Be careful not to confuse *track* or *tack* with *tract*, a pamphlet or a piece of land.

transitive/intransitive

Explain the difference between a transitive and an intransitive verb.
A transitive verb is one in which the action goes from the doer to the receiver and thus takes a direct object ("I *ate* an *apple*"). An intransitive verb takes no object ("I *sat* on the sofa"; "Arthur *jumped* high"), the action ending with the verb. The prepositional phrase "on the sofa" and the adverb "high" modify the verbs.

Note: Transitive verbs may be expressed in the passive voice ("The apple *was eaten* by me"). In this construction there is no direct object, and the subject receives the action of the verb. A passive form consists of the verb *be* plus a past participle. An intransitive verb cannot be put in the passive form.

transpire

A favorite word of my history teacher is *transpire*. Nothing happens or takes place; it always transpires. Is such an elegant word a desir-

able replacement for more ordinary diction?

Flatly, no. The word *transpire* is not elegant; it is pretentious when used for "happen," "occur," or "take place" — and also incorrect. *Transpire* means to leak out or become known.

> **Note:** The forebears of *transpire* are Latin *trans* and *spirare*, which literally mean "to breathe through," "to exhale." (In botany *transpire* refers to the emission of vapor by plants through the pores of their leaves.) With time, however, many writers have come to use it to mean happen or occur, although the reason for this change has never been documented ("Everyone had a different version of what *transpired* at the meeting"). In that sense, *transpire* is still widely used by those reaching for a fancier word than ordinary *happen*. Strictly speaking, *transpire* in general usage means, or should mean, to come to light or to become known gradually — a leaking out, so to speak ("The news of the disaster did not *transpire* until a month after the ship was sunk"; "As a result of the investigation it *transpired* that the treasurer had been embezzling"). Although the erosion of the meaning of *transpire* is deep, one need not be a party to its worsening condition. If fearful that the word *transpire* when accurately used will be misunderstood, or sneered at, sidestep those possibilities by not using it.

trigger

Is *trigger*, when meaning to set something off or to initiate, a desirable word?

It is a crisp word and may serve well, primarily in informal discourse. But be careful not to overuse it. Consider as substitutes *begin*, *cause*, *initiate*, *produce*, and even plain *start*.

> **Note:** Verb *trigger*, it is said, became a popular term after the first atom bomb was discharged. The bomb apparently set off certain mechanisms that were put into operation seriatim. Each mechanism sequentially set off, or triggered, the next one.

trivia

The speaker said, "All this trivia was just a waste of time." Please comment.

The word *trivia*, which means trifles, is a plural. The speaker should therefore have said, "These *trivia were*. . . ." *Trivia* has no working singular form. Be sure to avoid statements such as "I don't want to talk about *this trivia*."

> **Note:** To convert *trivia* to a singular idea, consider recasting. For example, in "Such a *trivial* matter was a waste of time," the adjective form *trivial* modifies a singular noun, although it can also modify a plural noun ("*a trivial* matter," "*some trivial* matters"). Or try *triviality*: "Such *triviality* was a waste of time."

trooper/trouper

Was it that we thought Grandpa was a good *trooper* or a good *trouper*, and when he cussed, did he swear like a *trouper* or a *trooper*?
A *trooper* is a cavalryman or a policeman; a *trouper*, a professional actor. A person who confronts the vicissitudes of life with strength and courage is said to be a good *trouper*. One who cusses long and loud is said to "swear like a *trooper*."

> Note: The basic noun and verb forms of the key words are *troop* and *troupe*. A *troop* is a group or band of persons (a Boy Scout *troop*). A *troupe* is also a band or company, but especially a group of actors (a *troupe* of strolling actors). To *troop* is to flock or assemble. To *troupe* is to travel with a company of actors.

truth/veracity

Are the words *truth* and *veracity* synonyms?
They are not. *Truth* refers to that which is true. It is a characteristic of a fact or a thing. *Veracity* is habitual truthfulness, a characteristic of a person. We may say that a person known for veracity is believed to be telling the truth.

try and

The expression *try and* was a favorite in my family. My mother frequently would say something like "Try and do right by your cousin." Is this usage sanctioned by current authorities?
There is no consensus among word-usage critics on the use of *and* for *to*. Some say that *and* in "Try *and* do right by your cousin" reinforces the verb, so that greater urgency is implied. Others say that using *and* instead of *to* makes the expression colloquial. Still others, that it is simply bad grammar, that *try* takes the infinitive and that *to* in this phrasing is therefore required. The recommendation here is that although *try and* may be a comfortable speech expression and acceptable in informal contexts, it should be avoided when writing formal prose.

All the foregoing matter applies to similar phrases: *come and*, as in "*Come and* eat now"; *be sure and*, as in "*Be sure and* work hard today"; and so forth.

turbid/turgid

How are the look-alikes *turbid* and *turgid* differentiated?
Turbid means not clear, cloudy, muddy, like a creek with the bottom stirred up. *Turgid* means bloated or swollen. It is often applied figuratively to a pretentious style of speaking or writing. As so used, it means inflated, grandiloquent, bombastic.

Note: Be careful of these look-alikes. They are particularly easy to confuse. Since they are used infrequently, their meanings are less likely to be cemented firmly in one's mind.

type

The personnel director said, "We need that type man in our department." What "type man" do you think is meant?
You are obviously speaking with tongue in cheek, recognizing that *type*, as a noun, must be followed by *of* before another noun. Therefore, *that type of man*, not *that type man*; *this type of machine*, not *this type machine*. Omitting the *of* is tantamount to using *type* as an adjective. Don't do it.
   Note: In "He has A-type blood," *type* is serving as an adjective and is joined to *A* by a hyphen. The hyphen justifies the construction. Observe this difference: "He is an athletic-*type* person (no *of*), but "He is the type *of* person who is athletic" (*of*). *Type* may be distinguished from *kind* or *sort* in that *type* refers to a specific, clearly defined class. The resemblance and difference between items or members in that group are noticeably and clearly implied from those of other groups. *Kind* and *sort* refer to categories that are less sharply delineated.

U

uncomparable/incomparable

If two things cannot be compared, are they *incomparable* or *uncomparable*?

Depends. Something that is peerless, beyond comparison, is *incomparable*. But golf balls and wallets are *uncomparable*, since the objects have no similarities. They cannot be compared. In grammar *uncomparable* is used of such words as *perfect*, *fatal*, and *complete*, words that are incapable of being compared because they express absolute notions.

> Note: An absolute term is said to be uncomparable because it cannot vary in degree or intensity. Hence such a term cannot be used in a comparative or superlative sense. Nothing can be *more* or *most* perfect any more than something can be *more* dead or the *deadest* of all. A latitude is permitted by grammarians, however, in that those words may be modified by *almost* or *nearly*, since they do not imply degree. Therefore it is permissible to say that an object is *more nearly round* or *square* than another and an animal may be *more nearly dead* than another. Something may be *almost equal* to something else.

unequivocally

Which word is correct: "We reject that notion *unequivocably* (or *unequivocally*)"?

The latter. Although *unequivocably* is often heard and seen in print, there is no such word. File it in the "Nonexistent Word File," where it will find such companions as *alot*, *alright*, and *irregardless*.

unique

What is wrong with saying, "This is the most unique vase I have ever seen"? The expression *most unique* is quite common.

Perhaps. But it is not justified. *Unique* means the only one of its kind or without an equal, and it therefore may not be qualified by *most*. One may rightly say, "Of all the vases I have ever seen, this one is *unique*," which means that the vase is not subject to comparison. It is uncomparable.

> Note: *Unique* is a unique word and should be kept so for the sake of precision. Since it is an absolute term, it cannot admit of degrees—that is, something cannot be *more unique* or *less unique* than something else. And it may not be the *most unique* of all. It cannot even be *rather unique* or *very unique*. Trying to raise *unique* to a higher level, or sending it off

on a tangent, actually destroys its basic sense. But those who find it necessary to weaken unique's sense of absoluteness may try modifying *unique* with *almost, perhaps*, or *truly*. Most authorities approve of those modifiers. And remember, such words as *different, unusual*, or *impressive* may sometimes serve instead of *unique* (they are not absolutes), thus obviating the need for converting *unique* into a comparative or superlative.

unless/except

Is a clause introduced by *unless* and *except* preceded by a comma?
Not if the clause is restrictive—necessary to the sense of the sentence ("You cannot claim a foul *unless* you declare it immediately"; "Take all with you *except* the blue shirts"). But "She must have gotten home by now, *unless* she lost her way."

Note: *Unless*, which means except on the condition that, introduces a conditional clause ("We will go *unless* it rains"). *Except*, which introduces an exclusion with the sense of omitting, may not replace *unless*. If *except* is substituted for preposition *but*, it must be followed by a pronoun in the objective case, not the nominative ("No one saw it *except me*," not "I").

A caveat is to avoid the expression *unless and until* (the sister of *if and when*). In "We will make no commitments *unless and until* the funds are available," either *unless* or *until* could be dropped with no loss in sense. This cliché is usually found in negative constructions.

until/till

I have seen the shortened form of *until* written *till*, *'til*, and *'till*. Are all these in good repute?
Not all. Only *till* is standard. The forms *'til* and *'till* are inappropriate, even though *'til* is sometimes seen in poetic diction.

Note: The meanings of *till* and *until* are the same, and the words are therefore interchangeable. Although *till* is commoner than *until* (except at the beginning of a sentence, where *until* predominates), the preference is to use *till* when referring to a specific point in time ("Let the project stand idle *till* we say otherwise"; "We didn't reach the office *till* two o'clock"). *Until* is preferred when the reference is to a duration of time ("She lived on the farm *until* she left for college"; "We will wait here *until* help arrives"). However, the consideration of rhythm must be taken into account when choosing one or the other.

Since *till* is not a contraction, but a single word, it must not be given an apostrophe.

up

Should one say, "We're going to *dress* (or *dress up*) for the occasion"?
Up is superfluous but idiomatic, which means that one will probably

say, "Let's dress *up* for the occasion." In serious writing, however, avoid unnecessary *up*'s, as in finish *up*, hurry *up*, fix *up*, sign *up*, pay *up*, and open *up*.

> **Note:** Many verbs idiomatically require *up* to complete the meaning. The verb and preposition are considered as one—a verbal phrase. Hence *start up* and *jump up* are legitimate expressions, as are *come up* and *get up*. Indeed, we *look up* words in the dictionary and *dig up* word origins. Numerous colloquial expressions include *up* ("It's *up* to the dean to decide"), and they too are acceptable on their level of usage.

An afterthought. In "We will keep the store open up till ten o'clock," what was the *up* doing there? Nothing. *Up* jumped on a train where it didn't belong.

used to

1. Is it correct to say,"Peter didn't used to read much"?
Colloquially, yes. But since *did* and *used to* produce a double redundancy (they are both auxiliary verbs), in literary prose one should say, "Peter *used not to* read much." If you think this construction sounds awkward, which it does, reconstruct: "Peter didn't *use* (not *used*) to read much." The caveat is that *use*, not *used*, may rightly be coupled with *did*.

2. Is "He use to do it that way before I came along" said correctly?
It is not. Make it "He *used* to do it. . . ." Idiom *used to* (not *use to*) represents regular practice or action customary in the past and is followed by an infinitive.

> **Note:** Interrogatives, as well as negatives, raise questions of construction about which not all critics agree. In fact there is no universally accepted form. Many reputable writers prefer *use to* when preceded by *did* (the recommendation here): "*Did* (or *Didn't*) you *use to* (not *used to*) work in Phoenix?" The best formula in negative questions is *didn't use to*. More formally, and strictly correct, is "*Used you not* to work in Phoenix?" But that locution is so clumsy that it ought to be changed. Try "Didn't you *formerly* (or *at one time*) work in Phoenix?"—less formal but more readable and still acceptable.

utter

We often hear the phrase *utter discord*. Why do we not hear of *utter harmony*?
Because adjective *utter* is most often used negatively. We speak of *utter* darkness, not of *utter* light; *utter* nonsense, not of *utter* sense; of *utter* defeat, not of *utter* victory.

Note: Adjective *utter*, meaning complete, is preferably used, as judged by the foregoing examples, in an unfavorable sense. You will not hear of *utter love*, but you might of *utter hate*. *Utter* is the comparative form of obsolete *ut*. Its superlative degree is either *uttermost* or *utmost*. The latter form predominates.

V

valued/valuable

How synonymous are the words *valued* and *valuable*?

Not at all. That which is *valuable* is of great value or has great monetary value. It may be a design for a new model of a dishwasher or a painting by a renowned artist. That which is *valued* is esteemed or held in high regard. It may command no price on the market. A picture of your father, though valued by you, may not be valuable as a sales item.

> **Note:** Something that has no value is not invaluable. *Invaluable* has a completely opposite meaning, "priceless or above value." Although prefix *in-* in many instances means not, when prefixed to *valuable*, it becomes an intensifier: "An *invaluable* painting can scarcely be purchased, its price is so high."

variety

How is the number of the verb following the word *variety* determined?

It depends on the article preceding it. *A variety* takes a plural verb ("*A variety* of planes *are* landing"); *the variety* takes a singular ("*The variety* of helicopters *is* small").

> **Note:** Just as the number of the verb following *variety* is determined by the article (*a* or *the*) that preceded it, so it is true with other words, many of which have been included in this book. See, for example, *number* and *total*.

various and sundry

Is the phrase *various and sundry* a good expression?

The phrase has two strikes against it. It is redundant and a cliché. Pitch another one and strike it out.

venal/venial

The words *venal* and *venial* look so much alike that I constantly confuse them. Can you help me solve this semantic puzzle?

True it is that these look-alikes are confusing. They must be, considering how often they are misused one for the other, even in edited writing. Further, they sound somewhat alike, the first syllable of both *venal* and *venial* rhyming with *he*. *Venal* means corrupt, capable of being bribed. A judge or politician who accepts a bribe is venal. *Venial* means trivial, excusable, something that could be easily forgiven. It refers to a minor offense (a *venial* error, a *venial* sin). A mnemonic aid is to remember that *venal* and *penal* rhyme—two words that should go together.

verdict

Is the word *verdict* used correctly in "The judge will render a verdict soon"?

Judges do not render verdicts. Juries do. A *verdict*, from its literal Latin, "true speech," is what a jury, in written form, hands to the judge at the end of a trial.

> **Note:** Humorously, *verdict* is sometimes used to mean opinion. A man surprises his wife with a new shirt and necktie. When she looks at them for the first time, he might say to her, "Well, what's your verdict?"—in effect, what do you think of my purchase?

very

My daughter uses the word *very* before every adjective. Is that usage objectionable, or does it make her meaning more emphatic?

It is best to use *very* sparingly. Newswriters avoid it because *very* creates a feeling of exaggeration. Since it tends to overstate, its effect is to weaken rather than to strengthen. It is better to say, "He was elated" than "*very* elated"; "It was a beautiful display" rather than "a *very* beautiful display"; "The meal was excellent" rather than "*very* excellent." A classic bit of advice concerning the use of *very* is said to have come from William Allen White, who, decrying the use of *very*, instructed his reporters to write *damn* instead of *very* whenever *very* appeared, and then to cross out the damns.

> **Note:** May *very* be used before a past participle? is a controversial question that has no answer that will satisfy everyone. Past participles are verbals and should not be modified by very, an adverb of degree. What is needed is the intervention of quantitative *much* to be modified by *very* ("Philip is *very much* displeased by the latest happening"). Adjectives may be modified by *very*. And therein lies the crux of the quandaries that disturb many writers. If a past participle has become an adjective, the problem is solved. But how does one know when a past participle has changed its status? Some combinations, because of frequent usage, have become idiomatic: *very interested; very pleased; very drunk; very tired*. The simplest thing to do, to avoid criticism from any source, is to use *much* (*very much*). Some authorities offer this guide: If *much* can be used, *very* by itself cannot be; if *much* cannot be used, then *very* alone is correct.

via

All post offices stamp their overseas envelopes "via airmail." Should the post office have its English corrected?

Strictly speaking, *via* means by way of. It should be used to describe only geographical routes ("Randy traveled to Chicago *via* Pittsburgh"). However, *via* commonly stands for by means of, as in the example, even though it is not a derivative meaning. Hence *via* airmail, *via* train or plane, and so on, are all technically incorrect. In these uses *via* is displacing *by* or *through*. One may say, correctly, "They shipped the goods to Paris *via* London," but not "They shipped the goods *via* airfreight."

> **Note:** Trying to change the post office's English is like swimming upstream. The term *via* has established itself in certain uses to mean by way of or by the medium of, a usage so widespread that it is fair to say that in those senses *via* is now idiomatic. All this, however, does not suggest that a writer should ignore the original meaning of *via* and follow the popular trend. It is better, still, to say, "We're going *by* bus" and "I learned it *through* the newspaper" than *via* bus or *via* the newspaper.
>
> One more point—pronunciation. *Via* is properly pronounced VIE-uh, with a long *i*, as in *identify*. But VEE-uh is often heard and has become a variant pronunciation.

vice versa

Would you give a clear definition and examples of *vice versa*?
Vice versa means conversely or, as it is said, "the other way around." "I will mow the lawn and then clean my room, or *vice versa*, as you wish."

> **Note:** The correct pronunciation of *vice versa* (which is spelled with no hyphen) is either VIE-suh VURH-suh or VIES VUHR-suh. The first pronunciation is favored.

victuals

How is the word *victuals* pronounced?
Victuals, meaning food fit for human consumption, is pronounced VIH-tls, and is often spelled phonetically, *vittles*. Its rarely used singular form is *victual*, which rhymes with "little." In fact, the plural form *victuals* is also rarely used. It is regarded as quaint.

view

I was once questioned about the preposition that follows *view*—*to* or *of*. I was trapped. Could you help me?
Will try. *View* may be followed by either *to* or *of*. Which to use depends on the meaning to be conveyed. The idiom *in view of* means considering, because of, or taking into account and is followed by a noun ("*In view of* the imminence of war, we are all fearful"). The phrase *with a view to* means with the purpose or intention of and is followed by a noun or gerund ("*With a view to* conciliating labor, management is making a new offer").

Note: *View* may be preceded by *on* (*on view*), in which case it means to be seen or displayed for public inspection ("Audrey's collages are *on view* at the church bazaar"), or by *in* (*in view*), meaning in sight ("There's no prospect *in view*").

A related matter involves the use of the term *viewpoint*, a place from which someone looks at something (but figuratively, a way of looking, an attitude of mind), as a substitute for the phrase *point of view*. Some grammarians reject the short form, saying *point of view* is the more accurate term. A point of view is the metaphorical spot where one stands to look at something. What he sees is his view. Therefore, a person conveying his conclusions expresses his opinions or views, not his point of views or his points of view.

voice, active and passive

I understand that, except in rare cases, we should use the active voice rather than the passive. Why is that?
The active voice is vigorous and vivid. "John *threw* the ball" rather than "The ball *was thrown* by John." The passive voice is static. In addition, the active voice is more economical. In the example it saves two words.

Note: If the subject is the doer of the action, the verb is in the active voice. The passive voice is preferable when the performer of the act is unknown or of little importance.

W

waiting on

Does this sentence make grammatical sense: "I'm waiting on the delivery boy"?

Not in the best English. When *wait on* means to wait for, it is colloquial or provincial. A homemaker waits *for* the delivery boy, not *on*. The phrase "wait on" is acceptable English only when it means to serve someone: "The waiter will *wait on* us shortly"; "I've been at this counter a long time. I wish someone would *wait on* me."

> **Note:** Although not all colloquial expressions are bad, and certainly not to be shunned (it is almost impossible to engage in general conversation without them), some colloquial expressions are on the low end and should be avoided. "Wait on" and "want in" or "want out" are such expressions. And so is *want for*, as in "We *want for* you to see that play." An attuned grammatical ear has no trouble selecting the appropriate combinations as replacements.

was

1. Grammatically, is this sentence acceptable: "The person I saw was him, no doubt"?

It is not. A pronoun following a form of the verb *be* (*am, are, is,* and so forth) must be put in the nominative, not the objective, case ("The person I saw was *he,* no doubt").

> **Note:** The expression "It is I/me" is discussed elsewhere in this book. Suffice it to say here that "It is I" is the grammatically correct construction (according to the foregoing rule) but "It's me" is the common reply to "Who's there?" given even by highly educated people.

2. My niece, pointing to a man nearby, said, "He was a former teacher of mine." She insisted that she spoke correctly. Was she right?

From a word usage stand, she was not. The verb *was* indicates what *former* means. Therefore, *former* should have been omitted. Or if retained, then *was* should have been changed to *is.*

way

Should one say, "It is a long way from here" or "a long ways from here"?

Choose *way.* Using *ways* as a noun for *way* is unacceptable; *way* is the required form when the reference is to distance. Also, avoid using *way*

as an adverb for *away*, with the meaning considerably or far—"The camp is *away* beyond the town." If *way*, as in the first example, sounds strange, try *far*: "It is *far* from here."

> **Note:** The commonest misusage of *way* (as posed in the question "It is a long *ways* from here") is one in which *way* is required. The commonest redundancy involving *way* is in *way, shape, or form* ("I will help in any *way, shape, or form* I can") in which *way* says it all. And for the cruise-minded, when the ship pulls up anchor, the ship is *under weigh*, not *under way*.

Welsh

1. Is it Welsh rabbit or Welsh rarebit that we eat?

This delicacy was originally named *rabbit* as a pun, but with time *rarebit* superseded it on most menus and in cookbooks. Today *rarebit* is the more usual term. In any event, there is no *rabbit* in this melted cheese served on toast.

2. Does a person *welsh* or *welch on a bet*?

Either verb may be used to mean to renege on a debt or to ignore a commitment. The spelling *welsh* predominates, but *welch* avoids a mistaken derogatory reference to the people of Wales.

wharf/dock/pier

Are the words *wharf*, *pier*, and *dock* interchangeable?

A *wharf* is a landing place. A *pier* is a platform extending from the shore over water. A *dock* is actually the area of water beside or between piers. In popular usage the terms are treated synonymously in the sense of pier. Technically, of course, they are not the same.

> **Note:** The plural of *wharf* is *wharves* or *wharfs*. The first term is preferred. *Dock* is the only one of the three key words that is also a verb. To *dock* is to cut down, as in "The company docked the men's wages for coming late." And most commonly, to maneuver a vessel into or next to a dock.

what

1. Should I say, "Let me whisper what *seem* (or *seems*) to be indiscretions committed by my secretary"?

Authorities are not in accord on the number to attribute to relative pronoun *what* when it serves as the subject of a sentence or clause. Most agree that *what* may be construed as a singular (meaning "that which" or "the thing which") or a plural (representing "those which" or "the things which") and therefore followed by either a singular or a plural verb, respectively. In the example, you may take your pick.

> **Note:** Fowler would criticize the sentence—"What *remains are* a few trees," preferring "What *remains is* a few trees" or "What *remain are* a few trees" to avoid *remains are*. But writers should choose the number

applicable to the *what* construction they feel most comfortable with. For example, the sentence "What really *sets* the pace *is* leadership and dedication," if bothersome, may be pluralized: "What really *set* the pace *are* leadership and dedication."

Caveat: If *what* is treated as a singular, the second verb must also be singular, although followed by a plural predicate nominative: "What *is* required *is* (not *are*) manuscripts written each season."

2. Is *what all* in "What all are you looking for?" a good construction?
Not at all; it is dialectal. The *all* is intended to intensify, but its use is not justified. Omit it.

whence

Is it wrong in today's writing to use the word *whence*?
No, except that it is old-fashioned. Be careful if you use it not to say *from whence*. The notion of *from* is already built in. The Biblical quotation—". . . from whence cometh my help"—was disparaged by Fowler as archaic. Today's writers would omit *from*.

Note: Thinking of *whence* brings to mind two other rhyming words: *hence* and *thence*. Both are bookish terms and, although not obsolete, should be employed, perhaps, only in poetic patterns. *Hence* means from here, from this source. *Thence* means from there, from that source. As with *whence*, *from* is implied in *hence* and *thence*, and so introducing either one with *from* is redundant. *Whence* means from which but may mean from where, in which case preposition *to* would be implied: "Arthur returned whence he came." Of course *hence* used as a conjunctive adverb is still in active use. It is a particularly useful word when a one-syllable word is needed to replace *consequently*, *accordingly*, or *therefore*.

where

1. What is wrong with adding *to* after *where*, as in "Where are we all going to"? It sounds natural to me.
The *to* should be omitted because it is superfluous. If *to* in that construction sounds natural, it is probably because you are accustomed to hearing it. If your friends would omit appending the *to*, the correct phrasing would then sound natural, too.

2. How should words *when*, *where*, *whether*, and *which* be pronounced?
They're properly pronounced hwen, hwere, and so forth. Incidentally, their original spelling began with *hw*. Today the *h* sound has all but vanished.

whether

I know that *whether* is preferred to *if* when alternatives are suggested. Are there any other special rules of usage applied to *whether*?

In formal English preferably use *whether* after such words as *ask*, *doubt*, *know*, *say*, *understand*, and *wonder* ("I wonder *whether* . . . ," "I doubt *whether* . . . ," "I don't know *whether* . . .").

Cautions. The combination *of whether* is undesirable and should be avoided. Do not say, "The court will take up the question *of whether* a change in venue is warranted." Omit *of*. Preceding *whether* with *as to* is equally undesirable. Rather than "The question *as to whether* the officer will be indicted must be answered soon," remove *as to*, improve the sentence, and save two words at the same time.

which

1. Why is this sentence objectionable: "Ralph was placed in charge of the committee, which angered the members"?
Which has no definite antecedent. It does not refer to Ralph or the nearest noun, *committee*. Recast: "Placing Ralph in charge of the committee angered . . ."; "The members were angered when Ralph was placed in charge . . . ."

2. What rule will help us use *which* correctly?
Be sure it refers to a noun. A reference to an entire sentence may be embarrassing. "Andy shouted at the class, *which* certainly was stupid." The class? Or the shouting? Improved: "Andy shouted at the class, which was a stupid thing to do."
> **Note:** It is a superstition to believe that *which* may not refer to a preceding statement. It may if it occasions no ambiguity.
> *Which* is a nonrestrictive relative pronoun that refers only to animals and things (its corresponding restrictive relative pronoun, *that*, refers to persons, animals, or things). A *which* clause is set off with commas because the clause could be removed without seriously affecting the sentence: "The brown house on our street, *which* is the third one on the left, is being put up for sale."

3. "He has a fine old villa in Spain, and which I would be delighted to own one day." Was that said in the King's English?
The construction of the sentence could be improved, without royal intervention. The use of *and which* is never justified unless a previous *which* has been used. The example could be rescued if *and* is removed.
> **Note:** This guideline applies to *but which* as well. The advice is not to use that combination unless it follows a parallel *which*. If there is none, cross out *but*. The sentence will be smoother.

while

May one say, properly, "Here is the dictionary, while there is the thesaurus"?
Not properly. *While*, which has a sense of time, may not replace *and*, a

coordinating conjunction that connects words, phrases, or clauses. Say, "Here is the dictionary, *and* there is the thesaurus."

Note: The predominant use of *while* is as a conjunction, its lexical definition being a space of time or during the time that ("*While* it was raining, we played dominoes"). It is sometimes used, but weakly, for *although* as a conjunction of concession ("*While* he ran as fast as he could, he couldn't get to the station on time"). Caveat. Be careful that a statement introduced by *while* is neither ambiguous nor ludicrous. Consider "*While* she had her first baby in Utah, she had her second in Ohio." Occasionally *while* stands for *whereas* to indicate opposition or difference ("The blue book is easier to read, *while* the red one is more authoritative"). *While* used in the conjunctive sense of *and*, as previously indicated, is viewed with disfavor. Not "My cousin likes fowl, my aunt likes fish, *while* I like steak," but "*and* I like steak." Not "The peas are on the right shelf, *while* the beans are on the left," but "*and* the beans are on the left."

While as a verb is not being considered here.

while/awhile

1. What alert applies when using the words *while* and *awhile*? How to spell and use them correctly in a given sentence is confusing.
Spell noun *while*, which is always introduced by a preposition, as a single word, never with *a* attached ("I'll study *for a while*"). Adverb *awhile* is a solid word ("We'll linger *awhile*").

Note: To repeat, if a preposition (*in, for*) precedes the key word, it must be the free-standing noun *while*: *in a while, for a while*, three separate words.

2. May the words *while* and *awhile* be interchanged?
Yes, if the sentence is properly constructed. Both *while* and *awhile* have the sense of time. We may say: "We'll sit and relax *for a while*" or "We'll sit and relax *awhile*."

Note: The thing that must be guarded against is the common misuse of *awhile* as a noun, as in "We'll sit and relax for *awhile*."

who/whom

1. Whenever I hear this question, "Who is this for?" it is invariably worded that way. Should it not now be considered standard English?
Perhaps, but *who* for *whom* has not been accepted by many critics. Until a change takes place, and a consensus is arrived at, prefer "*Whom* is it for?" Certainly if inverted, the need for *whom* becomes apparent — "This is *for whom*?" In good grammar the object of a preposition takes the objective case; hence *whom*.

Note: Many linguists believe that the relative pronoun *whom* is obsolescent and will disappear entirely from use except when it is preceded by a preposition: *for whom* it will be done; *to whom* it may concern. But until that day arrives, most writers protect their work against criticism by using *whom*, and *who*, correctly.

When the pronoun is the object of a preposition or of a verb, the form required is *whom*: "*Whom* did you go *with*?" "*Whom* did you meet?" When we say, "He's the person I paid the money to," we have omitted *whom* ("He's the person *whom* I have paid the money to"). Pronoun *whom* may be left out whenever its omission does not affect the sense of the sentence.

Be careful of overrefinement—that is, using the omnipotent *whom* where *who* belongs. In "This is the artist whom I am told is the best one to paint my portrait," *who* should replace *whom*, for *who* is the subject of the clause "*who* is to paint my portrait." The phrase "I am told" is purely parenthetical and may be omitted.

To conclude: In colloquial language the interrogative *who* is regularly used for *whom*: "*Who* did you buy it for?" "*Who* are you going with?" Speech aside, in writing switch to *whom*. One cannot go wrong by using correct grammar.

2. What guideline can you offer for this sentence: "The doctor *who* (or *whom*) I consulted left town."
The correct word there is *whom*. Whether to use *who* or *whom* can be determined by omitting both words. If neither is needed, the word must be *whom*: "The doctor (no *who* or *whom*) I consulted . . . ." *Who*, as the subject, may never be omitted.

Note: Use *whom* as the object of a preposition ("for *whom* the bell tolls") or as the object of a verb ("the girl *whom* I love") or as the subject of an infinitive ("the one *whom* he thought to be the teacher"). In all other instances, use *who*.

3. Is it grammatically correct to say, "Who do you want?"
Indeed not. *Whom* is still the required form when the objective case of this relative pronoun is called for. Therefore, "*Whom* do you want?"

Note: This kind of grammatical error can be laid at the doorstep of usual sentence constructions; that is, a noun beginning, or near the beginning, of a sentence should be in the nominative case. It is not in this instance. *Who* in the example has been incorrectly used for *whom*.

whoever/who ever

My son insists that *ever* in *who ever* is unacceptable. Is he right?
Two-word *who ever* is standard English. True, some formalists decry the addition of *ever*, but many writers use it to gain emphasis—"*Who ever* would think otherwise?"—the sense being "who in the world."

Note: One-word *whoever* is usually found in interrogatives ("*Whoever* issued those orders?"), and two-word *who ever* is usually employed to gain emphasis, as in, as was given, "*Who ever* in the world would think otherwise?" Clearly, *ever* is merely an intensive, for it can be omitted without destroying the sense of the sentence.

Whether to use *whoever* or *whomever* can be confusing. The easiest guideline to follow is to mentally supply the word *anybody who* before the key word and then see whether *whoever* or *whomever* reads better. For example, "This is for him or *whoever* (not *whomever*) comes early," meaning "This is for him or for *anybody who* comes early." "To *whoever* (not *whomever*) asks for one, we'll send one free," means "To *anybody who* asks . . . ." But "To *whomever* (not *whoever*) they designate, Gussie will mail the books," meaning "To *anybody whom* they designate . . . ."

whose

1. Do good writers now use *whose* rather than *of which* for things?
They do. The rule that *of which* should be applied to animals and things and *whose* to people has long been discountenanced ("The book *whose* cover is red . . . ," "The flower *whose* petals are drooping . . . ," "The motor *whose* pistons are . . ."). No *of which*.

> **Note:** Today relative pronoun *whose* is accepted as the possessive form of *who*, *which*, and *that*, and may refer to animate or inaminate things. Although *of which* when used as a reference to nonpersonal and inanimate things is traditional and is grammatically correct, using *whose* avoids the postponed and cumbersome *of which*. Consider: "He ran through the woods *whose* paths were covered with underbrush" and "He ran through the woods the paths *of which* were covered with underbrush." The former makes for smoother writing, gets to the point quicker, and is the better choice.
>
> *Whose* and *who's* are pronounced alike and possibly for that reason are sometimes confused. *Who's* is a contraction of *who is* ("*Who's* going to do it?") or *who has* ("*Who's* been knocking at my door?"). In "He's a man who's possessions are valuable and whose thought to be a generous benefactor," *who's* and *whose* should be switched to find out who's who and what's what.

2. "Who's house will you be visiting next?" Why is the error in that sentence so common?
Probably because of carelessness. Clearly the contraction *who's* makes no sense in the example. And just as clearly *whose*, the possessive form of *who*, is called for in "*Whose* house . . . ."

3. When are commas required when using *whose*?
If *whose* introduces a parenthetical thought, use commas to set it off ("The brown house, *whose* roof looks shabby, is the oldest on the street"). But no commas otherwise ("Employees *whose* work has been completed may leave early").

-wise/-ways

Is there any preference when choosing between the suffixes -*wise* and -*ways*?
Although both denote attitude or direction, -*wise* is generally pre-

ferred: *anywise, clockwise, edgewise*. *Lengthwise* and *lengthways* are equally acceptable, but the former has the edge. Neither *sidewise* nor *sideways* has an advantage in usage over the other, but *sideways* predominates.

Note: In the sense used here, suffix *-wise* means in the manner of. Almost any noun can have *-wise* appended to it and, presto, be converted into an adverbial modifier. There is nothing wrong with constructing an adverb with *-wise*, but the caution is, first, be sure that it is not displacing more readily understood words, and second, be sure that it doesn't sound or look silly ("Teamwise we are in good shape because pitcherwise we are well staffed"). Wordwise, that example is abominable, languagewise.

Suffix *-wise* may also mean possessing wisdom (*pennywise, worldlywise*). This usage is well accepted.

witness

My friend always says something like "I witnessed an exciting football game today." Is the word *witnessed* used properly?
Your friend's statement would improve if he were to say "I saw," rather than "I witnessed." Using a form of *witness* for a form of *see* in ordinary contexts is inappropriate. It sounds as though your friend were reaching for a fancy *see*. Plainer words than *witness*, in addition to *see*, are *watch* and *observe*.

Note: Verb *witness* should be reserved for use in a courtroom. There, in the dock, people testify to what they saw and heard. That is, what they witnessed.

worst

We often hear a statement like "I need it in the worst way." What do you think of it?
Not much. I'm not sure what the worst way is. I know what the intended meaning is — very much, exceedingly, or greatly, any of which phrasing would sound better. I would grade the expression *in the worst way* low informal.

Note: Another use of the word *worst* appears in the expression *if worst comes to worst*. This expression has been idiomatic in the English language for centuries. It is, of course, illogical because *worst* to *worst* shows no gradation. What is worse than what had been, can, in time, become the worst. The expression was borrowed from Cervantes, who said, in *Don Quixote*, published in 1594, "Let the worst come to the worst," which displays the same illogicality.

worth-while/worthwhile

Which spelling is correct: *worth-while, worthwhile,* or *worth while*?
There is no uniformity of opinion among authorities. Each form has its supporters, but the hyphenated combination is fast disappearing.

Some stylists lay down a fiat that *worthwhile* is the proper way to spell it. Others are not in complete agreement.

> **Note:** The prevailing style, and the one recommended by most critics, is that this adjective be written solid (*worthwhile*) when it precedes a noun, as an attributive adjective (a *worthwhile* project), and be written open (*worth while*) when it follows a noun, as a predicate complement ("The project is *worth while*"). Possibly the best way to remember the form to follow is this: If a noun is not being modified ("It is *worth while* to consider his plan"), use two-word *worth while*.

would have

Would this sentence pass muster in a course on English: "If Tina would have cooked her meal on time, her husband would not have missed his poker game"?

I think not. The combination *would have* should never be used after the word *if*. Since *if* expresses a condition that refers to past action, *would have*, serving as a conditional perfect auxiliary to *cooked*, is incorrect. It should be replaced by *had*: "If Tina *had* cooked . . . , her husband *would* not *have* . . . ." Let's take another example. "If they would have asked, we could have referred them to the right place" should read: "If they *had* asked, we *could have* referred them to the right place."

> **Note:** When expressing a wish, do not use *would have* for *had* or *might have*. "Angela wishes she would have gone" needs correcting: "Angela wishes she *had gone*." "I wish Rose *might have been* at home," and not "I wish Rose *would have been* home." To repeat, the auxiliary to use in clauses following the word *wish* is *had*.

wrack

The report said, "The wracking problem of today will confront us for a long time." Is *wracking* the right word?

Problems that seem to put us on a rack are racking, not wracking. Which also means that when trying to remember, you *rack* your brains, not *wrack*. *Wrack* means to wreck or ruin.

> **Note:** Think of a torture rack when reaching for the word to represent mental torture or a straining with great effort. Hence the correct combination is *nerve-racking*, not *nerve-wracking*. A rack is a frame, often used for stretching. A person who is put on a rack is being stretched and tortured. And this we say is what might happen to a person's nerves. Dictionaries, however, allow *nerve-wracking*, as well as *nerve-racking*, and *wrack and ruin*, as well as *rack and ruin*. Since *wrack* means ruin, the phrase *wrack and ruin* is redundant.

wrong/wrongly

Is it wrong to say, "I was quoted wrongly"?

It is not, but *wrongly* as used in the example is not the preferred form. *Wrong* is both an adjective ("He made a *wrong* turn") and an adverb ("He did it *wrong*"). *Wrongly* is an adverb only. Its accepted usage is before the verb it modifies ("The fabric was *wrongly* cut"). Coming back to the original example, "I was quoted *wrong*" is the right way to say it.

X

Xerox

May you rightly say you xeroxed your report? Or must you say you photocopied or duplicated it?

Technically, *Xerox,* a trade name, is wrongly used. One should say that the document was photocopied or a copy made on a duplicating machine. In spite of the company's best efforts to preserve its trademark, *xerox* is in danger of becoming a common word, as happened with Victrola and Kleenex. But *xerox* is different in that it is used as a verb.

> **Note:** Dictionaries list *victrola* in lower case, defining it as a kind of phonograph. A capital letter is used only if the trademark *Victrola* is being referred to. *Kleenex* is defined as disposable paper tissue. As a generic term, it is spelled with no capital letter: *kleenex.* The trademark *Kleenex* naturally is capitalized.

Xmas

May Christmas properly be spelled Xmas?

The spelling *Xmas* is quite common. But some people think it irreverent. It is best to spell *Christmas* this way, taking no shortcuts and no chance of offending anyone. Some newspapers will not print *Xmas* as a reference to Christmas.

X-ray

Should I write X ray or X-ray or x ray or x-ray?

How you write that term is just a matter of style, and so you may choose what appeals to you. Used as a noun either X ray or X-ray is standard, but the former predominates (preferably the hyphen should be omitted). When used as an adjective ("John is an X-ray specialist") or a verb ("Tony's left arm was X-rayed"), the prevailing style is to hyphenate. The capital X is used more often than the lowercase x.

Y

yet

My son insisted that I was wrong when I said, "Bob did not call you yet." Was he right?

He was. Negative constructions in which *yet* as a temporal adverb means up to now or thus far take a perfect-tense verb rather than the simple past tense. The example, correctly put, would have been "Bob *has not called* yet."

> **Note:** Although the expression *as yet* is used by some reputable writers, it is invariably inferior to *yet* alone. Omit *as* or recast with *thus far* or some other appropriate phrase. And be careful of possible ambiguity with *yet*. For example, "Are the boys here *yet*?" may be asking "Are they *still* here?" or "Have they arrived?"

Yiddish

Are *Hebrew* and *Yiddish* similar languages?

They are as far apart as English and Chinese. *Hebrew* is a semitic language. *Yiddish* is a German dialect and is a derivative of the Indo-European family of languages.

> **Note:** Many Yiddish words have become an established part of the American vocabulary. In fact, some such words are so customary in almost everyone's speech and are so expressive that it is difficult to communicate without them. For example, *chutzpah* has no English counterpart. It represents incredible gall. A *kibitzer* is one who is constantly offering unwanted advice. A *klutz* is a clumsy, stupid person; a *maven* is an expert.

you

1. When talking to my child, why do I say, "You *are* to leave now"?

Good question. We say "I *am*," "He *is*," but "You *are*." Centuries ago *thee* and *thou* were the singular forms. But the idea arose that *you*, with a plural verb, is a mark of respect. The language has been saddled with this anomaly ever since.

> **Note:** Although *you* may be used when referring to one person, the word is grammatically plural and must be followed by a plural verb.

2. At a college seminar on career planning, I heard this sentence: "If you attend a technical high school, you will learn a trade." Was *you* used correctly?

I think not. Apparently the seminar was attended by students past the high school level. The statement, therefore, referred to young people in general, which makes the use of *you* inappropriate. What was called for was the indefinite *one:* "If *one* attends a technical high school, he will learn a trade" or, if a recast is in order, "*Students* who attend a technical high school will learn a trade."

> **Note:** *You* is frequently used as an indefinite pronoun. It lends a familiar touch and is less formal and more direct than *one*. In more structured writing, when a reference is made to anyone or to any person, appropriate pronouns, rather than *you*, are the indefinite pronouns *one* or *anyone*. Be alert to consistency. A sentence may not begin with *one* and then aimlessly switch to *you*, as in "If *one* wants to work here, what *you* must do is apply in person." Make it "what *one* must do" or "what *he* must do." It is proper, and sometimes desirable, to shift from *one* to *he*.

you've got

What do you think of the license plate that says, "You've got a friend in Pennsylvania"?

Technically, "You have a friend" is all that is required. The unnecessary *got* is redundant. But so many people say, "*You* (or *I*) *have got* to do it," or whatever (perhaps because *got* adds a gutteral emphasis) that, except in formal writing, *have got* is widely accepted.

> **Note:** The combination *have got* is more suitable in conversation than in writing. Bearing in mind that economy of words is a gainful attribute, drop *got* wherever *have* will serve alone.

Z

zero

In the articles I write I am never sure whether zeros follow a dollar amount and the time of day. What is the preferred style?
Except in tabulations, do not use the decimal point and ciphers after an even amount of money ($95, not $95.00) or an exact hour of time (3 p.m., not 3:00 p.m.)

zoom

Which is correct: (1) the plane zoomed up, (2) the car zoomed along the highway, (3) the vulture zoomed down on its prey?
Zoom, a term in aeronautics, means climb steeply or rapidly. Airplanes and balloons that ascend quickly are said to zoom. Technically, (1) in the example is correct except that *up* is redundant and should be dropped. In general usage (2) is acceptable. Informally *zoom* may apply to fast movement along a level course. But (3) is nonstandard and should not be used on any level of usage. *Zoom* is not a synonym for plunge or swoop.

Index